Praise for *Stay-at-Work Mom*

Previously published as *Don't Wait Up*

T0085568

"A hilarious and heartfelt ess̶̶̶̶̶̶̶̶̶̶̶ Astrof's
collection is often trenchant ir̶̶̶̶̶̶̶̶̶̶̶ it is also
permeated with a sense of lov̶̶̶̶̶̶̶̶̶̶̶ eeply."

—*Publishers Weekly*

"The author delivers one punch line after another . . . Droll wit and profundity swirl together in a revealing memoir from a successful comedy writer."

—*Kirkus Reviews*

"Successful comedy writer and television producer Astrof has put together a forthright, laugh-out-loud collection of essays that lets you in on a little of what makes her shows like *2 Broke Girls* or *The King of Queens* so much fun . . . Hilarious and, of course, as well written as any good sitcom episode."

—*Booklist*

"*Don't Wait Up* is a funny, fascinating memoir of mothering that will definitely keep readers up way past their bedtime, laughing and sometimes crying page after page."

—*BookPage*

"An exceptionally funny and charismatic voice . . . Written with a sharp pen and an open heart, Astrof's work is heartbreakingly poignant and funny as hell."

—*Shelf Awareness*

"[Astrof's] love for her family shines through as she offers a brutally honest look at motherhood, marriage, and work, rarely losing her sense of humor even while totally exasperated . . . [She] is gorgeously shameless, honest, and funny, and manages to be insightful and poignant at the same time."

—*The New York Post*

Stay-at-Work Mom

Marriage, Kids, and Other Disasters

LIZ ASTROF

Gallery Books

New York   London   Toronto   Sydney   New Delhi

G

Gallery Books
An Imprint of Simon & Schuster, Inc.
1230 Avenue of the Americas
New York, NY 10020

First Gallery Books trade paperback edition September 2022

Previously published in 2019 as *Don't Wait Up*

GALLERY BOOKS and colophon are registered trademarks of Simon & Schuster, Inc.

For information about special discounts for bulk purchases, please contact Simon & Schuster Special Sales at 1-866-506-1949 or business@simonandschuster.com.

The Simon & Schuster Speakers Bureau can bring authors to your live event. For more information or to book an event, contact the Simon & Schuster Speakers Bureau at 1-866-248-3049 or visit our website at www.simonspeakers.com.

Manufactured in the United States of America

10 9 8 7 6 5 4 3 2 1

Library of Congress Control Number: 2018050181

ISBN 978-1-9821-0695-9
ISBN 978-1-9821-0696-6 (pbk)
ISBN 978-1-9821-0697-3 (ebook)

For Todd, Jesse, and Phoebe

List of Chapters

Introduction: The Stay-at-Work Mom   ix

Guilt Trip   1

Rules of Estrangement   27

No More Monsters   49

The Stain   73

The Year of the Turtle   93

Happy New Year   111

Out of the Basement, Into the Fire   129

The Kids in the Orange Shirts   143

Little Royalty   155

The Typhoid Mary of Playa Blanca   169

Water Is for Writers   189

It's Not Brain Surgery   205

Are You There, God . . . ? It's Me, Jeff's Sister   225

Tim Allen Tried to Kill Me   243

The Love Bracelet   261

I've Got This   279

Epilogue: One Flying Leap   289

Screwed   299

Acknowledgments   319

Introduction:
The Stay-at-Work Mom

Every Mother's Day, I'm reminded of what a . . . unique mother I had. There isn't a single card that captures my experience. And the dread I feel about that while heading into my local Rite Aid is profound.

To be fair, it would be hard for even the most seasoned card-poet to find decent couplets for Even Though You Left When I Was Five, You Continue to Haunt Me. Or I Know You Never Wanted Children, But . . . Or My Kids Can Never Have Enough Clothes or Shoes Because I Had to Share Mine with Your Ventriloquist Dummy.

That said, I'd settle for a simple On This Day and All Days, I'm Terrified of Becoming You. It wouldn't even need to rhyme. Maybe there could just be a fun illustration of a scared little girl with the shadow of her big scary mother chasing her.

Hallmark or no, though, my upbringing made me who I am today—a successful television comedy writer, a loved wife, a "competent" mother, and a complete mess of a person whose very first role model was a disaster. I can come up with jokes, storylines, and wacky characters inside a New York minute. While being yelled at by a narcissistic asshole boss at midnight, I can deliver rewrites on a forty-five-page script without breaking a sweat, bleary-eyed and bloated, as coffee and SweeTarts eat away at my stomach lining.

But the idea of taking care of my children for any extended period of time, facing their neediness and all that entails—how they get so . . . thirsty and hungry—well, that thought alone simply brings me to my knees.

So I stay at work. I am a Stay-at-Work Mom.

You would think in this "You go, girl," "She persisted," pussy-hat day and age that being a Stay-at-Work Mom would be roundly supported, wouldn't you? You'd be wrong. Truth is, there's still a stigma attached to working mothers—and nowhere more, I'm sad to report, than among the Stay-at-Home Moms.

Case in point: one Saturday a few years back I was at my son's football game, and this gal festooned with babies approached me before I could escape her line of fire.

She smiled and pointed to the *2 Broke Girls* patch on my jacket. "Oh my God," she exclaimed. "Does your husband work on *2 Broke Girls*? We love that show!"

I looked around to make sure it wasn't 1955 and then said, "No, you dumb twat, *I* work on *2 Broke Girls*—I'm a writer."

I didn't really call her a dumb twat. But my tone for sure implied it.

What followed was the telltale, unmistakable, and super judge-y head tilt. "Wow," the Mom said. "I could never be away from my kids like that."

I wanted to say: "Yes, you could—it's probably all you think about. You lie awake wondering why you let these small people who can't even wipe themselves or appreciate a good joke take your life from you. You don't even recognize yourself anymore under those maternity sweatpants. You fantasize about getting in your minivan, running away from all of it, getting involved in a *Bridges of Madison County*–type romance and never coming home again. There is no way any adult enjoys spending time with a toddler, even if it's 'brilliant' or 'hilarious,' and frankly, if you really do enjoy them that much, there is something seriously wrong with you."

But I didn't say any of that because deep down, I *do* feel guilty about the unrivaled joy I get leaving my house in the morning. I feel ashamed for needing more to fulfill me than fostering the growth of these beautiful human beings I created. I fear it's a shortcoming that I'm unwilling to surrender myself to Jesse and Phoebe (those are my kids) 100 percent of the time.

That unrivaled joy I feel when I leave the house? I wish I could bottle it. You know who would buy it by the case? Stay-at-Home Moms.

Some nights I do go straight home. But then there are the nights where I crawl on my elbows under my kids' bedroom windows to the garage where we keep an elliptical machine, so I can get enough endorphins coursing through my system to see them. Or other nights when, while other mothers are making their children pasta made from non-GMO lentils, I'll be in a yoga class full of twenty-four-year-olds. Or, just walking around the mall aimlessly until a voice in my head says, "Go home, already." Or, best of all (worst of all?), the nights I sit in my car around the corner from the house gathering the courage to face the bedtime routine all in the hope of missing it, and usually walking through the door just after they've fallen asleep, kissing them on their sweet, blissful, unconscious foreheads. Foreheads that my poor husband bathed while I was "stuck in traffic."

I can never confess these hard truths to Stay-at-Home Moms, though. No admitting my failings or my guilt, I must appear strong when my choices are challenged or judged—which I usually accomplish by throwing my husband, Todd, under the bus.

"I have to work," I said to that mom at the football game, feigning frustration and envy. "I'd love to stay home with my kids—God, if only! You're so lucky you're not the primary bread-winner!"

Occasionally, however, encouragement comes—often at the most unexpected times and from the unlikeliest of people. One day on the *2 Broke Girls* set, I was showing Jennifer Coolidge pictures on my phone, and she landed on one of my family on vacation, smiling and splashing in the pool.

"You have such a beautiful family," she gushed.

"I think I made a mistake," I heard myself blurt.

Her stunned silence was followed by a burst of laughter. I asked her what was so funny.

"It's just that nobody ever says stuff like that," she said.

I went on to tell her how, while in the delivery room delivering my firstborn, Jesse, I suddenly remembered I didn't even like kids, and that what I remembered most about childbirth was screaming "I hated babysitting!" to my doctor. I also told her how I cautioned Todd as he counted Jesse's fingers and toes not to get attached to his son, that the very first words Jesse heard from his mother were, "Don't take the tags off—we may not be keeping him," which cracked up the nurses but infuriated me.

"You don't get it," I'd wailed, as Jesse let out his first cry. "What if I lose him?"

The doctor assured me he was very healthy, and Todd had to explain that I was talking about losing him like at a mall. "She actually really loses her wallet a lot," he said.

Todd gets me.

Jennifer had grown quiet, and I realized I'd probably freaked her out—the crazy writer who wished her kids came with return shipping labels.

But no. "See, that's just so honest," she said. "I thought all mothers were so happy."

Then it was my turn to laugh. I told her there isn't a mother out there who pushes a human being out of her body and doesn't think, *Holy shit, I've ruined my life*, and if you get one glass of Chardonnay in them, they'll tell you as much themselves.

"Well, your kids look great," Jennifer said. "You must be doing something right."

Beneath my "who cares about them, they're just kids" expression, I was beaming. Beaming! Because someone I respected, one of the most talented comedians I'd ever worked with, thought I "must be doing something right"—which is basically the grail of compliments for SAWMs like me.

I'm a Stay-at-Work Mom not because I don't love my kids, but because I do love them—I love them more than I ever imagined I could. And I'm terrified of messing up their lives.

Guilt Trip

Being a working mom—especially a Stay-at-Work Mom—means you don't have to be home for a lot of the bad shit like homework and dinnertime.

You don't have to drag your cherubs to karate or gymnastics or any other things they once begged you to let them do and now have to be dragged to.

You don't have to sit in a folding chair or watch them through windows, unable to zone out on your phone on the off-chance that they glance over to make sure you saw their cartwheel or base hit, your non-scrolling hand locked into "thumbs-up" duty. Likewise, you don't have to deal with the meltdown after the event because they're overscheduled or be the bad guy and say no when they want a candy bar from the vending machine, standing your ground so they don't grow up to be assholes.

Instead, you get to see them when they're bathed, cried out, and drifting off to sleep, kissing them on the head at the stroke of wine o'clock.

Being a working mom also means, however, that you have to make up for all that time away, so your kids don't resent you so much that, instead of caring for you in your old age, they throw you in a home the first time you put your phone in the dishwasher. Which I've already done.

I make up for my lost time by taking the whole family away for a few days the minute my current show wraps for the season. Also, every spring break I go solo and take my kids on what I call a "Guilt Trip." This is mostly my way of making it up to Todd, who picks up the slack when I'm working late, or on weekends, or when I need to go to yoga after working late, or on weekends because I just spent the week working late. I don't want *him* to throw me in a home, either. It's all about planning for the future.

This past spring break, I decided the kids and I would spend three days and two nights at Great Wolf Lodge, an indoor water-park-slash-hotel not too far away from where we live. It's a pretty big resort chain that you probably don't know about—and one you definitely would never stay at—unless you have kids. To me, it looked like a pretty good deal—a hotel with enough activities to entertain the kids without me? I was IN.

Of course, I had come to that conclusion through a discount booking website at three-thirty in the morning. In retrospect, daylight hours are preferable for making travel plans.

But at the time, I felt more than up to the challenge, because while I wasn't bringing Todd, I was bringing Julie to help shoulder the parenting. Julie is a Stay-at-Home Mom I met when our kids were in preschool together—her son Luke is Jesse's age, and her daughter Quinn is the same age as Phoebe. When your kids are the same age and sex as your friend's kids, it's like hitting the playdate jackpot.

We'd first bonded over a mutual friend in New York who I knew from growing up and who Julie knew from her life as a "person" before kids.

"Tara Newman?!" she'd squealed. "I worked with her when I was in publicity! Oh my God, she's great!"

"Can't stand her," I said flatly. "Awful person. Truly hateful."

We've been close ever since.

Julie had many qualities I didn't like—she'd given up a career and pants with zippers to dedicate her life to her children and took actual pleasure in organizing their Legos. She always had wet wipes and Neosporin in her bag and a "Momgenda" calendar on her kitchen wall (I have one, too, but it remains open to January 2014). But Julie didn't pretend to be happy with every single one of her choices. She was bored, she was unfulfilled, and she ate stale Halloween candy in the middle of the night like a civilian.

On top of all that, our kids were ages where they could go off and invade a kid-centric contained space like Great Wolf Lodge while we got to sit back, relax, and complain to each other—me about the burdens of supporting a family, Julie about the crushing depression caused by spending her days immersed in children.

"I'm so jealous of you," she'd say.

"I'm so jealous of you," I'd say.

Julie was the secret weapon in my quest to survive the Great Wolf Lodge expedition, and I was damned proud of myself for coming up with the strategy—so proud, in fact, that when a class email went around about a lice epidemic a week before school let out, I decided to cast the net even wider—safety in numbers, after all.

"Phoebe had two eggs behind one ear and the mama behind the other, but the mobile lice lady came and fried them off her head for thirty bucks," I replied to all, adding, "By the way, I'm taking my kids to Great Wolf Lodge over spring break—if anyone is going to be there."

The response I got was overwhelming—not about the lice eggs, but about Great Wolf Lodge.

I was called brave and a better person than I. Quite a few moms responded, "You couldn't pay me enough money to go there" and "Please tell your kids not to tell my kids that place really exists!"

That should have been all I needed to know. Did I really think that I—who can't survive a trip to the mall without losing my car, my wallet, my mind, and/or at least one child—was a match for a world where even the most intrepid of über-moms feared to tread?

But you're not going alone, I reminded myself. This gave me strength, as did my standard mantra on Guilt Trips: This is for them, not you. We may not have been legion, Julie and I, but we were a team. Hell, it worked for Thelma and Louise. Until the over-the-cliff thing.

THE MORNING OF our trip, Jesse, Phoebe, and I loaded into the car while Todd—his slightly above-average good looks enhanced by euphoria at the prospect of a weekend to himself—heaved our suitcases into the trunk with one arm, demonstrating a strength and determination he usually reserves for adjusting the satellite dish. He hovered, grinning from ear to ear as he wished me luck—he'd been copied on the email tree about the lice and seen the ominous warnings against Great Wolf Lodge.

"Are you sure about this?" he asked, his attempt at concern a pathetic cover for the elated smile he couldn't suppress.

"I'm not that inept a mother," I snapped, slamming my door; I needed more Starbucks, two cup holders full was not enough. "I can handle a night away with my own children."

"It's two nights, Liz," he corrected me.

I put the car in reverse and had that sudden twinge of panic—two nights?! Could I do this? Could I actually keep a seven- and nine-year-old alive for two nights?!

Of course I could. I was their mother, they came from me. Phoebe had my thighs and stink-eye, and Jesse, my anxiety—what more proof did I need? We are apiece. We'd be fine.

That said, I immediately called Julie to make sure she was on her way—I didn't want to arrive before she did.

She was on the road, she said, she'd see me soon. I smiled into the rearview mirror at my kids.

"I'm so excited to spend time with you guys!" I said.

"You're going to come in the water, right?" Phoebe asked from the backseat.

Um . . . "No, Sweet Pea."

"What about the water slide?" Jesse asked.

Ummmm . . . "No, Doodle-Bug. But we are going to spend a lot of time together!" I cheered. "Or at least near each other," I mumbled into my coffee.

". . . What do you mean, 'near each other,' Mama?" Phoebe asked.

I glanced back at my daughter. She can't hear when I tell her to bring her soccer cleats inside before it rains or not to use an entire roll of toilet paper every time she wipes, but when I don't want her to hear something, Phoebe's a Doberman. She gets this from her father.

"I mean that I'll be near you because we're gonna all be together," I said, turning the music up to drown out any future utterances.

"Can you just give me a little bit of space?" Jesse hollered, his hands by his ears, gesticulating wildly in frustration. "For once in my life?"

"Jesse's looking at me!" I heard Phoebe scream.

Jesse and Phoebe were in that developmental stage where siblings become like a married couple, who have ironically become like siblings who can't stand each other. They commenced lunging for each other as far as their seatbelts allowed. I let them fight, safe in the knowledge that Luke and Quinn would be great distractions in a matter of hours.

WE PULLED UP to Great Wolf Lodge, which from the outside looked more like an industrial park than a hotel, only with giant boulders on either side of the entrance. Maybe they were kidding about the "lodge" theme. I wondered if the rest of the place was going to be a corporate cavern, which made me suddenly nervous about the food. Would it be amusement park fare, with fish battered and not a vegetable besides French fries in sight? I was trying to be healthy and avoid saturated fats—an instinct forged and buffed to a high paranoia by a lifetime of food-related traumas and subsequent eating disorders. Parking the car, I reminded myself that the trip wasn't about me, but about spending quality time with my children.

The kids, finally free to smack each other, left me to drag our luggage across the lot, along with my purse packed to bursting with goggles, water bottles, snacks, my wallet, and the various pills I would need to keep me sane when required and unconscious at the end of the day.

My fears of Great Wolf Lodge not having committed to the "lodge" theme were quickly assuaged. The giant lobby was lodge themed, as conceived in the mind of a meth addict. Faux log walls appeared haphazardly around un-upholstered log chairs, moose antler chandeliers, and lamps in the shape of bears either hugging or humping foliage. Trees sprouted out of nowhere amongst indoor-patio furniture, fireplaces, and one giant clock to remind me that it was still very early in the day.

The décor turned out to be the least of my concerns. That's because hotels made Jesse anxious. We'd been involved in exactly ONE MINOR hotel fire years earlier, which inconveniently happened in the middle of the night, and ever since then, my son had been terrified beyond reason every time we stayed anywhere another fire might break out. It's like he didn't realize that our house could catch on fire, too. Easily. I leave candles burning constantly. Even ablaze, though, that hotel had been an order of magnitude nicer than GWL. They had great salads, too.

In an attempt to soothe himself in the forest primordial that was his current surroundings, Jesse launched into a series of rapid-fire questions, pausing for neither answers nor air.

"How many rooms are there How many people can stay here What's the fire department limit What if the fire alarm goes off Can that fire get out of the fireplace Are there ample emergency exits . . .?"

Seizing a break when he paused to inhale, I assured him that we were in a water park and that there was definitely enough water to put any fire out.

Which didn't bring the result I hoped for. "So, there's going to be a fire?!" he shrieked, stricken.

Afraid of doing more damage, I left him to his panic and took in my cellmates. The line to check in extended from the reservation desk, snaking all the way to the little boy cubs' and little girl cubs' rooms on the other side of the lobby, and folding in on itself about six times. Order was maintained via those plastic rope things they have in banks and airports; I wondered when the next flight out was. Crying babies, clingy children, sweaty teenagers, and weary mothers and fathers all squeezed together. By choice, mind you—

we'd all paid for this, and even on Expedia, places like this didn't come cheap.

"Mama, look . . ." Phoebe called to me. She was a few feet away, smiling proudly under a five-foot squirrel.

"Wow!" I said, pretending to be impressed by it.

"Mama, look!" Phoebe shouted from the same spot. Still smiling.

"I see!" I said, wondering what the hell I was supposed to be looking at.

"Mama, look!"

Nothing had changed. She was even still smiling.

"I SEE you, PHOEBEEEE!" I snapped, drawing judgmental stares from everyone within earshot. Even the lady with the kid on a leash raised her eyebrows, though my guess was that if she had her kid on a leash, she'd probably done her share of yelling in public.

Regardless, I was immediately ashamed. The big bear paw on the clock hadn't even moved one minute, and I was already losing my shit. *This is for them, not you*, I reminded myself. *You love them.*

"I'm sorry, Phoebe," I offered, for her benefit and everyone else's. "It's just that I saw you already once and I didn't know what more you wanted me to see—"

"—I was standing under a squirrel!" she said cheerily.

"Yes, but you were standing under the squirrel the first time, and I already saw you, so why did you need me to . . . you know what? Never mind." No sense in reasoning with a seven-year-old. I should just be happy she wanted me to look at her. And that the line was moving.

I scanned the crowd looking for Julie, praying she hadn't gotten a flat tire or into an accident—because then I'd have to be alone for even longer. I texted her: Are you here? Where are you? She didn't respond right away. I sent again. And again. My daughter's impulse to confirm her need for attention didn't come from nowhere.

Phoebe and Jesse were now actually fighting on me. She was biting him, and he was squeezing her head. She's a biter. He's a head squeezer. I told them both through gritted teeth to stop it or else. Jesse, feeling badly for making me upset, hugged me and licked my arm. I pushed him off me and then—because my anxiety was triggering my need for symmetry—I asked him to lick the other arm discreetly and then to stop for real.

Arms evenly licked, Jesse went back to questions. "What if someone in a loose-fitting shirt sits too close to a fire and runs around spreading it?"

"Don't worry," I answered—if the people on line were any indicator, there wasn't a flowing garment for miles. I stared at the back of the gentleman in front of us, sweating profusely through his mesh tank top. The scorpion tattooed on his neck had the word *Daddy* in one of its pincers, blood dripping off the *Y* for some reason. The guy's girlfriend was wearing the merest suggestion of a string bikini, her triple-D's straining against the top in a way that I think alarmed even her. They had no children with them, so I could only assume they were into some sick shit that was enhanced by a log cabin–type backdrop. I stepped back as they started making out, backed right into a third party's sweaty appendage, and froze, too scared to look and see who it belonged to.

Just then, like an un-perspiring ray of light from heaven, I spotted Julie approaching, Quinn and Luke in tow. Like Jesse and Phoebe, Quinn and Luke were also headed for divorce. Julie and I hugged. I clung to Julie for too long, and she let me—God, did I look that traumatized?

Our kids ran off together. Julie was completely unfazed by the lobby décor—a happy, positive reminder of why I'd come.

"You look beautiful," I told her. She did—a vision in sweat-pants. She didn't tell me I looked pretty, but I was okay with it. Kind of.

We finally got to the front of the line, and the Park Ranger who was checking people in. I now saw why it took so long: it wasn't a check-in, it was an orientation. There were "wands" to distribute, and "Paw Passes" for each guest, as well as lanyards with barcoded tags that doubled as both room keys and Mommy's credit card (so nothing stood between your kids and anything retail). The Paw Passes, we learned, entitled each kid to a free stuffed animal, a cup of Mike and Ikes, and a liter of soda. The passes also came with barcodes that could be used to buy things just in case the lanyard barcode got lost or gnawed on. Great Wolf Lodge, it seemed, was the most genius consumer marketing plan ever.

"The wands are for the room," the Park Ranger said, handing over the last of the swag.

"Wands?" I blurted. "Cool—I forgot my light-up dildo." This resulted in my first "shush" from Julie. Clearly, I'd forgotten I wasn't in a room full of comedy writers.

Equipped with our armfuls of barcoded money-sucking plastics, we corralled the kids and headed to our rooms, passing the restaurant on the way. A giant grizzly bear stood outside the entrance, leaning on a sandwich board with the menu written on it. Turned out I hadn't been too far off in my dietary projections—the only vegetable listed was a double-stuffed potato.

"Ooh, double-stuffed potatoes!" Julie said, "I'm getting two. I'm on vacation!"

To me, this was a vacation like I was a virgin. But for my kids, this . . . actually, was a vacation. And this was for them. Not me. *You love them. You love them that much.*

Our room, or Wolf Den, kept with the log cabin theme—God

forbid we forget we are trapped in a plastic forest while we sleep. There were bunk beds, which I knew would be the source of endless "top bunk" fighting, and the walls boasted a painted mural with fairies and woodland creatures. Jesse, anxious to get to the waterpark and pretty much just anxious in general, changed quickly into his swimsuit and met Luke in the hall outside Julie's room. I heard him saying something about a fire alarm and asking whether there was one in Luke's room, but as Jesse began rattling off hotel fire death statistics, I was distracted by Quinn, who came crashing into our room, wand in hand, and did something that I still think Julie should have punished her for.

"Watch," she said to Phoebe, and pointed her wand at one of the fairies and it . . . came alive—that's really the only way to describe what that fairy did. Its head, which I could have sworn was painted onto the wall, moved side to side and its wings, which had also seemed painted . . . flapped. Same with the woodland creatures—with each wave of Quinn's wand, they came alive. With a second wave, they started speaking to us in high-pitched cartoon voices.

It was your basic terror shit, in a Karen-Black-devil-doll-movie way, only with demons stuck to walls. In an indoor waterpark/hotel. I had two questions: Why? and Is this how I am going to die?

"Mama, look . . ." Phoebe called to me. She was by the bed, smiling proudly pointing her wand at a butterfly that flapped its wings before running to another butterfly. And another. More flapping. So many flapping wings. And I was paying for this. And Julie was calling it a "vacation."

I struggled to breathe and fumbled for a Klonopin. *This is for them*, I thought, *not you. You love them. You can eat a potato for your children. You can sleep in a nightmare room.*

Once changed, we took several elevators for what felt like several hours down to a lower-lower-sub-subterranean level of the building, working our way past sweaty traffic through a loud and teeming arcade of shops and kiosks—all accepting Paw Passes from children as currency, no parent required. Genius.

We reached the end of the arcade and paused by the set of glass doors. Behind them lay Valhalla—the indoor waterpark itself. The moment we entered, I was hit with a blast of thick, wet "air," the smell of chlorine so strong I knew that whatever murder Great Wolf Lodge was trying to cover up, they'd succeeded. I gave my eyes a minute to stop stinging and tearing up (some of this was crying), after which I was confronted with absolute, soaking wet, lodge-themed bedlam.

The sound hit me in that instant, much as the "air" had moments before—a cacophony of rushing water, feet slapping on wet cement, screaming, crying, squealing, and every few seconds a weird grinding sound, followed by a bell coming from a gigantic, eight-million-gallon water pail near the ceiling that tipped over, threatening to fall and crush about a hundred people before it would (yay!) dump water on them instead.

There was a giant wave pool, where masses of children bobbed up and down. It reminded me of the end of the movie *Titanic*—and, I guess, the real-life one, too. There were also big colored tubes suspended in the air that made up an elaborate maze of water slides that emptied into pools, all of them surrounded by a lazy river.

A line of fun-seekers, just like the ones in the lobby except with fewer clothes on, meandered up a huge set of stairs to the top, where the slides begin. There were splash pads, slip 'n' slides, a chute that just dropped brave people out of the sky into the middle of all the chaos, and—of course—a concession stand serving overpriced, damp food. Paw Passes accepted.

Between the ill-fitting bathing suits and the complimentary

towels—which were postage stamp–sized—a real fuck-you if you ask me—I found myself pretty much at a nudist colony with no one who should ever be naked, ever.

"Why would grown adults run around in public looking like this . . . ?!" I shouted, earning my second Julie-issued *shush* of the trip.

I turned back to the doors (just to make sure they still opened) and next to them saw a sign that read:

PERSONS CURRENTLY HAVING ACTIVE DIARRHEA
OR WHO HAVE HAD ACTIVE DIARRHEA IN THE
PREVIOUS 14 DAYS SHALL NOT BE ALLOWED TO
ENTER THE POOL WATER

I could only speculate as to what "active" meant to the legal team behind Great Wolf Lodge, but it was safe to assume that even formal-sounding words like *shall* and *previous* weren't going to stop this crowd from going in the water with, presumably, shit. I was horrified. But mostly, I was grateful that I wouldn't have to so much as dip a toe in that shit river. I wasn't too worried about my kids, either, because their systems were newer and stronger than mine, and I'd prepared them for situations just like this one by not making people sanitize their hands before holding them when they were newborns and allowing them to eat stuff off the kitchen floor.

I waded through the fog and saw that Julie had already secured a table. She pointed to where our kids were—Quinn and Phoebe on the splash pad, laughing and jumping, and Jesse and Luke in the wave pool.

"Did you see the diarrhea sign?" Julie asked.

"I know!" I said, settling into the soaking wet chair next to her. "Thank God we don't have to go in that fucking water."

"Isn't this great?" She meant it, too.

"You know what? It is. For them," I said and meant it, too. Our kids were having a blast, and that was what mattered.

This is about them. Not you. You love them. You can sleep in a nightmare room for them. You can breathe in toxic swamp air.

We grabbed the kids some damp chicken tenders and fries from the concession stand. Then we sat together and talked and laughed, reminiscing about all the preschool parties I'd forgotten to bring paper plates to. Jesse waved to me happily, and Phoebe even came over to check in. I took advantage of this precious moment and hugged her tightly, careful not to get any water in my mouth. I even found myself starting to get sad that the weekend would soon be over and almost felt guilty that this guilt trip was turning out so pleasant.

Then out of the fog, Quinn appeared, shoulders slumped.

"What's wrong, honey?" Julie asked, concerned.

Quinn said something inaudible, her head on Julie's shoulder.

"Oh no, really . . .? You just rest, sweetheart," Julie soothed. ". . . Do you want something to eat? Chicken tenders, fries?"

Quinn mumbled something else, as Julie looked at me, concerned. "She's not hungry," Julie mouthed.

A sopping Phoebe approached, looking for Quinn. I told her Quinn would be there in a minute, that she was just taking a little break.

That was when Julie announced she was taking Quinn back to the room, to lie down—it was a headache, she'd give her some Tylenol, she was sure it would pass. I was sure it would pass, too. It had to.

They disappeared.

Phoebe got sad. Her lower lip pouted out, followed by huge crocodile tears that formed giant pools in her lower lids, just before flying out of her face. She wiped them away with one chubby little prune-y hand. I could handle Sad Phoebe with a hug and a few tickles. But her eyes quickly narrowed, her hands balled up into fists, and she turned into Mad Phoebe.

"This is the worst day EVER! I am not going to play by myself NO MATTER WHAT!" she shouted over the sound of rushing water while stomping in place, purposely splashing me with indoor puddle water. I was going to need to talk to her "feelings doctor" about her spitefulness. But for the moment, I just gently steered her into the shallow end of the puddle and asked her what she would like me to do.

She wanted me to go on the big slide with her—the highest one, the death-defying one. I wasn't doing that. I told her maybe tomorrow. I also wasn't doing that.

Jesse and Luke passed the table, and I told them to take Phoebe on the slide. Luke was going on it, but Jesse didn't want to, he was afraid, he wanted Dippin' Dots instead. I told him to knock himself out, that's what the Paw Pass was there for. Luke and Phoebe hit the slide. Jesse was mainlining sugar and feeling like a baller.

My right hand hurt. I looked down and saw that in the short time since Julie had skipped out on me, I'd dug four bleeding half-moons into my right palm with my nails.

"Mama! Look at me!" Phoebe called from the top of the slide.

"Wow!" I shouted, pretending to be impressed, wondering if Stay-at-Home Moms had to look at their kids as often or if it was a "making up for lost time" kind of a thing. Either way, it was almost dinnertime, and I had made it through the first day without having to go in the water. Success.

When we got to the restaurant, Julie flagged me down from a table in the back corner. I assumed that the afternoon's headache was gone, and we could get on with our trip. But when we got closer, I saw what had been obscured by a bus station in the form of a treehouse—Quinn, face down on her bread plate. I tried to pretend I didn't notice, not making a big deal out of it and hoping Julie would forget about the fact that her daughter's hair had butter in it. But Julie was obsessed, constantly fussing over Quinn. She was that kind of mother. She was also the kind of mother who, if her kid was sick, would take them home, even if it meant her friend would be left alone at an indoor waterpark with whatever "active diarrhea" was.

I looked at Quinn—the side of her face that was exposed, at least. It was pale and slightly green. I got an idea.

I was regarded by Julie's kids as the "funny Mom," the "silly Mom." I'd earned the title about five years earlier, when our kids were toddlers and we were all at a playground. Julie and I had been watching them from a nearby park bench. I had to work later and would be no doubt pulling an all-nighter or close to it. Julie was saddled with her kids' grueling bedtime routine but didn't have a deadline for a script looming.

"Ugh, you're so lucky," I said.

"Ugh, you're so lucky," she said.

Suddenly the sky got dark, thunder boomed, and the kids came running over to us. Jesse, sensitive to sound, was inconsolable. This was when, as I often do when I don't know what to do to calm a child, I improvised. Standing up, I broke into a random imperson-ation of a large, grumpy, orange cartoon fish named Mr. Grouper from a popular show at the time called *Bubble Guppies*. Singing loudly, shamelessly, I got Jesse and all the kids to forget the thun-der and the bolt of lightning that had just lit up the monkey bars. Before we knew it, they were all laughing hysterically while Julie and I hauled ass to the car.

Back at Great Wolf Lodge, sitting at dinner, I figured that Mr.

Grouper might be the only thing that was going to bring Quinn back to life. I stood up and hunched forward, assuming Mr. Grouper's signature stance—hands (fins) on hips—and started to sing, loudly.

Sadly, in the five years since the lightning episode, the children had unfortunately and mysteriously grown older (go figure). Mr. Grouper not only didn't help Quinn feel better, it made her face sink deeper into the plate she was resting it on. She was now feeling worse. And so was I. All seemed lost.

Until Luke moved in on his sister's untouched crayons. Sensing this, Quinn suddenly and miraculously perked up, grabbed her fork, and lunged at her brother. My heart leapt at the sight of them rolling around on the floor in a fist fight. Had I known something like that would make her rally, I'd've grabbed her crayons earlier, instead of her potato (Julie had been right: two double-stuffed potatoes was the way to go). I didn't even notice or care that Phoebe and Jesse were now going at it—him squeezing her head, Phoebe biting him back—or that the whole restaurant was staring.

"Maybe I should take her temperature?" Julie pondered.

"Let's just take them for a walk and burn off the energy," I advised in a rush. "And we can talk about tomorrow, because you guys'll definitely be here." It was not the time for subtlety. This was a crisis.

This is about them. Not you. You love them. You can sleep in a nightmare room for them. You can breathe in toxic swamp air for them. And you can risk the health and well-being of a child.

We had walked around the hotel and past the arcade, where Julie and I presented a united front on not spending money on video games, a united front on not buying the kids wizard hats (which had no place in a "Lodge" and shame on this hotel for trying to make Harry Potter money), and a united front on no fourth desserts for anybody. I needed Julie—I wasn't present enough to my children to spoil this quality time by saying no to them. That would negate the whole point of our Guilt Trip. But if Julie laid down the law, I could piggyback on it and not be the bad guy. United front.

Finally, like we had done hours before at the pool, Julie and I were able to sit in the chlorinated air and catch up, free once again to complain about our lives to each other. It was turning into a beautiful night under the fluorescent lights of the window-less waterpark/hotel, when Quinn started to plummet. Again. Her headache came back, her shoulders slumped, her face went pink.

No no no no no no no no no. *Come on, Quinn*, I thought, *you activated demons in my room—you don't want me to hate you! Come on, Quinn!*

"Come on, Quinn," I hissed.

Quinn put her head in Julie's chest. I suggested a fourth dessert might perk her up, after all.

Julie got that concerned mama face: furrowed brow and the kind of deep frown the lady at the Estée Lauder counter told me causes irreversible aging. But Julie appeared to be more worried about her child than aging. Something I personally thought she would regret someday. I was definitely regretting it already. Before I could say anything, though, I heard her start to say, "Maybe I should just take her home—"

"No!!!" I almost screamed. "Get a good night's sleep. Maybe all the . . . lack of sun wore her out. Maybe she just needs to pass active diarrhea!" I was frantic. But Julie took my advice, and they headed up to bed.

"Sleep well!" I called to the elevators, a little threateningly, pointedly at Quinn. "See you tomorrow—it's gonna be great!!!"

"Is Quinn sick?" Jesse asked, in his genuinely caring way.

"She's fine," I snapped.

"Can I get a toy?" Phoebe asked, in her genuinely not-giving-one-shit way.

I assured both of them, but mostly myself, that Quinn would be fine. She'd be fine.

The good news was that there was no fighting over the bunk beds. That was because when we opened the door to the room, a phantom frog on the wall was activated, its loud and sudden cartoon croak sending Jesse running down the hall, screaming "FIRE!!!!"

In the end, both kids slept with me in my bigger-than-a-twin, smaller-than-a-full-sized bed with tall but narrow irregular pillows, Jesse softly wiggling his toes on my legs and snoring, Phoebe smacking her lips in a way that made me almost violent. There was only a thin corner of blanket reserved for me, and I couldn't get any of it to me because Phoebe was on it.

This is about them, I thought to myself, *not you. You love them. You can sleep in a nightmare room for them. You can sit in a toxic swamp for them. You can risk the health and well-being of a child for them. And you can go without sleep for two nights for them.*

I must have slept some, however, because I woke to a text. From Julie.

We are leaving after breakfast.

I looked at the text again. I could barely type back.

No! What's wrong?! I wrote, trying to sound oblivious because if I acted like Quinn being sick yesterday wasn't a big deal, then maybe Julie would think it wasn't a big deal either and stay.

Quinn was up all night on and off, she wrote, adding a teary emoji.

I fought the urge to flush my phone down the toilet. Me too! I wrote back, adding, I think maybe there's something wrong with the AC . . . I was getting desperate. Texting wasn't going to cut it—I needed to persuade Julie in person.

I got the kids ready, and we hustled down to the same restaurant as the night before, now laid out with an all-you-can-devour, saturated-fat buffet. I didn't tell them our friends might leave. I didn't want to upset . . . me.

Jesse raced off and filled four plates with pancakes, chocolate sauce, marshmallows, and syrup. Phoebe dove into the communal scrambled egg platter with her hands and face. I clocked the fact that there wasn't a single egg-white option.

Finally, Julie appeared with her kids, all dragging suitcases behind them. No denying it—Quinn looked like shit.

Julie said they were leaving. I reminded her that she had said they were leaving after breakfast, not mentioning I was planning on keeping the kids munching till three in the afternoon.

No, they were going to grab something to go, she wanted to get Quinn home, it looked like strep throat.

I told her I thought that was a mistake, that she was coddling Quinn. Pulling out the big guns, I said I'd read as much in a parenting book. Written by . . . experts. The experts talked all about how indulging kids over every little strep infection sent a message that they could just leave vacations every time they were sick and looked awful, and GOD, Quinn really looked AWFUL.

But Julie wasn't interested in experts, she was listening to her maternal instincts, much like the Botticelli-esque painting by the elevator bank of the mama bear with the huge ass, tending to her cub. Julie was a mama bear. Quinn was her cub. I was furious.

"Would you stop trying to control my entire life?!" I heard Jesse yelling.

"Mom!!!! Jesse's being meeeeaaaan!" I heard Phoebe keening.

I wished they would just get a divorce, already.

The next thirty hours played out in my imagination like one of the fever dreams I hoped Quinn would have the entire ride home. I loved her, but right now I was very angry. She was abandoning me in an indoor water park with these people—"these people" being my kids, who wouldn't give me a moment's peace. And would deny me any real estate in my own bed. And make me go in the water and swim in active diarrhea.

I was desperate.

"Nobody leaves!" I shouted, no longer fucking around. "We all agreed—we promised—to stay at Great Wolf Lodge until check-out tomorrow"—I gestured to the giant clock—"when the little paw is on three and the big paw is on—"

"Liz, Quinn is sick," Julie laughed. Sort of. She made a break for the door, waving her good-byes to Jesse and Phoebe.

Miracle of miracles, Luke announced that he wanted to stay. He was mad at his sister for being sick. I was too. I'd always liked him more than Quinn.

Miracle of miracles, Quinn then mustered up the little bit of non-infected energy she had left to say she wanted to stay, too. She was kind of having trouble walking anyway, so leaving would have been cruel.

Silently, I was begging. The kids were not-silently begging and getting louder by the moment.

Then Quinn threw up.

"Ugh, you're so lucky," Julie said.

"Ugh, you're so lucky," I said.

Then they were gone.

I turned to Jesse and Phoebe, who stared at me expectantly. I told them I wouldn't be mad if they wanted to go home. They didn't want to go home. I promised I wouldn't be mad. No luck. I shooed them back to the buffet and called Todd.

I told him the place was actually great and that he should meet us. I told him about the whole camping theme—I think I even called it a "motif"—and said I felt bad that he was missing out on the trip of a lifetime. Also, I said we could do sex things in the bunk bed after the kids were asleep, as long as we were quick and I could keep my sweatpants on.

He said no. He couldn't come. Because he didn't want to.

I started to pretend-cry and told him how gross the place was. I real-cried a little, appealing to his sympathy for the kids—with Quinn and Luke gone, they had no one now.

"They have you," he said, and told me he thought that was great. He told me how much the kids loved being with me, something that continued to boggle my mind. I could never understand why they followed me around and got happy when I came home. Why Jesse was always asking me questions. Why Phoebe always wanted me to look at her. When I was a kid . . . I never wanted my parents to look at me. Mostly because it usually resulted in forced exercise or a bowl haircut.

"I can't go in the water, Todd." I was full-on fake sobbing now. But he'd already wished me luck and hung up.

Dipping a waffle in chocolate sauce with my free hand, I called every mom friend I could think of and offered them a free night's stay at Great Wolf Lodge. And anything else of mine they wanted. I even called an immature writer friend who loves Disney World and secretly plays with Barbie Dolls. No takers.

It came down to me, the last mom standing. Time to sink or (not) swim. I whipped out my trusty Paw Pass, and we headed for the arcade.

Stuffed animals, rubber bracelets with their names, a wizard hat, arcade cards—you name it, I charged it. I broke a sweat trying to win Phoebe a stuffed pickle in the claw machine—to everyone's delight, I succeeded. I let Jesse go on a motorcycle ride so many times he's definitely going to be infertile, but desperate times.

It was inevitable, however. Eventually they tired of the arcade and wanted to go to the waterpark. I suggested a mini golf course just thirty minutes away.

But Jesse wanted to go back in the wave pool—as my luck would have it, something about the pressure of the water against his chest soothed his nerves. Phoebe wanted to hit the giant slide. With me.

I told her that Jesse would take her. Jesse turned pale.

"The wooden structure isn't strong enough to hold that many people," he said. "Especially with all the moisture in the air." He made a good point.

"Please, Mama?" Phoebe begged. "Please, will you go with me?"

About to stay strong in my no, Jesse suddenly announced that if I went on the giant slide, he would face his fear of rotting wood structures and come with us. Phoebe jumped up and down, delighted. The two of them were suddenly, actually getting along. For the first time maybe ever.

I took it in.

This is about them, I thought to myself, *not you. You love them. You can sleep in a nightmare room. You can breathe toxic swamp air. You can risk a child's health. You can go without sleep.*

And you can go in the shit-water for them.

Minutes later, in a bright orange, children's extra-extra-large one-piece bathing suit from the Bear Essentials Swim Shop, I entered the waterpark. Once inside, I grabbed a pile of teeny beach towels and attempted to spread them over my body. Even together, they amounted to the size of a washcloth. It took both hands to hold them in place—one over each thigh. (Unlike Jesse and Phoebe and seemingly everyone else in the place, I didn't have that childlike innocence that would make me unaware of what my body looked like in comparison to other people's. I hadn't even had that when I was an actual child.)

We slowly ascended the wooden staircase for the tallest water slide. It was the longest and slowest line in the park, in the hotel, and quite possibly in California. Adding insult to panic, everyone in the line carried a giant inner tube. I carried three, one over each shoulder and one around my neck that I could barely see over. My mouth and nose were both pressed up against what I was certain was diseased rubber, my hands still clutching the two washcloths over my thighs.

I tried not to breathe through my nose. I tried not to breathe through my mouth. Somewhere around my legs, my son (I hoped it was my son; there was no way to check) was clinging to me for dear life. Terrified with every shake of the staircase, he started pulling on me—where he thought we could go was anybody's guess. We were trapped in every sense. I lifted the inner tube every so often to yell, "CALM DOWN!" in his general direction, wondering how long I'd be able to set an example, surrounded by sagging bathing suits and body parts, my eyes watering from chlorine fumes and sweat and claustrophobia. I was about to mingle with all that hair. All those toes. All that . . . toe hair. The guy with the *Daddy* tattoo with blood dripping off the *Y*, who I'd just spotted ahead of us . . .

I was about to lose it completely, suffocating for real, when we suddenly found ourselves at the top of the steps on a slick platform. Jesse whooped with relief, having faced and conquered his fear. I'd've been more excited for him if I wasn't about to face my own fear—being shot into a pool of doody water in an itchy children's bathing suit.

Like an assembly line, we were separated and sent to separate slide openings, where we were instructed to place our inner tubes in the water and sit in them with our legs spread.

"You must see some horrible things," I half-joked to one poor young employee, who closed her eyes and solemnly nodded. In a way that suggested future PTSD. I dropped my towels reluctantly and took my place.

"Mama, look!" Phoebe called to me, joyous.

I looked at her on one side of me. "Wow!"

"Mom, look!" Jesse called to me.

I look at him on my other side. "Wow!"

"Mama, LOOK!" Phoebe screamed.

"For FUCK's SAKE, I'm LOOKING, PHOEBE!" I screamed back, just as—with a giant PUSH—I was starting my descent through the chute.

Swishing around, I knocked into the walls, I was upside down, I was right side up, I was completely out of my comfort zone . . .

. . . And I was laughing my ass off.

All three of us seemed to shoot out the bottom of our holes at the same time into what was no doubt a pool of shit. Our inner tubes banged against each other's as, laughing hysterically, we spit water out of our mouths and decided to go again.

And again and again.

I didn't even slow down for tiny towels. My thighs—a shade of pale only seen in a morgue—were exposed. I was a sea of cellulite breaking over sagging knee skin. It had been so long since I'd shaved my legs, I looked like I was making some kind of a political statement. All of this in the bathing suit I'd put on backwards— I don't know why I'd assumed the image of the wolf went in front, but seeing its long snout ending in a wet, black nose at my crotch, it was suddenly obvious to me I'd been mistaken.

I didn't care. I'd found a lack of awareness and self-consciousness about my body that I'd never known. I was free—in this prison of a waterpark/hotel, I was freer than I'd ever been.

The next morning, I had the kids up an hour before the water-park opened. We spent the whole day immersed in rotavirus and joy. Taking on one slide, then another slide and another and another. Another and another. We went on the thing that dropped you from the sky—I'm pretty sure in hindsight that this was a ride they just never finished constructing. They never had to; it was perfect the way it was. We couldn't get enough of it.

BY THE TIME the little paw was on the four and the big paw on the six, the kids were waterlogged and pooped—literally. And I was on the slides myself while they maxed out their Paw Passes. They were finally ready to leave Great Wolf Lodge.

I was the one who begged them to go on one last slide, promising it would be my last. I promised. But I was lying, and I got to go back up and down and back again. Because I'm their mother, and I said so.

And this was my Guilt Trip, too.

Rules of Estrangement

For a long time, it was impossible for me to be estranged from my mother. And that wasn't for a lack of trying. Years after deciding that for my own mental well-being I needed to put some serious distance between us, my mother continued to email me constantly, call me relentlessly, and send me countless friend requests on Facebook. (Social media, by the way, makes it very, very hard to shake a person. Even with "privacy settings.")

Instead of ignoring her pestering however, which is what you're supposed to do, I felt the need to make it clear that I wasn't ignoring her because I was rude, but because we were estranged. So, I would call her to tell her as much, thus breaking the rules of estrangement.

Also, she did other shit that made me have to reach out. Like the time she stole my identity and got a credit card in my name ("Just for the Marriott points," she told me, when I was forced to contact her). Or when, more recently, she tried to OD on Vicodin and what she claimed was cleaning fluid but of course wasn't cleaning fluid because she's never held a cleaning product in her hands. Being a person, I called and left a just-checking-in-to-make-sure-you're-alive-but-don't-call-me-back-because-we're-estranged message. Which isn't the best way to be estranged.

After the overdose, however, she was at long last deemed unable to care for herself, and it fell to my older brother, Jeff, to put her in an assisted living situation in Los Angeles, where all three of us live. Jeff is also a comedy writer—and my best friend. He's hilariously funny, sublimely sarcastic, and, at times, a competitive asshole. This is due in no small part to my father placing him on a pedestal during his formative years, as did his teachers and principals. He was far and away the smartest kid in his class and got straight A's, but only because there was nothing higher. Given our town's proximity to potato farms, as well as the popularity of psychedelic drugs among his peers, Jeff's graduating class of 1982 didn't have a ton of . . . graduates. Jeff went on to an Ivy League school where he continued to soar and, well, now can't handle failure as a result of it all. He is also a survivor of our childhood, with challenges different from, but no less challenging than, my own. I love him for it all.

I hadn't wanted to visit our mother but, like my mother, Jeff doesn't fully understand the rules of estrangement, so he asked me to come with him. I couldn't say no. Not when he needed me. Not when I, too, don't fully understand the rules of estrangement. Which was how I found myself at the Jewish Home for the Aged on a Sunday afternoon.

Jeff and I met her in the facility's dining room. I hadn't seen my mother in several years and she was barely recognizable. She was old for seventy-three—hunched over and drugged out of her mind.

Her skin was sallow, her eyes sagged, her nose job . . . actually the nose job still looked pretty good. She wore a short, dirty-blond wig that sat crookedly on her head.

She looked up from her lunch, which was four globs of some sort of Chinese-themed food. "Hi, sweetheart," she mumbled.

I leaned in, patted her shoulder, and kissed the air near her face, surprised that she didn't smell too much like her lunch. I had to fight any feelings of compassion I had for this former-terrorist-turned-old-woman. I also had to fight my nausea.

Sitting at her table, Jeff made small talk with her while I took in the atmosphere, the thin carpeting and plastic tables—nothing matching but who cared, no one stayed here long anyway. The wheelchairs, the oxygen tanks, the stale, medicinal, and weirdly cheese-and-cracker smell. The old people, diminished versions of their younger selves, some unable to hold up their heads, some surrounded by family that looked like they just wanted to get the hell out of there and get on with their day.

All this led me to a decision I needed to share with my husband immediately. I texted Todd:

I'm going to kill myself the minute I start showing signs of old age or sickness.

Okay, he shot back.

I loved him so much.

Seriously, Todd, I continued. "So brave," "soldiered on in spite of her condition," or even "put up a good fight" will not be said about me.

Cool, I'll help, he responded immediately. He knew where I was, why I was saying what I was saying, and he also knew I meant it.

So, we went back and forth, planning my Todd-assisted suicide. Todd was super helpful; I had no idea he was so creative that way. He told me that jumping off a building or roof wasn't a great idea because there's the possibility that I would survive and have to wear whatever the nurses put me in. He knows me so well.

We were about to land on exactly how I would die (something involving a pillow and smothering, but enough pills so I wouldn't fight him—again, his idea) when I heard a cell phone ring. I looked up from my own phone, to see Jeff checking his. He won't take it, I thought, he wouldn't possibly leave me here at the table.

He stood up. "I have to take this," he said.

The asshole was actually going to take the call and leave me with our mother. I grabbed his shirt.

"Don't go," I pleaded, grabbing his shorts as well. "Take the call here—put them on speaker!" It was understood (because I'd said it at least five times that morning) that Jeff and I would not leave each other's sides during our visit.

"I'm right around the corner," Jeff said and took off.

I looked across the table at my mother. Her once-nimble body, able to clear an ottoman in a single bound to grab Jeff and me by our legs, was now frail. Those sharp and bony fingers, now too arthritic and bent to inflict the sort of damage she'd made a career of. I could definitely take her in a physical fight (oy, what would that look like in this place?), so I knew I wasn't in any physical danger.

So, what was I afraid of? Why was I so angry—furious, really— as I sat there trying not to focus on the smell of her lunch, which I had thought was Chinese-themed food but now I wasn't so sure? Maybe Mexican?

I realized, this was the first time I was alone with her since I was six.

"HIT THE BOMB shelters!" Jeff would call each night around five, which was when our mother would start out on one of her hair-pulling, scratching, pinching, and biting rampages. Wherever I was in our split-level house, I would hear my big brother sound the alarm and head for the bomb shelter, and I'd race to meet him under my bed where, panting, our heads against the orange shag carpeting, we'd wait until our father came home to save us from her, usually bearing pizza and greasy donuts from Manhattan where he worked (because on the rare nights she attempted a meal, our mother's cooking was a horror movie on a plate).

Lost in junk food, I'd sit at the kitchen table, sowing the seeds for the comfort-eating that would soon make my life a delicious misery and watch as Dad would shove Mom against the wall and scream in her face while she scratched and kicked him. Every family has their dinnertime routine. This was ours.

I was five and my brother was nine when our parents split up and our mother moved out. But it was while she lived with us, and her attacks were a regular event, that a tradition was born between me and my brother that continues to this day. During her rampages, when one of us needed to venture out from under Jeff's bed to pee (Jeff) or to find a snack (me), we would say the words *safe-safe* to each other. Saying those words was our talisman, because our world was anything but safe-safe. Our safe-safe incantation continued into our adulthoods, and to this day it's the last thing we say to each other before hanging up, as a reminder of what we survived and what we mean to each other. None of which was on display in the nursing home as Jeff continued his phone call and I sat alone with our mother, feeling not very safe-safe around her and getting increasingly pissed-pissed at my brother for leaving me there.

My supposed-to-be-estranged mother and I sat in silence while I watched the door, waiting for Jeff to return. I couldn't understand why he'd insisted on coming to visit her. It wasn't like she'd ever given him any reason to justify his loyalty, and he'd lived with her four years longer than I had. But my brother was the only member of our family who had remained loyal to our mother when Cathy moved in with our dad, shortly after the divorce.

Beautiful, kind, clean Cathy. Thirteen years younger than my dad, twenty-four when they met, with bouncy blond hair, rosy pink skin, and blue eyes, she looked like a princess. She was a "shiksa," according to my Grandma Ethel. *Shiksa* is the Yiddish word for a gentile woman, meaning, not plagued with Jewish thighs or untamable curly hair. She arrived like a Fairy Godmother to me, always cooking and reading me bedtime stories, even making hot chocolate and gently brushing tangles out of my hair without getting even a little violent. She made me feel special. She made me feel cared for. She made me feel safe-safe without having to hide under a bed. It was one of the best times I could, or would, remember in my entire childhood.

I now think that the reason Jeff stayed so fiercely loyal to our mother was because for all of the insanity and violence she directed our way, it was clear that I was her favorite, and he still craves her approval. Approval that he should pray never comes. I should know.

Because being our mother's favorite was nothing even close to a perk. And that was a big part of the reason I couldn't breathe in her presence at that table in LA all those years later.

A year after my parents divorced, Mom was living in Philadelphia with her mother, my Grandma Bea. Although (or perhaps because) Grandma Bea had spent time in a mental institution—complete with shock treatments—she was still unstable.

Mother's Day was coming up, and I was looking forward to spending it with Beautiful Kind Clean Cathy and my dad. My plans went into the shitter, however, when my mother—or "that witch," as my dad called her—decided to come from Philadelphia with Grandma Bea to spend the weekend with Jeff and me. Her plans included an overnight with us at a nearby motel. I begged my father not to make me go. But from what I heard him say to Beautiful Kind Clean Cathy through his bedroom door, he didn't have this thing called "custody" that he would need to say no to her, so I was screwed.

That Saturday, my mother pulled up in her beat-up two-door, navy Dodge Dart (she had returned the Cadillac the year before). Jeff eagerly got inside. My mother looked and smelled exactly as I remembered—kind of sour, her black hair greasy and flecked with lint and dandruff. She wore a black turtleneck and dark-green puffy coat covered in patchy food stains. Grandma Bea was in the passenger seat, more put together with her bright red lipstick, and what looked like some kind of an animal sitting on her head. Leaning in to kiss me, she instructed me not to touch her "mink" hat. Not a problem. Not even out of the driveway yet, and I wanted to go home.

Jeff, now ten, wasted no time telling them about how he made it to the final round in the statewide spelling bee by correctly spelling the word *agenda*. Even though he lost for the county in the next round, with the word *incarcerate*. Thanks to him our school was in Long Island's biggest newspaper, *Newsday*, for something other than vulgar graffiti on a teacher's car.

We stopped for dinner at a restaurant and after a near-brawl with the manager over their "No Sharing" policy, we all ate from a single plate of meatballs and spaghetti when no one was looking. When we left, I noticed the salt and pepper shakers that had been on the table were now gone and knew they were in my mother's pockets. How many salt and pepper shakers did one woman need? I wondered. We drove to a motel, where we had another near-brawl with the guy at the front desk, who refused to honor my mother's expired coupon, which also happened to be for a different motel, and we finally got settled into our room.

I went right to sleep—I didn't even want to watch TV. I figured the sooner I slept, the sooner I'd be reunited with Beautiful Kind Clean Cathy. But in the middle of the night, I made the grave error of getting up to pee. It wasn't until I stood up that, aided by a sliver of blinking light coming through the curtains, I saw my mother sitting on the floor, crying. Instead of asking her what was wrong, I decided to get back into bed and hold it in. Callous, maybe. Definitely smart. But also too late—she'd spotted me.

"Sweetheart?" she called into the dark.

I stood frozen. Maybe she would think I was sleep-standing and leave me alone. I swayed a little for effect.

Next thing I knew, she was next to me. Her long, bony fingers softly touched my hair, tucked it behind my ear. To this day, I flinch whenever I am being touched softly. I'd much prefer a punch in the face than a gentle caress. And don't even go NEAR my ears.

"Sweetheart . . . I want you to come live with me."

Oh shit. No no no.

She said she wanted me. Not Jeff, just me.

"A little girl should be with her mother," she said.

She added, for incentive, that if I lived with her, she'd give me Jimmy, which was not exactly a selling point. Jimmy was her dummy that she used during a short-lived career as a ventriloquist. He was a porcelain doll with a white face, bright red cheeks, and brown lacquered hair that came to a swirl on top. He had big blue eyes that rolled around in different directions, with lids that opened and closed at will. In short, Jimmy scared the living shit out of me. If my mother's invitation to live with her had been unpalatable to that point, her invitation to make Jimmy my new brother was the ultimate deal breaker.

My heart beating fast, I told her in my most grown-up voice, the one I'd modeled after Carol Brady, from *The Brady Bunch*, that I wanted to stay with Daddy. "I just think it's better," I said.

She flipped on the lamp. Before my eyes could adjust to the light, she had lifted her dingy, coral nightgown with one hand and lowered the waistband of her giant, faded underwear with the other. Then she took my chin, held it tightly between her fingers, and directed my face to within inches of a large, puckered pink scar that ran the length of the rippled, loose skin of her lower abdomen.

"You did this to me," she said.

What was THAT?! How did I do . . . whatever the fuck it was I was supposed to have done? Could I have forgotten maiming somebody like that? Was she sure it was me?

She said it was because I was a "C-section" and that was the scar I'd caused. I could only figure that had something to do with my report card, but I was confused because the lowest grade I'd gotten so far was a B. Nonetheless, I apologized profusely for causing her . . . that.

Which was when she asked me again to come to Philadelphia and live with her. Once again, I used my most grown-up voice. But this time, using the no bullshit one I'd modeled after Loretta Swit in *MASH*—I stood my ground about not wanting to live with her.

She watched me get back into bed. She went to turn off the light but stopped, her hand on the switch.

"Sweetheart . . ." she said again, "there's a thing in this world called 'retribution'—and you'll get yours for abandoning your mother."

I didn't know what retribution was. I just hoped it wasn't anything like a C-section.

The next day, the four of us made a hurried trip through some museum. My mother pulled us kids by our arms and shouted at Grandma Bea to keep up, all the time cutting Jeff off every time he started to spout facts about what we were seeing.

"Butterflies are part of the class of insects in the order *Lepidop-tera*," he all but pleaded, "along with the moths and adult butterflies. Mom, adult butterflies—"

"Let's go, Jeffrey," she snapped, yanking him into the next room.

I wondered what the rush was but just assumed she'd stolen something pretty expensive, like a crown jewel or a dinosaur bone. That was usually why we rushed out of places.

Finally, we were on our way home. With each familiar sight— the Busy Bee Flea Market, 7-Eleven, the mall, the local homeless guy—I got more excited. Beautiful Kind Clean Cathy, here I come.

But my hopes were dashed by my mother's announcement that we were "going visiting."

"Going visiting" meant seeing old friends of hers in her old neighborhood and inevitably included Betty, whom I only remem-bered as having hair that was very big, very brown, and very hard, as well as her mentally ill son named Jared, who licked his hands a lot.

This was too much for Jeff, who hated visiting more than any-thing and wasn't as adept as I was at tuning out his surroundings. My mother knew this, and in what seemed a rare moment of kind-ness, she said she'd drop him off at our house and we'd be back in an hour to take him for Baskin-Robbins ice cream. Baskin-Robbins was Jeff's favorite thing ever, so he jumped out of the car and planted himself on our stoop to await our return.

I tried to catch his eyes. Safe-safe, I prayed. Come on, Jeff— safe-safe. He didn't look at me as we drove away, and I guess I was tired from the museum and from lying awake all night after seeing that scar-thing, because I fell asleep.

When I woke up, it was dark outside. The car was cold. I sat up and looked out the window. There was this foreign city, with tall buildings and lots of traffic, and my mother was arguing with Grandma Bea.

"Yes, I'm sure about this," my mother shrieked. "She's my daughter, I can take care of her—I have a towel for her!"

Where was I? Where was Jeff? Had I missed the ice cream?

"She's up," Grandma Bea said, turning to me. Her face pale, her head seemingly floating above the neck of her coat, her red lipstick just as red as before. Maybe redder.

My mother looked into the rearview mirror. "Welcome home, sweetheart," she said happily. "You're in Philadelphia!"

What?

Grandma Bea nudged the arm of her puffy coat. "Paulette, give her something to eat."

Agitated, my mother reached into her pocket. She retrieved a packet of saltines and the salt shaker from the night before and shoved them at me.

Grandma Bea told my mother that she'd better know what she was doing because her own condition left her unable to help.

"I'm her mother," my mom shrieked again, and I really wished she'd stop saying that. I also really wondered why either one of them would need to take care of me—I had Beautiful Kind Clean Cathy for that.

We sped into an underground garage. My mother stopped the car short and got out, leaving Grandma Bea to help me out of the backseat, which apparently wasn't good for whatever "condition" she had. Or my condition, which was having no tangible idea what the fuck I was doing in Philadelphia.

We took the elevator up to a high floor in a fancy apartment building, like the "de-luxe apartment in the sky" on the *The Jeffersons*, with shimmery white walls and plush mint green carpeted hallways. We got to Grandma Bea's apartment, which I had never seen. Despite it smelling like tomato soup, it was immaculate in a sterile way, replete with hard-looking couches and chairs covered in plastic, which is what old people did to their furniture to keep it nice. I knew as much because my dad's mom, my Grandma Ethel—or Ettie Apple, as we called her, because she had a housecoat with apples on it—did the same thing with her furniture. I loved Ettie Apple—she baked us cookies and took us on a city bus in the Bronx when we visited her. I missed her so much now I got a knot in my stomach. I also missed the Baskin-Robbins, I was sure of it.

Grandma Bea took off her dead animal hat and announced she'd had a long day and she was going to lie down. She started down the hall to one of the two bedrooms, warning me not to touch anything with sticky hands before closing the door behind her.

I turned to see my mother pick up a black rotary phone. "We're going to call your father," she said as she dialed.

The knot in my stomach started to loosen. I was going home.

"We're going to tell him you're living here now," she continued, and the stomach knot tightened up again so fast I almost threw up.

If there had been any doubt up to then that missing ice cream was the least of my worries, that was over. I wondered about my brother—if I was in Philadelphia and Jeff wasn't with me, who would warn me when it was time to hit the bomb shelter? Where was the bomb shelter in this place? Who would keep me safe-safe? And would there really be no ice cream? Because food is comfort, and I needed comfort badly at that moment, and also promising ice cream and not getting ice cream was a mean thing even for a mean person to do.

I heard my father answer the phone in a faint but frantic voice.

"Les, it's Paulette," my mother said calmly.

This was going to be bad. Calm was the only thing worse for my mother to be than not calm.

After a lot of muffled screaming from the other end of the line, she told him where we were.

A volley of expletives was exchanged in all kinds of tones, cul-minating in her screaming "I did not 'take her'!"

But she did, I wanted to scream even louder. Don't believe her, Dad, she took me! She stole the salt and pepper shakers at the diner and now she stole me! Come get me! Let's stop for ice cream on the way home!

"It's not kidnapping," my mother hollered and shoved the phone at me.

"Sweetheart," she snapped, menacingly close to my face, "tell your father you want to live with me."

For the first time that night, I was afraid. Telling him that would be lying and, even though I was only six, I was keenly aware of how saying it would hurt my father, who had brought home Beautiful Kind Clean Cathy to take this witch's place. Also, the word *sweetheart* was at this point officially dead to me.

Holding the phone to my ear, I could hear my father telling Cathy to get Jeff inside already, that his piece-of-shit mother wasn't coming back to take him for ice cream. Apparently, my brother was still sitting outside on our stoop waiting for us to take him to Baskin-Robbins.

My father was back on the line. ". . . Elizabeth?"

He sounded scared. Which scared me more. "Hi, Daddy," I said.

"I'm going to come get you," he said breathlessly.

Oh, thank God, I thought. But my mother was glaring at me. It was the cold, dead, dark stare of a woman who never should have had children. A woman who would lie about ice cream. A woman who was really good at pinching and biting and hair-pulling and possibly having Jimmy the ventriloquist dummy kill me, so I did what she told me to.

"I want to live with Mommy," I mumbled into the phone, tears streaming down my face, praying my father could tell I was lying.

"Put her back on the phone," he said. His voice was tight, his tone the same as it was back when our neighbor Mr. Andretta poured hot turkey grease on our lawn as retaliation for our dog, Schnoodle, peeing on his bush. (Schnoodle hated Mr. A. He also hated my mother and growled whenever she went near him because dogs smell assholes. In every way.)

I held the receiver out to my mother tentatively. She grabbed it and listened for a moment.

"You can't," she said, in a teasing singsongy voice. "No, you can't . . . No, you can't—"

Suddenly, she screamed.

"Because you don't have custody, Lester!"

She slammed the phone down and stormed down the hall where Grandma Bea had gone.

I sat on the plastic-covered couch. Unable to get any traction, I slid down to the edge and then to the floor. I did this over and over. Just like at Grandma Ethel's, but scary instead of fun.

Eventually my mother returned with a worn plastic shopping bag that was coming apart in places. "I bought you some new things you'll need for living here," she said, putting the bag on the couch between us and dumping out the contents. There was a towel covered with tiny sailboats. One of the sailboats had a rust-colored stain on it. Obviously, this was the famous towel she had been talking about in the car, the towel that made her a good mother. There were also some shirts and pants and a package of four pairs of underwear, each of which looked like they'd been worn before.

There was also a black-and-white marble composition notebook bent at the corners, and a fountain pen that had leaked into one of the shirts. "Those are for school," she said.

It was obvious that this dirty, hysterical woman didn't know or care that I already had a *Charlie's Angels* backpack and notebook at home that Beautiful Kind Clean Cathy had gotten me at the beginning of the school year when we did a thing called "school shopping" that normal people did and which were my prized possessions. It was equally clear to me that this mean bitch didn't care about the purple puffy heart stickers Sandy Kanopka had given me at her birthday party that were safely stored in my pencil case in the front zipper pocket back at home. In my room.

This was when it hit me that I really wasn't going home.

I started to cry. The knot in my stomach came undone, and I cried and cried.

"Why are you crying?" my mother asked, offended. "I just gave you all of these new things—how can you be so ungrateful?"

I finally said the words. "I want to go home."

Her eyes narrowed. "You are home," she said. "And you belong with your mother."

I sobbed. She put her face up close to mine.

"I'm part of you," she said, softly putting my hair behind my ear. "I'll always be part of you, and you can't deny that."

I sobbed harder. Why couldn't beautiful, kind, clean Cathy be part of me?

At her order, I followed her to her bedroom—it was that or have her touch me softly again. In stark contrast to the rest of the place, her room was a complete shithole, with blankets in piles and the floor covered in clothes, trash, and empty food containers. Amidst the clutter, I spotted a broken umbrella, a flattened sun visor—but no Jimmy. I scanned the corners, all piled high with dirty laundry and junk, but couldn't spot her demon dummy. The unclean and slightly rancid smell my mother gave off permeated the space. I breathed in sharp, short breaths to try and see if any of Beautiful Kind Clean Cathy's fresh smell was left in my nose. It wasn't.

As she changed into the same nightgown from the night

before, my mother, now angry again, told me that I'd been "brain-washed" by my father and his side of the family. And that Cathy was a "whore." Another new word. I missed that whore.

My mother shut the lights and motioned for me to join her in her smelly bed. Against my better judgment, I did, and once next to her she hugged me tight and told me how much fun we were going to have.

She slept. I lay awake, clinging to the edge of the bed, waiting for Jimmy to emerge from the filth and darkness and kill me. Weirdly, he didn't try it, which was a shame because if ever there was a day I wished I were dead, this was it.

THE NEXT MORNING, in the same clothes I thought I'd be having ice cream in, my mother took me to a nearby public school to enroll me.

I sat in the principal's office in a big red leather chair and looked out on the playground. Instead of grass like at my Long Island elementary school, there was a blacktop with two bare swing sets—just cold-looking metal. It was recess, and kids were playing outside, a sea of puffy jackets in different colors. Were these the kids I was going to grow up with, instead of the kids I thought I was going to grow up with? I wondered which of them would be my friends, and what they served for hot lunch, whether pizza day would still be Friday and if their grilled cheese also came with chilled fruit, and if I would have to change in front of other people for gym class.

I was snapped back to reality by my mother's signature shrieking, directed this time at the principal, an older-looking guy (he literally looked older than he had looked when we first got there) who was telling her, for what must've been the fifth time judging by the fact that he looked like he was on the verge of losing his shit, to send me back to my father. But my mother was resolute in her keeping me, the word *custody* piercing through the screaming. For all her ranting and raving and shouting and crying and a good amount of spitting, however, the principal wouldn't let me into the school, and we left.

It's all a bit of a blur for a while after that. For my mother, the novelty of taking care of her daughter wore off almost immediately, and my Grandma Bea's condition made her unable to help and required her to lie down and worry about her furniture a lot. My mom was angry that the clothes she'd bought for me didn't fit and complained that I was "too tubby" for them. As for the famous towel, it was so old that it was no longer absorbent. It didn't take long for my mother to revert back to her old self, enraged at the idea of feeding, dressing, bathing, or caring for a child in general and me in particular.

I wondered if my dad was getting that "custody" thing, even though my mother said that no court in the world would award it to a father over a mother. Maybe they would give it to Beautiful Kind Clean Cathy. She would fight for me.

By day we visited schools, with me looking out on a series of urban playgrounds while my mother got into shouting matches with a series of principals, all of whom told her to send me back to my father. By night I would eat Grandma Bea's high-fiber old-people cereal and look down at the traffic from her high-rise dining room window, wondering if my father's car was among the headlights. If he was coming to save me, or if he'd given up on trying.

This was the routine for several weeks, until one afternoon, after we'd driven to the outskirts of Philadelphia in traffic only to face yet another principal—a woman no less—who had taken my father's side. More screaming, even some crying, and, if I remember correctly, an attempt to pinch the lady.

We got back to Grandma Bea's, and my mother told me to go into the bedroom we shared and close the door. I did as I was told, then pressed my ear against my side of the bedroom door and listened to my mother dial the phone; clearly, I'd gotten brave during my sojourn, as hardened as any other POW, daring enough to eavesdrop.

At first, I couldn't hear much, but it didn't take long before she was screaming. Repeated *fuck you*s (no surprise there) cleared the door, followed by "This isn't over, Lester," after which I heard the phone slam and her stomping toward the bedroom.

She was coming for me. This was it.

Head for the bomb shelter, I thought to myself (I wasn't that brave) and dove under the bed. Or tried to—it was a disaster under there, too. I wedged my way in between the musty boxes and rotten food, only to catch sight of a lifeless blue eye inches from my face.

The rest of Jimmy was obscured by clothes and shoes and take-out containers, but the demon dummy had found me at last.

I don't know what made me scream, Jimmy or the door crashing open and bouncing off the wall. I turned away from the doll and saw my mother's feet kicking my suitcase, the one Beautiful Kind Clean Cathy had packed for the overnight that seemed to have taken place years before.

"You're going back to live with your father," my mother spat, kicking the suitcase again. Better the suitcase than me (though I knew I could be next). But holy shit, I was going home.

I'm going home. I kept saying it to myself over and over, with each repetition feeling myself getting stronger and her getting weaker and Jimmy—Jimmy couldn't hurt me now. I was going home!

That night, one of the cars on the street below pulled into my Grandma Bea's building to come and get me. My own personal chariot home. It turned out it wasn't driven by my father, who was prevented from picking me up by the terms of the "custody" thing. Instead it was my Dad's friend Chaim, a small and extremely kind man with a head of black hair as big as his red track suit was loud.

He came into the bedroom to introduce himself, which was when I finally came out from under the bed. I'd never met Chaim, but from that moment forward I loved him. Chaim was my Prince Charming in nylon.

My mother wouldn't say good-bye to me. She stormed up and down the hall shouting that she didn't deserve this.

I did say good-bye to Jimmy. The poor bastard didn't choose his life, and it was a life I wouldn't even wish on a demon-dummy.

EVENTUALLY I LEARNED why no school in Philadelphia would admit me, leaving my mother with no choice but to send me back home. It turned out that the principal of our school on Long Island, Mr. DeBonis, had taken up my cause. It wasn't because of me, though— Jeff's winning the county spelling bee was the first bit of good publicity our white-trash school had gotten in years, which of course made our family's cause a personal one for our principal and compelled him to withhold my school records and explain my family situation to anyone who asked for them. Mr. DeBonis also called all the schools in the Philadelphia school system for us and told them not only what my mother had done, but how batshit crazy she was.

So even from two states away, my brother had inadvertently saved me. Kept me safe-safe. His mother left him on a porch waiting for ice cream and fucked him over—and in return, he fucked her back. Talk about "just desserts."

Many years later, sitting across from her at the Los Angeles Jewish Home for the Aged, a mother myself, I was no longer afraid of what she could do to me anymore. But I was still afraid—afraid because I came from a woman capable of kidnapping her daughter and (even worse) not kidnapping her son, too. It's not like there wasn't room in the car!

"I'll always be part of you, and you can't deny that," she said, softly putting my hair behind my ear.

That curse would inform every decision I made as a person and as a mother. Including the terrible decisions. Like the one I was about to make on my way home from the "home."

I called Todd, who was getting Jesse and Phoebe ready for bed, and told him to put me on speaker—which he did, thinking I was saying good night to the kids.

Instead I announced that I was taking them for ice cream. Jesse and Phoebe were going to get the ice cream Jeff and I never did.

Todd turned off the speaker, reminding me that it was eight o'clock on a school night and telling me that taking the kids for ice cream was about the dumbest thing I could do at that moment.

But I'd said it, and they'd heard me. I had to take them. Otherwise, I would be doing what she'd done when she promised ice cream and there was no ice cream. I reminded Todd of the day's suicide texts and that I'd probably be dead someday soon anyway. Placating me, he relented—but not before telling me I would be in charge of putting the kids to bed. No problem, I told him—I was their mother, and I didn't need a towel to prove it.

When we got home from ice cream an hour later, Jesse went to his room, leaving me to get my very hyped-up daughter to go to sleep. Phoebe was five—the same age I was when my mother had first left, and as strong-willed and confident as I had been insecure at that age.

She started doing cartwheels around her room. I told her to stop doing cartwheels. She did more cartwheels, then switched to dancing. I told her to stop dancing. She danced more, then jumped on the bed. I told her to stop jumping on her bed or else there would be consequences. She jumped higher. I screamed at her to get into her bed. She refused until, finally succumbing to exhaustion, she crapped out on her own terms and got under her blanket.

I watched her as she started to fall asleep, her fingers in her mouth. Then, just as she drifted off, I leaned over her and asked a question that couldn't wait until morning.

"Phoebe . . .?" I asked. "Why aren't you afraid of me?"

She opened her eyes.

"Because you're my mommy," she said, as if it were the silliest question in the world.

And in that moment, Phoebe let me know that I had not become my mother, but her mother.

I tucked her blanket around her, smoothed her hair, kissed her softly on her forehead, and whispered, "You can be a little afraid of me."

But I'd always keep her safe-safe.

No More Monsters

My father was seventy-five—youthful, despite, or maybe because of, hanging up his hairpieces—and Cathy was as *shiksa*-gorgeous as ever at sixty when they moved out of our old house on Long Island. Before leaving, they shipped me what was left there from my childhood: a small leather yearbook from elementary school and the mirror that hung in my bedroom growing up.

I was never sure why they sent the mirror. It wasn't anything extraordinary, antique-wise—if anything it was pretty beat up. A wooden frame measuring three feet by two, there are decorative swirls carved into the wood that meet in the middle in a flower, the white paint still sticky from years of humidity. A typical girl's mirror from a run-of-the-mill kids' furniture store on Jericho Turnpike, no doubt long out of business.

It arrived one day like a family member who traveled two thousand miles via UPS ground, unannounced and looking for a place to stay. Todd and I were living in an apartment at the time. I couldn't hang the mirror up, because I'd told Todd there wasn't enough wall space for his framed movie poster for *Jaws*, which was about the same size. That had clearly been a lie, but I'd used the word *aesthetic*, so I won. Knowing nothing could be gained by revisiting that particular battle and feeling guilty at even the thought of breaking the mirror in two over my knee and throwing it away—I mean, it had traveled all that way—I settled for leaning the thing up against our bedroom wall, to be dealt with later.

From its new perch, my mirror served as a lone spectator to our ongoing struggle to conceive a baby. We'd become slaves to my temperature chart prior to its arrival, but the new drugs my fertility doctor had put me on were making me fucking crazy, as did the herbs my fertility acupuncturist had put inside my ears that could not be jostled. Never a huge fan of sex—it's so *naked*—the experience was now on a par with a root canal: a necessary task I endured with my sweatpants mostly on. Plus, I wasn't even sure I liked kids.

I'd certainly avoided babysitting whenever possible growing up. My chosen after-school profession had been working behind the counter of the clothing store Benetton in the Sunrise Mall, where I'd chain-smoke and moon over Don Jaconi, who wore Calvin Klein's Obsession for Men and worked in the cassette aisle at Sam Goody across the way. I'd blow puffs of smoke in his direction, sort of . . . reaching out to him. At twenty-eight, Don was a man—super-pale, his jet-black hair even hinting at a little premature gray. He had piercing brown(ish) eyes, earrings in both ears, and I was in love with him—so in love that I still remember telling my friend Dina, a greeter at The Gap who had stopped by Benetton to chat, that I wanted to "have all of Don's babies" while ringing up a rugby sweater through a cloud of smoke.

I guess I *had* wanted kids at some point. Though possibly only if they were Don's.

But years later, far away from the Sunrise Mall and the smoke-filled merino wool sweaters I sold to Don Jaconi at a massive discount, I was married and living in Los Angeles. Todd and I were spending six nights a month, pre-, mid-, and post-ovulation, trying to get pregnant. One night, I lie on my side in the dark, I was looking through my childhood mirror at Todd, lit by the porn on the TV that allowed him to be attracted to me enough to do the deed and go back to his football game in the other room.

To be fair, my mirror had seen a lot worse. From the time it showed up with my new bedroom furniture (including a canopy bed) when I was eight, it watched me grow up, suspended over my little girl's vanity that later doubled as a desk, flanked in time by my poster of John Travolta in *Grease* on one side and my signed photo of Janet from *Three's Company* on the other.

Many a night the mirror had borne silent witness to my flinching at the sound of my father's approaching footsteps and subsequent blasting open the door waving a bad report card, or a pair of shoes I'd left out in the rain, or, one memorable evening, an empty package of Cathy's favorite cookies that I'd put back in the rear of the cabinet, where they were hiding it from me (my strategy was to just hope the house would burn down before she went looking for a snack and noticed the package was empty).

In retrospect, it's a miracle the mirror survived the fury-fueled trashings of my room on those occasions, the air peppered with condemnations of me as a *pig* or *slob* and always, always, a huge disappointment to my father, as out of control as my mother, just like her in fact, and not nearly as smart or good as my older brother, Jeff.

For what would feel like hours, he would rage: I was going to fail out of school. I was going to be a nothing. My mirror never suffered so much as a crack or a paint chip from where it hung, watching— me red-faced and crying, Jeff and Cathy hovering in the doorway, trying halfheartedly to calm my father down, too afraid to step in.

My mirror would watch my nine-, ten-, and eleven-year-old self promise my father to be better, to beg for my keep. It would watch my father not believe me, tell me that he was done with me and how much he hated me, all before mercifully leaving me to sit in the wreckage that he left my room. Clothes, pictures, stuffed animals, everywhere— all stuff my father paid for that I knew I was lucky to have.

The mirror would watch him come back into my room later, calmer and contrite. He would hug me, telling me that I knew he loved me, that he just got so frustrated because he wanted me to be happy. And thinner. And smarter. And more like my brother. And just a completely different person.

My mirror saw me after fat camp, which left me twelve pounds lighter and four inches thinner. Proud and tan, admiring my new thigh gap, and so, so hungry as I swore I'd never gain weight again, my mirror watched me gain all of the weight back. Watched me desperately try to zip my jeans, flailing, gasping for air, cursing myself, my thigh gap long gone, then giving up and stretching my (also tight) sweatshirt down to cover the fact that the jeans weren't buttoned. I knew, even if Dad and Cathy didn't, that fat camp hadn't been about teaching me to eat healthy. Fat camp was simply about starving kids like me and then releasing us—more cynical, less trusting, so, so hungry and with the souls of hardened criminals— back into our old lives, with a 7-Eleven (Freedom was waiting!) on every corner. Until the next year, of course, when our parents would deliver us back to be starved once again. The camp knew what it was doing. Failing us kids was how they made their money.

My mirror knew this and never judged me. Quite the opposite—it served as my appreciative audience, not only when I would put off doing my homework, instead reading my history book as a news anchor for the Channel 4 news, but when I hosted my "Talk Shows," and did my impressions of guests like Carol Burnett, Penny Marshall, and *The Facts of Life*'s Mindy Cohn speaking into my hairbrush and me reading "viewer questions" off index cards. In between segments I'd act out commercials—back then you HAD to stop for commercials. Putting Dove soap on one side of my face and Zest deodorant soap on the other, I'd look straight into my mirror—the only time I could do it without hating myself. "The Dove side feels smooth and soft. The Zest side is burning . . ." I'd say in a sultry grown-up lady voice. I'd do taste tests with crunchy peanut butter on one spoon and creamy on the other. "Well, this is just nuts! I love them both equally!" I'd say in a kid voice.

Then I would carelessly leave the spoons in my desk drawer and get ants. Then my room would get trashed again, at which point my father would sometimes discover some of the cash I'd stolen from him, at which point I'd really catch hell.

Mercifully, no one ever found Cathy's white angora sweater that I borrowed without asking and a BIC pen accidentally exploded all over. Trying to clean it with that same bar of Dove soap just . . . spread the ink around the sweater. The mirror witnessed me put it in a plastic bag before hiding it in the nook above my closet like a dead body.

It saw me after I'd gone on my first voluntary jog around the neighborhood—I'd meant to go only a block to satisfy Cathy's request that I "just go get out of here," but I got lost and wound up running four miles. Sweaty, breathless, and exhilarated, endorphins rushing through my system. Freed by my own two feet, I'd felt empowered, having literally run away from my problems.

The mirror saw me shed weight, through running and a diet

of turkey breast, grapes, and Trident gum. It saw the return of the thigh gap—bigger this time. It saw me model new designer jeans my father had only dreamt I'd fit into someday. It saw me beam when I earned his approval, saw the pride I felt. Enough joy to make me forget the bad stuff.

It saw my first attempt at putting on makeup. Blue eye shadow. It saw my severe allergy to eye shadow.

It saw my shame. My pride. My perms. My acne. My Molly Ringwald *Breakfast Club* phase. My Molly Ringwald *Sixteen Candles* phase. My Molly Ringwald *Pretty in Pink* phase.

Then, shortly before I left home, my mirror saw me sneak into my bedroom at sunrise, reeking of Calvin Klein's Obsession for Men after my first date with Don Jaconi. We'd each paid for our own food at a deli, and he had driven me to a cemetery. We sat in his car and made out, and he told me his dream of becoming floor manager at Sam Goody and maybe, just maybe, someday moving out of his mother's house because his stepfather really bummed him out. He told me he was really thirty-six, not twenty-six, and showed me where his grandfather was buried.

A few weeks later, my mirror saw me bawl my eyes out when I found out Don was dating a girl who worked in Victoria's Secret. He'd gotten us the same Christmas presents—a thin gold-plated bracelet and a bottle of Shalimar perfume.

My mirror had seen the good, the bad, and the ugly. And now, across the country, it saw a married me with my legs in the air, trying to increase my chances of pregnancy, searching for the TV remote so I didn't have to see that the porn Todd needed involved lady wrestlers.

WHEN TODD AND I moved from that apartment into our first house, there was still no baby on the horizon. I was disappointed and frustrated. But just when I went into the spare bedroom and lamented to Todd about what a great nursery it would make, if it were not for my "unreliable ovaries"—the doctor's words, seriously—the realtor poked her head in and told me that the two families who'd lived in the house before us conceived within the first month of moving in. So, we bought the house at slightly above market price.

I tried to sell my childhood mirror at a garage sale in the hope of finding it a good home. At the end of the day it was the only item that remained—someone had even bought the blanket it had been lying on. Even Todd's brown, leatherette football-watching chair—another thing we "didn't have room for aesthetically"—had been sold. I wondered if people sensed the shit my mirror had seen and didn't want it.

SO, THE MIRROR wound up coming with us to our first house, where it sat in the garage for ten years.

EVENTUALLY, THE KID thing happened—Jesse, as the realtor had promised, having been conceived within a month of moving in. Two years later, Phoebe was born. And as it turned out, I did want children—though I was grateful that my kids hadn't been sired by Don Jaconi, because he was forty-six when we dated when I was sixteen. His hair hadn't been prematurely graying, but on-time graying, and far as I know he never made floor manager of Sam Goody or moved out of his mother's house.

When we moved to a bigger house, the one we live in now, I left the mirror at our old place with a bunch of other stuff I didn't know what to do with. But when we were unpacking . . . there it was, staring at me. Well, I was staring at me in it. It had followed me to California, then from apartment to apartment to my first house. And finally, my second house.

My spiritual friend, Kristin, suggested that night that the universe wanted me to have it, that it was a character in my life story and that it would reveal itself eventually. I told her to stop acting like the universe is a thing.

At the time of that move, Jesse was eight and Phoebe was five. I was worried my son would be anxious about the change—all the new creaks and drips, the different outside sounds, the noise the air-conditioning made when it's turned on. Any of it could cause severe panic in him, I knew.

I didn't think for a second that Phoebe would be fazed by her new home, however. My fearless, brave child—the one who had barreled out of me six days early and was almost born in my new car—had been on a rampage, brave as hell ever since. She was the kid who would climb to the bow of a fast-moving boat during a whale-watching excursion, the kid who jumped into the pool before she could swim, and who kicked me out of Mommy and Me, preferring to be just "Me."

Which was why I was so surprised to find the kids' roles reversed at their new address. Jesse was calm, even excited about having a staircase—not quoting me so much as a single staircase death statistic. Phoebe, on the other hand, refused to go to sleep in her room, terrified that monsters were living under her bed. I told her that was dumb.

"But Nora said there are monsters!" she yelled at me. Nora was her friend who spewed "facts" about shit she knew nothing about. Like that McDonald's food had plastic in it (which ruined my previously foolproof bribing strategy).

I was insulted that Phoebe trusted a five-year-old more than her own mother. I told her that Nora knew nothing, that she was a compulsive liar and not even that cute. I also refused my daughter's demand that I check under her bed one last time.

"It's three in the morning, Phoebe," I said as I kissed her forehead, "and I have to go to sleep and be awake tomorrow because I happen to work for an actual monster."

In retrospect, I shouldn't have said that last part.

"You work with a monster?!" Jesse was rooted to the doorway. Apparently, he'd overheard.

"Okay, yes, he's a sort of monster," I explained. "But he's a monster who paid for this amazing new house and your school and all your toys."

Now, they were both terrified. They stared at me as if they were seeing me for the last time.

"I'm saying he's a different kind of monster!" I insisted. "A mean man! Not the monsters that eat you! I mean, okay, yes, he eats people alive in a verbal abuse sense, but he doesn't actually chew people up and spit them out . . . well, he *has* been physical in the past, but—"

I had yet to understand that my children were too young to get the finer points of metaphor. Or sarcasm. Now everyone was inconsolable. Including me.

I put the kid's vaporizer on high, pumping lavender into the air. The woman who had sold it to me said it was soothing. She had also gotten me involved in a pyramid scheme, and now I was selling artisanal oils to fellow desperate parents.

"Okay, listen up," I said firmly. "The monster I work for is just one of many very successful men in television who've been rewarded for treating people terribly. His bosses think that's a small price to pay in return for their 'genius,' so they get giant development deals and lots of money, and Mommy gets a job!" I said it all a little condescendingly, as if they read the entertainment trades.

"You're talking about Tony, aren't you?" Jesse asked.

"Yes!" I enthused, proud of my son. "He's the monster! And that's what we call the 'cycle of abuse.'" It was an odd time for a teaching moment, but you call them as you see them.

"I'm NEVER sleeping in my room EVER!" Phoebe yelled, not giving a shit what kind of monster I worked for.

Though in pictures, Tony looked "happy" and "fun" with his bright-green eyes, chiseled features, and truly great smile (it always appeared as if he'd been caught midlaughter), his reputation for being a monster preceded him. Stories about his outbursts, firings, one about him knocking a plate of food out of a writer's hands . . . accounts of his nastiness spread through writers' rooms all over LA. Even my therapist knew of him and thought my taking the job was a bad idea.

So did my brother. Jeff had preceded me in our chosen careers as TV comedy writers by a bunch of years. Which made me take his thoughts on the matter pretty seriously.

"You can't work for that guy!" Jeff had exclaimed when I called him with the news. "My friend was about to be deported and still didn't take a job there. He works in a diner now, Liz. In Canada!"

I'd told him I didn't have the luxury of choosing jobs based on whether or not my boss was abusive. It was a show I loved and really wanted to write for, an established hit, meaning job security. So long as I didn't fuck up, of course.

"Safe not getting fired by a monster?" I asked him.

"Safe not getting fired by a monster," he sighed.

"Safe-safe, safe-safe, safe-safe," we said over each other, as we always did before hanging up the phone.

I learned on my first day that my assigned seat at the conference table in the writers' room had been occupied twice before—both times by writers who, among others, had been fired. No one expected me to last. I was basically sitting on an Eject button, and everyone would be surprised when I broke the curse by staying on.

The writers on the show were shells of their former selves. Several had skin rashes, a couple had gone completely gray, one had developed a tic where he looked like he was about to speak but never did. They looked like war refugees, not like the staff of a hit show with good hours and high-end snacks. There were alliances among them, and I sensed immediately that I was being watched to see which side I would join. Every friendly "Where you from?" or "I love your shirt!" or "Want my coleslaw?" propelled me into a different loyalty camp.

I set out to make sure I was nice to everyone at the same time, while being not nice to anyone at the same time. Basically, I stayed in my office during breaks.

Maybe I'd dealt with so much worse in the past at the hands of other authority figures like my father. Maybe I was more of a survivor than I realized as a result. Maybe I was just seeing a different person than everyone else did, but Tony seemed delightful to me. He was charismatic, funny, and a great listener who really seemed to care about his staff's lives and emotional baggage. He wanted to know all about us. I started to think maybe he was a reformed monster, that maybe he'd spent his most recent hiatus floating in a lithium pool. Maybe he'd never been all that bad, and the stories about him were embellished.

If anything, as it turned out, the stories about him had been under-bellished.

I was about a week in when this young female writer who just hours earlier Tony had proclaimed a magical genius and "the voice of the show" stood up to pitch a story. He'd put her on such a pedestal that he made her actually stand when she spoke—in fluent Hipster, of course—so we could admire more of her.

For whatever reason—probably a Millennial thing—or because she looked great in them—she put on a pair of large sunglasses as she stood up. Tony stood up as well. I thought maybe out of respect. Would he be saluting her? He would not.

Red-faced, his formerly kind, bright-green eyes bulging, he started screaming at her. I didn't know which of them I was supposed to look at, or if I was supposed to stand, too, or go with my gut and just crawl out the door. I decided to do what the rest of the room was doing and stared at my thumb as if it had just sprouted out of my hand.

Tony went after this girl in a way I'd never seen in a writers' room before. He made it deeply and viciously personal, attacking everything from her character and personality to her clothes, from her car to her private life. He used all the things she'd opened up to him about against her. I didn't know if he was once beaten with a pair of sunglasses, or if his mother had been beaten in front of him with a pair of sunglasses, or if he even had a mother, rather than having been spawned in some primordial and toxic ooze.

Afterward, exhausted from his tantrum and (it seemed) just a tiny bit pleased with himself, he sent us all home at noon.

No one but me seemed thrown by what the fuck had just happened. Everyone just acted like this was normal. No one talked about it. The guy who looked like he'd go to say something and then not went to say something, and then didn't.

That's when I knew: this workplace was open season for Tony's rage.

I wasn't wrong; we went home at noon a lot. I gleaned from hushed snippets that he'd been bullied when he was a kid and seemed to have a score to settle. As he'd also been treated badly by past bosses, he had a second score to settle. And those were just the scores we knew about.

His outbursts weren't reserved for the privacy of the writers' room. A former actor, he was forever in search of an audience— sometimes even a studio audience. It's fairly common when taping a show for writers to gather between scenes on the floor to rewrite jokes that don't "land" the first time around. Tony would get so frustrated and impatient when this happened that he would cause his own scene. The audience would stop watching the actors they'd waited all day to see to take in the other performance—the writers being screamed at and shamed by an unhinged man in a very expensive suit with everyone scrambling to make him happy. His writers would rattle off jokes, one after another—he'd shoot every one down, usually accompanied by a crushing insult. "That's not a joke, it's a sentence!" he would seethe, knowing that statement was like a knife to the heart for a comedy writer.

He was petty, mean, and immature. He made fun of people and preyed on their weaknesses. He was the most dangerous type of person with power. He was unpredictable. As a result, so were the lives of everyone who worked for him.

Having been a writer for many sitcoms, the learning curve on this show was easy for me. I was quick with jokes and story fixes. I didn't even own sunglasses. I managed to remain above the fray for the longest time.

Until I ate an apple. A small, seemingly harmless Fuji apple that I brought into the writers' room one day.

Just as I took my first bite, I heard an enormous groan to my left. I looked around the table at my fellow writers to see who had put on sunglasses or, worse, complimented the work of one of Tony's peers. But they were all looking at me. I turned to Tony. His eyes narrowed as he glared at me, nostrils flaring as he exhaled sharply for a full minute.

"What? You want some?" I asked, holding my apple out to him. Trying to keep it light.

He told me, in a measured, singsong tone, trying to remain calm, but fury verrrrry close to the surface, that he was poor growing up and though his father had money for beer, the only thing they had to eat was . . . apples. And so, apples trigger him.

I almost laughed—I would have laughed. I should have laughed and told him to shove an apple up his ass and roast himself before turning in my parking pass and walking out on that job forever.

But I didn't do that.

I looked around. Everyone's eyes were on me. And then on their thumbs.

I went to throw the apple away—it was a little mealy anyway. But he stopped me, demanding in an even more singsongy, cartoon villain-voice that I finish the apple.

"That's okay. I don't want it," I said.

"Go ahead. Finish it," he said.

"I don't want to."

"I want you to," he insisted. One of the most successful men in television desperately wanted me to eat an apple. And he wanted to watch. It was like S&M, but with fruit.

I looked down at what remained of the evil, offending apple— it still had its sticker on—and stuffed it in my mouth. It was so large that I could only breathe through my nose. It almost took out my two front teeth. I'd spent a lot on porcelain veneers, and in order to keep them safe, I tried to shimmy the apple to the back of my mouth with my tongue. Thanks to a great gag reflex—the same one that made me a terrible bulimic in high school—I was able to rest it at my throat and, as soundlessly as possible, suck enough juice out of it to make it small enough to manage as it broke down. The rotten part actually helped speed things along.

Seemingly satisfied, Tony returned his focus to the dry-erase board where we'd been working out a story. Blood rushing to my head, a veil of dots shimmering across my eyes, I took a deep breath in and swallowed—the sticker the last thing to go down, scraping my throat.

The groan Tony let out was even more giant than the first.

I think his words were, "Do you really swallow like that?! Really?!" after which, to further legitimize his contempt, he did a five-minute impromptu stand-up set on my loud swallowing.

Trying to deflect, wanting the attention off me, wanting to let everyone know I was okay, I sat back in my chair, casually resting the bottoms of my feet on the edge of the table, a defensive posture for sure. Putting a leg's length between myself and what just happened with the apple.

This, too, caught Tony's attention. "There's one thing I hate," he said through gritted teeth, and I got the feeling it was more than apples. And my swallowing.

"Genocide?" I joked. "Flat soda? Adam Sandler?"

He raised his chin toward my shoes, his nostrils flared. "Feet on the table." And then with sheer disdain . . . "And now you're going to try and slam Adam Sandler?!"

I gazed over at the propped-up feet of another writer, a comedian with semi-famous friends whom Tony adored because of his closeness to semi-famousness. The guy's black boots were splayed across his station, with either gum or dog shit stuck to the bottom of the left one.

I removed my offending feet from the starfucker's view, but the damage was done.

From then on, almost everything I did annoyed him to an explosive degree. He went after me almost constantly. I couldn't have an opinion on a movie or television show or my own relationships without being "Completely wrong."

Any story pitch of mine would get shot down to the tune of him accusing me of everything from trying to "destroy our characters" to "taking down the series" and even on some occasions trying to "ruin television itself"—after which he'd often pitch the same story idea I'd pitched that just seconds ago threatened to ruin television.

All day long, little digs, insults, throwaway jokes at my expense. It was like being hit with a bag of oranges over and over and over.

Of course, like any abusive relationship, at least the ones I'd been in, praise and acceptance were showered on me in between the "beatings."

"You are SO talented," he'd gush after I turned a script in, leaving me riding high until the next outburst, further locking me into that horrible and toxic job, and before I knew it, earning my keep and keeping a relentless, manipulative monster happy became the same thing.

His approval mattered more than anything, including my own son's safety—a point that was hammered home when Tony, in a moment of confusing generosity, announced that he was taking the staff to a Dodger game, where we watched from a giant suite owned by the studio.

I never would have brought my child into what I now considered a war zone, but one of my best friends—also a writer on the show and my life raft there—was bringing her son and suggested during a work session that I bring Jesse.

It was at this point that I regretted having a son at all. If Tony hated the way I swallowed, he certainly wasn't going to like the way Jesse threw up without warning from as little as a whiff of onion. The only good thing about bringing Jesse (having a son) would be that I could focus my attention on him and avoid stepping on any landmines with Tony.

I still was weighing the pros and cons of bringing him (having a son), when it had been decided that Jesse would be joining us. Tony rolled his eyes but gave his permission.

Knowing the man hated kids even more than apples and my feet, I had initially tried to keep Jesse as far from Tony as the skybox allowed. But Tony seemed taken with Jesse—engaging with him, even playing with him. Not minding my son's tendency to touch the earlobes of people he liked, Tony instead responded to it by goofing around good-naturedly, wrestling a little with my son, and even draping a rally towel across Jesse's shoulders. Jesse seemed to be enjoying it, based on the amount of Tony's earlobe he had between his fingers.

It was only later in the bathroom, where Jesse was hunched over the toilet, and I was assisting his wiping—he was getting better, but still not winning any awards—when he looked over his shoulder at me and told me Tony was being a little rough with the towel. It was bothering him.

As far as the news made my stomach drop, it was about to fall further. "If it's just a little rough play, can you just be cool with it?" I heard myself say over the first flush.

"Can't you tell him to be gentler?" Jesse asked.

"That man pays for our lives!" I said in a panic—a hushed one, in case someone might overhear and know what a terrible mother I was. "Be cool, Jesse! Just be . . . cool!"

In fairness to me, Jesse did say he was hurting him a "little."

This was how Jesse came to know Tony by name. It was also just around the time I started crying in my office a lot, losing a considerable amount of hair, and stress-buying enough dog beds, bath towels, car phone chargers, and hoodies from Amazon to have my own designated drone. It's also around the time that I became an integral part of the show, with Tony including me in hiring decisions and casting. He started confiding in me with such mean-spirited gossip that I had to take a shower and donate to charities after hearing it.

Even then, as "in" with him as I was, he would turn on me, often in the most unexpected, deep-seated, and ugliest of ways.

Like the time he mentioned to the staff that he couldn't go home because there was an incident happening in his neighborhood, which I mistakenly referred to as West Hollywood. Tony went pale.

"I live in Hollywood!" he spat. "You think I live in West Hollywood because I'm gay!"

I tried to explain that I'd made a mistake, that I had a terrible sense of geography, that I didn't even know where we were working at that moment.

He told me to repeat what he'd told the room. I did as I was told.

"I can't go home," I said, "there's something going on in my neighborhood—"

"Where's that? Fat *Jew* Town?"

Silence. Silence everywhere in the building. Silence next door. You couldn't hear a pin drop because even the pins were being silent.

"I can't believe you think I'm fat," I said in a small voice, once I regained any composure.

"*You* think you're fat." Tony grabbed my hand tightly with his large, bony fingers and squeezed it. Hard. "You think you're fat," he repeated, in case I didn't hear him the first time.

I was having a skinny week, too. I even had my thigh gap back, having lost even more of my sense of reality along with the weight.

Expectedly, the writing staff had a quicker turnover than the IHOP in Ventura on a Sunday morning. By this point, the Hipster Millennial and the comedian with the famous friends and dog shit on his boots were both long gone. Seeing the way Tony treated me, what I unleashed in him, the other writers were afraid to speak. The one who would go to speak and then not speak went to speak less and less. They all became catatonic and eventually got fired.

By the end of my second season working on the show, we were down to maybe four people from the original team. One of them stuttered so badly that we didn't have the time for her to finish a sentence, so it was really maybe only three people.

Walking to the soundstage one afternoon, a new writer we'd just hired (who wouldn't last either) told me she studied me and tried to do what I did. I asked her what that was.

"He beats you down, and you just keep going," she explained. "Over and over and over. But you never run out of jokes or pitches. He shits on you, and you come up with more! You're like a Whack-a-mole—how do you do it?"

"I just had a shitty childhood," I said, blushing at what felt like a really great compliment instead of the observations of a sane person.

It was true, I had my childhood to thank for providing me with pretty much all the tools I needed to succeed in television. You could just ask that mirror I couldn't get rid of. My resilience in the face of derision and men who couldn't stand me, coupled with my ability to bury my pain under jokes, had seasoned me for sitcoms better than any of the Thanksgiving turkeys I used to eat all the skin off of, much to my father's disgust.

Tony was a monster. But he was no match for the ones who had come before him. And, like them, he did pay for my house.

It was what I knew—monsters and jokes.

TONY'S APPRECIATION OF me was as wildly inconsistent as his contempt. Like when, at a party celebrating the show's long-running success, he made an effusive speech thanking a room full of hundreds—from the cast, crew, executives, and assistants to anyone and everyone who had darkened our soundstage up to and including the water delivery guy—everyone, except for me. Glaringly.

Then there was the time when he caught wind of the fact that my brother and I were going to try to create a show together—based on us, about adult siblings who were forever bonded by a shared shitty childhood who now lived in an unhealthy codependent relationship from which hilarity would ensue. On that occasion—as our final season together was winding down and everyone was looking for their next job—Tony decided to bestow upon me the ultimate praise, in the form of changing my contract to prohibit me from taking on outside projects until after we wrapped. The story was good, though, and Jeff and I both wanted to see it move forward, even though that meant my brother would have to find someone else to write about us with.

Enter another very successful, temperamental, high-strung, and notorious monster named Dean.

It was only through his magnanimity (and my brother's insistence) that I was eventually brought on board to help out with the pilot. Based on my own life. That I had helped create. So, I was one of the few writers allowed at the cast read of the pilot script. Dean didn't want too many writers "breathing near him." I sat behind him and my brother, off to the side, out of the way, keeping my breathing to a minimum.

Though I'd read it many times, hearing our script aloud was surreal to me. Two much better-looking and younger versions of Jeff and me were speaking our words, saying "safe-safe" to each other without any understanding as to what those words meant, not knowing what they were borne of or how they kept me from falling apart completely. I found myself praying the actors had experienced enough trauma in their lives to really sell ours.

After a table read, the network executives—the people who ultimately decide whether to put the show on TV—leave the room to talk amongst themselves about what they've just seen. Basically, they tear apart what they had approved of up until that moment.

Anxiously waiting to hear what the network would have to say, and before anyone could speak, Dean snapped in a loud, angry tone that he wasn't changing anything. The director casually mentioned a huge flaw in the story—the character's actions weren't warranted and led to an unsatisfying ending. Much like Tony always had in the face of criticism, Dean went to "ten" immediately. Refusing to listen to reason, he became a runaway train. Nothing I wasn't used to—but I had a fix for the story snag in my head. Yet, while it was my life story, it wasn't my show. It wasn't my place to speak up. Or breathe.

But I couldn't help myself.

"You could have them go to—" I started to say, and before I could finish the sentence, Dean had wheeled around in his chair. Not two inches from my face he screamed at the top of his lungs, "DON'T TALK, LIZ!"

Everything stopped.

I started to shake, my lip started to quiver. I told myself to hold it together. That I was used to this. I was a Whack-a-mole who could withstand abuse. I was a professional who needed to be taken seriously. A man wouldn't cry. I couldn't be the woman who cried, I thought, wiping the tears away as quickly as they rolled out of my eyes.

My defenses weren't up, that was for sure. I wasn't expecting what had come at me. Or maybe the situation had been emotionally charged to begin with, and I'd missed the signs. I looked over at Jeff; he was just sitting there, staring at his new thumb, looking down at his shoe, waiting for the moment to pass. Dean's yelling wasn't Jeff's fault, I reminded myself. This rage was customary, it was sanctioned by the powers that be, by everyone who knew about Dean's temper (and Tony's temper and that of so many others) and still hired them to make shows.

Abuse like what had just befallen me was a small price to pay for the "genius." We weren't making art for art's sake, after all: we were doing it for money. And it was understood that if a few eggs needed to get broken to make a good omelet that hopefully went into syndication, so be it.

I'd survive. Hadn't I always?

Or . . .

Had I?

Dean screaming at me, not letting me get a word out, Jeff looking on but doing nothing, I was once again my eleven-year-old self, broken in my bedroom, begging the monster to let me stay in my house. Then, like now, I wasn't safe-safe.

The difference was, I wasn't eleven anymore. I didn't have to "earn my keep."

The monsters didn't buy my house, or my kids' toys—I did.

I didn't have to put up with this. I was an adult who could stand up and walk out.

So, I did.

I drove home and went straight to the garage. I dragged my childhood mirror out from behind some shelves, breaking a few things in the process—very dramatic—and brought it into the house.

Dean had a daughter, same age as mine. What would he do if someone screamed in his daughter's face? What would I do if someone screamed in my daughter's face?

What kind of behavior would she accept as the price of doing business?

I had a responsibility now to be a role model for my fearless daughter. At least if I wanted her to stay fearless.

That afternoon, I enlisted Todd to help hang my childhood mirror in Phoebe's room, on the wall across from her bed. The same place it occupied in another little girl's room a lifetime before. I told Phoebe that with the mirror hanging this way, she would always be able to see for herself that there were no monsters under her bed. I had found the mirror's purpose, why it had followed me this far. My spiritual friend was right, it was a character in my life.

"No more monsters," I told her. "Okay?"

"No more monsters," she repeated, then asked if she could get another panda backpack.

And I took her to the mall for a present for no reason, but not before standing in front of the mirror and saying it to myself.

No more monsters.

The Stain

There's a great saying that "when life hands you lemons, make lemonade." Having been given the mother of all lemons in the lemon of all mothers, I tried to find lemonade. Though Cathy was decent step-lemonade—on top of helping to raise me, she taught me how to behave like a person—like, to always use a top sheet, and whenever I'm invited to someone's home, *always* bring a (wrapped, non-regifted) hostess gift—I needed someone who would accept me, warts and all. And Cathy had seen more warts than any step-lemonade should see. So, for years, I continued to search for a mother figure I could start fresh with. Fresh lemonade.

And just like when people see Jesus' face in a potato chip or cloud formation, I saw my mother figure in the form of a raised paint stain on the wall of my yoga class.

This paint stain bore an uncanny resemblance to a wise-looking woman complete with a strong jaw, a small upturned nose, deep-set eyes, and hair that billowed behind her, falling just below her long, elegant neck, after which the rest of her disappeared into the wall. She resembled Wilma Flintstone . . . after she took the bones out of her hair. Like Wilma, she conveyed a serenity and wisdom, and I knew instantly I could trust her advice and I would continue to appreciate her company. Until they painted over her.

I was comfortable with her from the start. I would stand in Warrior Two for eight breaths and telepathically ask my paint stain image of a mother if it was okay to drug my kids to knock them out when I wanted to watch a movie, and by the time I'd move into Downward Dog, she would not only give her blessing but praise my stance. I'd move into a headstand and share my concerns about perimenopause, asking if she knew when I could expect to start the change. My paint stain mother had no answer for that one, of course, as she was a paint stain and therefore never went through menopause. But from her perfect little mouth came no scorn or dismissal, as I'd been used to with all my other parental figures. All she offered were sympathy and support—like Wilma Flintstone offered to Pebbles.

One time as class was winding down, I asked my paint stain mother if Todd and I should take our kids on a trip to Hawaii with my best friend Amy and her family.

It was no easy decision. First, we'd never indulged in a family vacation, not counting the time we went back east for four days, staying in a cousin's finished basement on Long Island. I wasn't sure if five-year-old Jesse and three-year-old Phoebe would even know how to appreciate a tropical paradise and poolside snacks. What would be the point of doing something extravagant if I couldn't hold it over their heads and threaten to cancel it or use it against them later in life?

Second—which probably should have been first, because it was a bigger deal—I sort of hated my best friend Amy.

My hatred didn't mean I wouldn't die for her, because I would. I would give her the shirt off my back if she needed it. But it would look so much better on her that I'd be mad, though I'd swallow the anger because I love her so much—and with good reason.

Because even though I often need to take a muscle relaxer and eat a jar of peanut butter before I start my car after spending time with her, Amy is and has always been the person who makes me laugh the hardest—that silent kind of laugh where I can't breathe and almost pee and then when I do pee, she doesn't call attention to it. I hope everyone has a friend like her. The friend who'll look at something on your back and tell you if it's a zit or maybe cancer, and if it's a zit, squeeze it. The one who will come with you to a liposuction consult, convince you that you totally don't need it, and then bring you frozen yogurt after the surgery.

So, I love her.

That said, her nose job is subtler than mine. Also, her knee skin hasn't been subjected to gravity and probably never will be. Even after babies, her stomach doesn't look like Munch's *Scream* every time she bends over. Her hair is thick and beautiful, whereas I've had a receding hairline since the age of fourteen.

There's more. Like me, she's also a comedy writer. She's been at it for as long as I have. Unlike me, however, she's achieved every TV writer's ultimate goal—the near impossible—getting her own show on network television. Twice. The characters and worlds *she* created were good enough to reach millions on network television.

With her success had come a beautiful, giant, 1920s house with an intercom and a staircase that was once used for servants. Her wedding—to her handsome, sweet, smart, charismatic, not one bit narcissistic even though he's an actor husband—was covered by *InStyle* magazine. The very edge of my arm can even be seen in one of the photos.

And where the rubber meets the road, I have to say it—she simply has better kids. Thanks to the fact that Amy has read every parenting book, they use "inside" voices when necessary, they self-soothe, they go to sleep when told, and they don't steal. Not that my kids steal—though if they're anything like me, they will eventually. In short, Amy is better than anyone I know on all fronts. Including me. Especially me.

On top of all of it, she had a helpful, loving mother who would fly to LA on a moment's notice if Amy had an emergency or even just needed to take a nap, one who'd drive her grandkids to all their after-school shit and pick up dinner for Amy on the way home. A mother who loved her unconditionally. Who supported her in every way. An angel mother.

So. I hate her.

I wasn't proud of hating my beloved friend so much. My paint stain mother knew this, and understood how loaded the proposition of vacationing with Amy and her perfect family was, how extended proximity to her platinum life risked tarnishing my own.

Do I go? I asked my paint stain mother.

Of course you do, she told me.

Even though she'll be walking around in a bikini, and I'll be in a Spandex burqa?

I love your sense of humor. Yes. You go and enjoy yourself, my paint stain mother insisted.

So, we went, surviving the flight and getting to our hotel, where Jesse and Phoebe were greeted by hula girls with leis. Jesse refused his, and I made the requisite jokes to Todd about Phoebe getting lei'd before Jesse, then shouted at them to "please, act like people" when they ran, shrieking with joy, through the lobby. It was as if they'd never been anywhere nice. They hadn't.

We got settled in our room, which was so small, containing two king-sized beds that took up so much space, we couldn't open the dresser drawers all the way.

But I couldn't get down about it. It was paradise, after all.

Well, a slice of paradise. A small slice.

While I tried to find a place for my suitcase in the bathroom, Todd unpacked all the cameras we would ruin and ultimately lose, and the kids fought over who was going to sleep where and with whom.

"Jesse rubs his toes on me when he sleeps!" Phoebe whined.

"Phoebe makes mouth sounds!" Jesse whimpered.

"How about we go home right now?! I'm calling the airport!" I said, making my first empty threat of the vacation.

Amy texted that she'd arrived. They had checked into their villa. I hadn't known they were staying in a villa. How cool? Good for her. Before long, I finally found myself sitting in a shallow lagoon talking with my best friend about life while our sons splashed in the water together and our daughters waited on us from the pretend restaurant they'd set up in the sand, our husbands off doing whatever husbands do. And as Amy's four-year-old handed me the imaginary peanut butter sandwich with pickles on it that I ordered, I was grateful to my paint stain mother for insisting I go on this trip.

Amy complained about the hotel's exorbitant prices—especially for a place that wasn't nearly as nice as her go-to (the Four Seasons). Fortunately for me, I'd never had a Four Seasons to compare our current digs to, and the accommodations seemed really nice—definitely worth using all of our miles getting there.

The Four Seasons comment was my first vacation reminder of the fact that Amy is *better*. Her standards were *higher*. What's fancy for me was *slumming* for her. I fished around for a muscle relaxer in my beach bag with one hand, accepting a cup of imaginary coffee from Phoebe with the other.

We had already made a plan to all meet up in the evening at our hotel restaurant, but Amy suggested that we just come to her place for dinner instead—that way the kids could run around and play while we hung out.

I chalked up her suggestion to the fact that having complained about the cost of the hotel, she probably didn't want to spend money on dinner.

I didn't want to sit in her gorgeous *villa* with the terrace and the view of all of Hawaii and field questions from my kids about why we were staying in a room with just two beds and a view of a parking lot instead of a mansion with several extra bedrooms. I didn't want to have to explain to them that Mommy's career wasn't as good as Amy's, how Amy wrote for a wider audience and Mommy's writing was too "specific" for the masses, after which my kids would judge me. Plus, I knew any meal at Amy's would require me to eat organic food because in addition to running a network TV show, Amy finds the time to make sure her kids don't ingest anything containing chemicals or nitrates. Whereas I buy food with the word "product" listed in the first ingredient or a warning that says, REMOVE PLASTIC FILM BEFORE HEATING. Just another example of how she has her shit together and I don't. And now, I would have to smuggle in a Diet Coke, like a junkie.

I didn't need that.

But mostly, I didn't want to be reminded of my own jealousy. I was on *vacation*, for fuck's sake.

Eating at a restaurant would clearly have been much better for my anxiety—especially as I'd taken my last muscle relaxer at the lagoon. But being a people pleaser—and more specifically, an Amy pleaser—I shoved my resentment down deep, said "Sure!" chirpily, then quietly seethed.

Later, on our way over, I had Todd stop at a store, so I could get Diet Coke and a hostess gift (organic avocados). Todd, Jesse, and Phoebe waited in the rental car. While in line I texted Amy to see if she needed anything, then immediately texted another friend back in LA to touch base. Amanda's life was pretty much in the shithouse. With three kids under the age of five, a true douchebag of a husband, and a herniated belly button that made it unbearably painful for her to laugh, her network of friends—myself included— were on high alert support-wise.

In an effort to downplay the good time we were having, I texted Amanda that the weather was bad, our hotel was kind of gross but nonetheless annoyingly expensive, and that even Amy was freaking out about how much we were all paying for the trip.

Amanda didn't believe me for a second. She shot back, There's no way Amy is freaking out about the price. She's rich, isn't she?

By now it was my turn at the register. While the checker rang me up, I texted back, Please. She's making us have dinner at her villa instead of going to a restaurant to save money. Cheap snob! I pressed Send, feeling a small sense of relief that I could complain to some- one.

Back on the road, I briefed the kids on good behavior at our friends' villa. I told Jesse to respect people's "bubble space" and that the other kids may not want to hear animal facts and to get them out of his system now. This was his cue to list enough moray eel characteristics to make me want to strangle myself with one. I told Phoebe that if she got angry and needed to bite something, don't let it be a person—or I WOULD call the airport and we WOULD go home (my second empty threat). I then went to text Amy to let her know we were en route. I looked at my phone and, under Amy's name, I saw the text: Please. She's making us have dinner at her villa instead of going to a restaurant to save money. Cheap snob!

Somehow, I'd sent Amy the text meant for Amanda.

Oh, Jesus Christ. No. No. *No.*

I turned my phone off, turned it back on. A fresh start?

But there it was. Right under Amy's reply that I'd missed about not needing anything from the store.

I started to feel my face get hot.

"I just sent Amy a text calling her a cheap snob," I told my husband.

Todd shook his head and sighed. "Why would you do that?" he asked.

"Because I have no attention to detail—you know that!" I choked out the words. My body was on fire as I was transported in an instant back to my first (brief) job after college, when I stood outside my office at *Bridal Guide* magazine in New York, where I was assistant to the Creative Affairs director. It was four degrees outside, but I was stripped down to a camisole and *still* burning up as I stared into the back of a truck stacked with two thousand copies of our magazine that were supposed to have gone to a convention center in Atlanta for the Hotlanta Bridal Expo but instead, because I'd gotten the return and send-to addresses mixed up, they'd shipped to our Lexington Avenue office instead.

Twenty-one years later, I was filled with the same feeling of dread and hot-faced panic I'd had then.

Only now, I wasn't going to lose my job. I was going to lose my best friend, who I hated. But also loved.

Maybe I could intercept the text, I thought. Maybe she hadn't read it yet. I frantically called Amy to beg her not to read her texts. Once, twice, three times I was sent straight to voicemail.

I looked up and saw Todd was looking at me instead of at the road. "Why did you call her a cheap snob?" he asked.

"Because I was being *nice* to *Amanda*," I said.

Ignoring Todd's confused look, I went back to redialing, and got through.

"*Hey Amy,*" I said, bright and cheery though my throat was closing. "I sent you this *cuh-razy* text. Obviously, it's not about *you* . . ."

I pressed 3, deleted, and rerecorded. "*Hey!* It's me. I got you *avocados!*"

Press 3, delete, rerecord. "*Amy* . . ."

My voice trailed off—what could I say? I hit Delete and hung up.

From the backseat, Phoebe asked when we'd be there. I told her Mommy was busy.

Jesse said, "Pretend I'm a zero-year-old German shepherd and you're my mother." I told him to pretend with his father. I had no time to be a German shepherd. I was in crisis mode. My best friend was about to see the real me. And it wasn't even true. I didn't even mean it!

Todd pulled into the steep driveway. I barely waited for him to stop the car before I got out. I told him to grab the laundry I'd brought—in case she hadn't gotten the text, it would be great to throw a load in while we were there.

I rang the doorbell. I was shaking and still on fire, not knowing what to expect, as the kids and Todd joined me on the porch. Maybe she'd been too busy cooking to check her phone or switched her phone off because she was in Paradise Mode. Or died.

Amy's husband, Matthew, finally opened the door, their kids Sam and Lily bounding down the stairs behind him. His giant smile made me think I was in the clear, that she hadn't seen the text. I searched his face for clues, but it remained blank and handsome.

"Welcome," he said as, overcome with a wave of hopefulness and relief, I kissed him way too hard and a little on the lips.

"Hiii!" I heard Amy happily call from somewhere. Suspicious as to what she could sound so happy about, aside from her life in general, I followed her voice to the second floor, past the elevator (the *elevator*) and into a breathtaking living room/dining room/kitchen situation with the views of the Hawaii I was afraid of.

I was so frantic I didn't even get jealous.

"Hey . . .!"

Showered, hair back in a low ponytail, and dressed in skinny jeans and a T-shirt, Amy was at the center island in the kitchen pouring a glass of wine. In my coffee-stained pink sweatpants and a T-shirt, my flyaway frizzies failing to conceal the fresh scar I gave myself picking a zit on the way over, I dropped my provisions on the counter.

"I brought organic avocados," I said, trying to match her enthusiasm. It couldn't be matched.

"Oh, that's so nice, thanks!" Amy gushed. "Want some wine?"

I don't drink, because when I lose inhibitions, I binge eat and get sad—*really* sad. Amy knows I don't drink and knows why. Did this mean she'd seen the text and figured inhibitions were in the trash anyway? That sadness was already on the horizon?

"I'd love some," I said. *I* knew sadness was on the horizon.

She handed me a glass and said the kids' dinner would be ready in a few minutes. I seized the moment and, telling her I'd take the time to give myself a tour of their house, set out in search of her phone.

I needed to delete that text.

I walked past Todd and Matthew chatting on the balcony and headed for the private wing and the master bedroom, where I immediately spotted Amy's phone on a nightstand. I rushed over, heart racing, and woke it.

There it was, right on the home screen. My text. *I could save this,* I thought, praising the lord and my dead grandmother Ethel, who I'm pretty sure reversed a possible HPV diagnosis a few years ago and stopped me from getting hit by a truck once.

But the phone was locked. I needed the passcode. *Dammit!* So close and yet so far.

Knowing we love all our children equally but that there's *always* a favorite, I guessed that Lily was Amy's favorite. I tried to remember Lily's birth date and of course failed. I remembered that she was born exactly seven weeks after Phoebe, but my brain was frying along with my body. I had five minutes, tops. I needed math. I needed memory.

I needed my husband.

"*Todd?!*" I called out at the top of my lungs. "Todd, you HAVE to see this bedroom! It's *insane!*"

"What are you doing?" Amy called.

"Freaking out over your room," I shrieked, "It's *a-mazing!*"

Todd appeared in the doorway. "What are you doing?" he said.

"When was Lily born?" I asked.

"*I* don't know," he answered.

"Then what's seven weeks after Phoebe's birthday?" I pressed him.

"When's Phoebe's birthday?" Todd asked.

I turned my scream of terror into a forced squeal of delight as, for Amy's benefit, I shouted, "Isn't this room SO nice?!" before turning back to Todd, waving the phone at him.

"There's a *code,*" I said. "How do I unlock this without her *code?*"

"If there's a code, there's nothing you can do," he replied.

I broke out in a whole new sweat. "Can't you do something to *bypass* it?" I hissed. "You work in *editing,* Todd!"

"You're just proving you don't know anything about my job," he said.

"Please do *not* make this about you!" I whisper-shouted.

Matthew called up that dinner was ready. Todd headed for the door, but I pulled him back by his shirt. "Where are you going?" I asked.

"To feed the kids," he said.

I'd forgotten them. Why did they always need our help eating? Shouldn't they have been able to feed themselves by now?

Before he could get away, I pulled him back by his shirt.

"Todd." I was scared. "Do you think Amy will forgive me? Was it bad, my text? It was *bad*, right?" I yanked at his shirt, hard enough to feel a few stitches pop. "*Was it bad?*"

"Yeah, it was bad."

"It *was* bad? Like, *bad* bad?" How could my own husband agree that it was bad?

"Yeah."

"But she'll *forgive* me, though—*right?*" I was suddenly terrified I'd piss myself from fear.

"Yeah. But you'll have to take your lumps," Todd said like it was the '50s. "She's said worse things to me to my face, by the way."

She *had*? Now I was kind of mad at *her*. I flashed to the time of Lily's heart surgery, when they needed blood donors and Amy didn't want my blood because she wanted her daughter to receive "happy, positive" blood that didn't have a ton of artificial sweeteners and Diet Coke in it.

Then again, she'd said that to my face. Not in a text to someone else.

Todd was right. I would have to take my lumps.

My stomach in knots, I followed him downstairs.

The kids were all on the back deck having the time of their little lives. It could have been a magical night, had I not ruined it. In the kitchen, Amy was filling their bowls with pasta. "What were you doing?" she asked.

"Just loving your place," I said and then, "Hey—when's Lily's birthday? I keep forgetting . . ."

The sound of the screen door opening and the cheers of the collective progeny swallowed her answer. Todd and I followed Amy out to her beautifully set table, right down to the hard butter in stick form for my son, because Amy remembered that butter in swirls sent Jesse into hysterics of *Rain Man* proportions. Amy could remember my son's dietary restrictions, and I couldn't remember her favorite daughter's birthday. There was even salmon for me, which I love—especially on a grill, which Matthew was seeing to.

My heart sank—she was being so very generous, as she always was. *Why did I have to be such an asshole?* I asked myself for the hundred thousandth time. *Because I was rotten.* But had I been born that way, or had it happened slowly? All I knew was that I seemed to always ruin everything.

I stared at Amy, spectacular in the Hawaiian moonlight, my shitty text awaiting her when she went to bed. I could throw the phone in the toilet, but what if it wasn't just water resistant, but waterproof?!

I *had* to find a way to spin this. For all my flaws, I was good at two things—online Boggle and lying.

I had nothing prepared but launched into a last-ditch effort.

"So, listen to this," I started. "Todd's mom is coming to visit us next month, did I tell you? She's staying in this place—she says it's a 'villa,' which—are you *kidding* me? *This* is a villa—!"

Matthew brought the platter of grilled salmon over from the barbecue. I grabbed a piece with my hand, stuffed it in my mouth. I felt like a gymnast on a balance beam. If the balance beam were on fire and gymnasts were liars.

"So, anyway, Amy, Todd's mom wants to *make dinner* for us at the villa she's staying in instead of us going out to eat at a restaurant, I mean . . . *She's such a cheap snob.*"

"Uh-huh," Amy said, walking back into the kitchen.

I followed her and forged ahead, even though my story made no sense even to me. Why would Todd's mother stay in a "villa" in Los Angeles, and not our house? And why would she cook when we were the ones who lived there? But there was no turning back now. I hung in the doorway, near the salmon (panic made me hungry), and got ready for my dismount, determined to stick the landing.

"So, I was texting with my brother-in-law—you know Jack, right? Todd's brother, Mark's partner—sorry, *husband* now—so *great* about gay marriage, isn't it? Anyway, I was texting with Jack, and I was texting a whole bunch of people at the same time—including you—saying how she's a cheap snob, meaning Todd's mother, so if you're the one who gets that text from me—"

"I saw the text," Amy said, avoiding eye contact.

The words hung there.

I started to get hot again.

Well, she could have said something and spared me the . . . gymnastics, but I guess I had to let that go.

"It wasn't about you," I stuttered, which is what I do when the shit hits the fan.

She cocked her head, not believing me, her eyes a green too beautiful to be named. I downed a glass of wine in one swallow, followed by a fistful of pita chips that were sitting on the center island. Sweat poured out of my head.

Amy swallowed hard. *"Liz—"* she started to say, but I cut her off.

"No, Amy, *listen* to me," I assured her in a rush. "Todd's mother *is* coming, you can ask him."

Matthew came into the kitchen and looked right at me. This time, his face was easy to read.

"Stop it, Liz," he said. "Just admit the text was about Amy."

Todd had now appeared in the doorway. He took one look at the desperation on my face and turned to leave.

"Todd!" I stopped him in his tracks. *"Tell* them how your mother is coming to stay with us." I gestured to Amy, who was looking into her wineglass. "And wants us to *cook* at her villa, because she's a *cheap snob,"* I said, leading him.

I shot him a pleading, "go with me" look—it was one of those times where I decided only *he* could see or hear me, like a sidebar between two characters on a sitcom. Instead of coming to my aid, Todd threw his hands up, shook his head in an *I don't know her* way, and moved to the other side of the kitchen with the others. I was ridiculous, and he knew it. I was outnumbered, and I knew it.

Just then, Jesse ran over, wanting more butter; the sourdough bread was warm, and it was melting too fast for the butter to hold its clumpiness. I grabbed the stick from the counter and handed it to him. "Just have the whole thing."

Watching him skip off, happily, I heard myself say, "I swear on Jesse's life, it wasn't about you, Amy."

All three of their jaws dropped in unison, as if choreographed. Amy's head jerked back a little so as to get a look at me from a farther distance; Todd's shoulders slumped, disappointed in me. Matthew shook his head quickly, like trying to get water out of his ears. He must have heard me wrong. There was no *way* I had just sworn on my child's life. And worse, on a very bad lie.

This, I would have to say, was my lowest point of the evening. Possibly the trip. Only time would tell.

I bit the inside of my mouth hard, trying to transfer all of my terror at the situation I'd created to the pain in my mouth. I felt a cold sensation and tasted blood.

"Fine," I said to Amy, willing the earth to swallow me. "It *was* about you. I'm *so* sorry."

Amy turned away, her gorgeous face flushed. She was hurt. I'd hurt Amy. Someone I never even knew *could* be hurt. Was I the first person to hurt her?! My heart broke at the realization, that I had caused her pain. I felt like crying. I *wanted* to cry. But I couldn't. I physically couldn't. The 30 milligrams of Prozac I was on combined with the Xanax I took that afternoon and the glass of wine I'd guzzled was making it impossible for me to access true emotion. And I couldn't even frown because of all the Botox. I just looked happy and vaguely surprised about everything.

Amy went outside to check on the kids. Todd silently picked from the bowl of pasta. I tried to appeal to handsome Matthew. "Matthew, you know I love Amy so much."

He shrugged and said, "Look—in all the years you guys have been friends, you were always true blue . . ."

I *was* true blue. But I wasn't.

". . . And with all the bullshit over the years, Amy could always count on you."

She *could* count on me.

But she couldn't.

Amy came back inside carrying the kids' empty plates over to the sink.

I went to help her, and she wouldn't let me. With her back to me, she said she wasn't surprised what had happened because it just confirmed what she'd always thought—that I talked shit about her.

"Why would you think *that*?" I asked her, shocked.

"Because you talk shit about everyone," she said.

"No, I don't!"

I do, though.

I really do. Most of the time I don't mean what I'm saying. Most of the time I don't even *know* what I'm saying. Sometimes I'll hear someone talking and think, *Man, she's catty,* and then realize it's me and I'm talking about someone. It's almost like a tic. But didn't everyone talk shit? Isn't that what reality TV is all about? This is America. It's our national pastime—talking shit while baseball's on.

So *yes*, I talked shit about people all the time. Usually because I'm nervous. Or desperate. Or maybe I hope that if I focus on everyone else's flaws, mine won't be so obvious.

"Amy. I would *never* say anything bad about you!" I insisted.

She said nothing. And in the silence, there was a chance for me to come clean. A chance to grow as a person. To tell Amy that I thought she was being a snob for complaining about the accommodations and then cheap to make us eat in at her villa. To tell her my text came from a place of my own insecurity. That I'm jealous of her on every level. She had a villa; I had to hear Phoebe's mouth sounds! She had a mother; I had a paint stain!

Do it, I thought. *Evolve. Grow.*

"Amanda hates you!" I blurted, throwing yet another friend under the bus. So much for evolving or growing.

I couldn't see him, but I could hear my husband's sigh.

"Amanda, your friend who I met once?" Amy asked, confused.

"Yes! She resents you because you're so pretty and your belly button isn't herniated, and you married such an amazing guy . . ." I gestured to Matthew. "Amazing guy. Truly the best."

"I thought we had a great conversation," Amy said, thinking back.

"Nope. She hates you," I said as if Amy was silly not to have realized that.

"Who's Amanda?" Matthew asked.

"My miserable friend. Amy, I was just trying to make her feel better about her sucky life by saying I was on vacation with a cheap snob, which obviously you are *not*. I would have called myself a cheap snob, but she's not jealous of me! Because why would anyone be jealous of me?!"

Amy turned back to me.

"Let's not discuss it. I know I'm not cheap—"

"You are *so* not cheap—"

"Liz, *please*. But this was an expensive vacation, and I'm not going to ruin it by being upset." She said this defiantly, decidedly, and then declared, "We can just deal with this after."

I knew what that meant. The minute she landed back in LA, she would tell our mutual friends what happened. They would, of course, take her side . . . even Amanda. I pictured all of Los Angeles lighting up with people finding out the truth about me—that I'm a bad person. That the lemon didn't fall far from the tree. And then, they would all leave me. Which I'd deserve. My paint stain mother might even slide off the wall, mortified to be associated with me. These would be . . . the lumps I had to take.

Todd left to go to the bathroom, and I suddenly realized that my lumps would probably also include Amy telling Todd the secrets she was keeping for me, from him. Amy was nothing if not thorough, and if everyone else in Los Angeles was going to abandon me, my husband probably would, too. Vows or not, Amy would win.

I followed my husband down the hallway. I needed to get to Todd before she did.

He'd closed the bathroom door. I opened it.

"It's just me," I said, wiggling my way in.

"Can't I pee in peace?" he asked, midstream.

No. No, he couldn't.

I took a deep breath. "I may as well tell you, because Amy is going to, I was still seeing Josh when I met you," I confessed.

My beautiful husband zipped his fly and looked at me, confused. "Who's Josh?" he asked, even more handsome now that I knew I could lose him.

"My ex-boyfriend. When we started dating, I slept with him like twice, before you and I went on that cruise," I confessed. "Actually, okay, once after—but not after we said, 'I love you.' And I *do* love you. I'm sorry."

"Okay," Todd replied, unsure of how to react.

But I wasn't finished.

"And I didn't *love* love you when we got married." The words were tumbling out now. "I *loved* you, but probably not as much as I should have and kind of had a nervous breakdown at my bachelorette party. And also I smoked in the apartment after you asked me not to. That's why the dog smelled like smoke all the time, not because she was hanging out with dog owners who were smoking at the dog park." I wasn't sure if Amy knew that. But just in case she did, he needed to hear it from me first.

Todd looked at me, blankly but not so blankly, then reached out and pulled me in. I put my head on his big, calming chest. Even though he shouldn't have—and I wouldn't have, if I were him—he put his arms around me and kind of patted my back. He loved me. But he'd had enough shit for the night.

I let him wash his hands in peace. It was the least I could do, after ruining our vacation.

In the living room, the kids were rubbing their eyes, falling asleep. It was time to go.

Before leaving, I grabbed Amy and hugged her hard.

"I'm so sorry," I said. "I'm so sorry, Amy. Can we give you money for dinner? Not that you'd want it, because you're not cheap. Not that that would be cheap!"

I wouldn't let go of her. I was afraid that once I did, she'd be gone forever. My only friend who made me pee-laugh.

Matthew held the door open for us. Todd grabbed our bag of dirty laundry and patted Matthew hard on the back in a way that said *Sorry, man.* And then he actually said it—"Sorry, man." The kids said their good-byes and headed for the car with their father.

With some struggling, Amy finally freed herself from my death-grip. "I'll see you at the lagoon tomorrow," she said, closing the door.

"You *will* . . .?" I asked, surprised, pushing the door back open.

"Yeah, I'll text you when I get up," she promised.

I couldn't believe it. "Don't you hate me . . .?"

"*Nooo!* Stop. Let's just laugh about it and move on."

I couldn't believe it. She'd seen the rotten, ugly, insane me, and she was okay. Because she also saw the good. There *was* good. My being there for her at the hospital when Lily was sick. My offering my toxic, unhappy blood or helping her with her scripts that would make it to national television. My driving across town to stash painkillers in her umbrella stand when I thought she could use a good Vicodin buzz. It all counted.

She didn't even hold a grudge. She's *that* perfect. Which really made me hate her. And love her.

I was never going to call Amy a cheap snob again. I was never going to invite Amanda and Amy to the same parties again. And I was *never* going to trust the advice of a paint stain again.

The Year of the Turtle

I used to wonder how families with eight hundred pets wound up that way.

You know those families. You've been to their houses—the ones where every bedroom has a fish tank and every bathroom has a (loaded) litter box. There's usually a fat and listless guinea pig ("He's the last . . .") living in the kitchen and a weird extinct bug in an overgrown terrarium that's way too close to wherever they keep the remotes. Their birdcages either have a dozen little birds that never shut up or one prehistoric parrot missing half its feathers who looks like he'd rip your face off if he could figure out how to pick the lock. Their ancient dog is morbidly obese, obsessed with crotches, and saves her incontinence trick for company.

Their houses smell a little. Even the people smell a little.

We've started to become one of those families.

Granted, we never really had far to go, what with the two dogs (both requiring their own crates) and the geckos. (Though to be fair, we've never had more than one gecko at once; we just replace the one every time it dies before Jesse finds out and melts down. Which is why they've all been named Taylor. I think we're on Taylor IV.) And the fish.

And now, our latest—and most frightening—acquisitions: the Turtles.

Phoebe's second-grade class had been studying China, and she became obsessed with visiting Chinatown in Los Angeles. While her interest in learning about different cultures and visiting a foreign land all of thirty minutes away impressed me, I really didn't feel like making the trek downtown. Who knew what the parking situation was going to be? What if there wasn't a Starbucks within twenty feet at all times? There were simply too many unknowns.

So, I waited for this obsession of Phoebe's to pass. I knew eventually she would forget about Chinatown. And just when I thought she had given up, that I had broken her, Chinese New Year hit, and she was back at it. This time, she was relentless. Seemingly overnight, my daughter had turned into one of those people who didn't give up (unlike, say, me).

And so it came to pass that on the first day of spring break Phoebe was headed to Chinatown. But not with me—with Angela, our long-suffering nanny who was one of the part-time residents in our Animal House and increasingly unhappy with the arrangement. Angela is twenty-five, close to six feet tall, and beautiful. So pretty, she can wear her blond hair short. Or with purple or green tips. I often wondered why she was wasting her time with us when she could have been America's Next Top Model. I wasn't about to bring that up, though—not when I needed her to do things like go to Chinatown.

Angela took on the task with quiet resignation. Jesse, on the other hand, was furious that he had to go with them. He'd had a day of playing on his Xbox and had some hard-earned relaxation time (his phrase) planned. I lectured him about the importance of getting out from behind his screens, out of his comfort zone and seeing the world, impressing on him how lucky and blessed he was to be healthy enough to experience life. The irony wasn't lost on me since this was one experience I refused to experience.

Before I left for work, Angela asked me what the souvenir policy for the day was. At some point, it had become routine that everywhere they went, we would buy the kids something. I made them promise to behave, to be good listeners, to neither whine nor melt down, and they could get one thing each. And we all went our separate ways.

A few hours later, Starbucks in hand, I watched from the comfort of my office a video Angela sent me of my kids at lunch. They were having an actual, honest-to-God blast. Phoebe's greasy, chubby fingers ripped her fortune cookie apart, while Jesse read his lucky numbers out loud, one dumpling speared on a single chopstick.

They were beautiful. Good, sweet kids, just being kids for that all-too-short childhood any of us get. It made my heart hurt—how much longer before my son lost that raspy little-boy voice of his? How long before my daughter's fingers lost that chubbiness I loved so much? How much of their childhood was I going to watch on an iPhone?

I felt disconnected. And guilty. I hated myself for not being the one to have taken them on their adventure.

About an hour later came a picture of the "souvenirs" they wanted.

I'd assumed Phoebe would get some Chinese fan that I'd find collecting dust under her bed that weekend and that Jesse would go for a plastic car that would break on the ride home and wind up in our graveyard of discarded toys. Instead, I found myself looking at a photo of two green turtles, each about the size of my thumb.

Turtles? Since when did they like turtles? We were the only family at our preschool that didn't host Fred, the class tortoise, for a weekend (one of our dog's appetites has been known to lean toward the exotic). At least two of the Taylors died on the kids' watch (not that we ever told them). My kids were less "animal kids" and more . . . animals.

But Phoebe and Jesse were clearly smitten over these little baby green things. And I was still under the guilt-inducing influence of that idyllic video. Desperate to make them happy, or at the very least to not be the person who ruined the moment, a part of this joy, I replied to the text:

Fine by me!

and figured Todd would of course do his part and reply:

No turtles!

This was our pattern. Due to my guilt at being a working mother and the fact that my intense need to be liked extends to my children, I'm the parent who gives in to their every whim, foisting on Todd the unfortunate task of denying their dreams and breaking their little hearts. This heartbreak is important because, according to the many parenting books I've read the backs of, parents who give their children everything they want ultimately release them into the world as lazy, greedy asshole adults who can't handle disappointment.

When Todd didn't respond within his usual thirty seconds, I called him. He didn't answer, either. I called again. Still no answer.

He always answers, so naturally I assumed he was dead. I tried him one more time in case he wasn't dead, which would be the only excuse I'd accept at that point.

And again.

And again.

He finally answered. "What's up?!" He sounded out of breath.

"I thought you died," I said. "Can you respond to the turtle text?"

"What 'turtle text'?"

Apparently, Todd was "busy" and hadn't seen the text, which left me wondering what he was so busy doing that he hadn't been following the day's events, including the subsequent texts from Angela, who had by now bought the turtles. Was Todd "busy" having an affair? The thought was taking over my entire brain— or would have, had Todd not immediately texted back a Teenage Mutant Ninja Turtles image.

It was then that Angela sent me a link to an article about the illegal sale of baby red-ear slider turtles in Chinatown, and while it was smart of her to do some research and see what we were getting into, I couldn't help but wonder if it was a little passive-aggressive that she didn't do the research until after purchasing exactly those turtles for the kids.

I read the article and was relieved to learn that the reason the turtles were illegal was not because they were gang related, stolen, or stuffed with drugs, but that they were merely riddled with diseases like salmonella, with 163 outbreaks reported in Los Angeles since their arrival.

These were the creatures my possibly vindictive nanny had purchased and my possibly cheating husband had approved. Two Baby Mutant E-Coli Turtles that were going to kill us all.

I called Angela and, over the gleeful, thankful shouts from the kids, I screamed, "Nobody touch the turtles with your bare hands!" I may be an absent mother, but I more than make up for that in neuroses.

Angela asked what they should put the turtles in when they got home. What did she mean, put them in—didn't they come in some sort of . . . turtle house?

They did not.

Didn't the people who sold them say what we should put them in?

They had not—the turtle smugglers, in fact, barely spoke English.

I shot Todd a new text, telling him to stop at Petco on his way home and ask (without asking) what someone (not him) would need for illegal baby red-ear slider turtles (that he definitely did not possess). I would have gone myself, but I really didn't want to go to jail, and he was the one probably having an affair, and this was all his fault anyway, so he deserved prison.

In person, the turtles weren't that gross. They were almost cute, even—tinier than in pictures, maybe the size of a quarter. Jesse, flush with excitement, introduced me to his turtle Janoris, who he named after a football player, and Phoebe's turtle she named Panda because she loves pandas. Naming an animal after another animal, however, is something that infuriates Jesse to no end. Phoebe clearly did this just to fuck with her brother.

The turtles were bopping around in their temporary housing— a Tupperware container with a rock in it and three turtle "pellets" that looked an awful lot like those fried Chinese noodles to me. Jesse was clearly smitten but was just as clearly growing anxious for them to "get settled into their permanent habitat." I promised him that his dad would be home soon with everything they needed, never imagining that two five-dollar black-market turtles could possibly need more than a few more rocks and a good flush at the end of the week.

Thirty minutes and four hundred dollars later (after Petco Member Discounts), Todd walked in the door with a 75-gallon tank, two lamps, all kinds of filters, and turtle food. That list wasn't even including tank décor and shrubbery. The tank was bigger than the dog's crates. Combined. It was bigger than my first apartment.

I couldn't understand why these teeny things needed an Olympic-sized pool. Todd explained to me how he learned at Petco that "his friend's" turtles were going to grow—because they were babies and babies grew into adults. My astonishment illustrates how little I dwell on what babies do.

It got better. As they grew into adulthood, Todd continued, the turtles would become territorial, so eventually we would need two tanks. Eventually? There was an eventually that went beyond, say, Memorial Day at the outside? How long did it take for them to go from butter beans to territorial adults to dead?!

"With proper care, the red-eared slider will live forty to seventy years," Jesse read from the red-ear slider brochure Todd had picked up.

Forty to seventy years.

Basically, the turtles were people. Illegal people who would grow up to hate each other and, possibly, us. We had two more insane people living under our roof. Except they wouldn't be going away to college or moving out at all. Ever. When we looked for retirement homes, we'd have to ask, "Where can we bring the turtles?"

That was when Angela regaled us with a story about her aunt who was survived by her sixty-five-year-old turtle, Hank, who could open the refrigerator himself and was still alive. Her "fuck you" well and truly complete, my nanny then grabbed her jacket and her copy of *In Cold Blood*, wishing us a good weekend as she closed the door behind her, sealing us up with our fate. Fates. For forty to seventy years.

Jesse was now on the verge of a nervous breakdown, terrified that the turtles would expire before being moved into their new home. Todd told him firmly that it was going to take a while to set up the tank and the filters, and that the guy at Petco promised that the turtles would be fine in the Tupperware until the morning.

Which was my cue for a nervous breakdown. "You didn't tell him we have these things—did you?!" I screamed.

He had. The guy had asked him point blank if he got them in Chinatown, and Todd had said yes. Because Todd couldn't lie about anything except being "busy" having an affair.

Neither of us slept much that night. I lay in bed thinking how every time the doorbell rang, I was going to think it was the Department of Environmental Conservation—basically, Turtle Immigration. I'd be like Lorraine Bracco in *Goodfellas*, except instead of cocaine, I'd be flushing turtles down the toilet.

I woke up the next morning to the sound of the bells on our backdoor jingling. This was Crash, our puppy, telling us he needed to go outside. We'd spent a lot of money having him trained to do this with his nose (and give high-fives). And it would have been worth it, if he didn't consistently shit on the carpet immediately after ringing the bells.

Still, I was up and decided to try and make an early yoga class.

I went downstairs, and was surprised to find Todd bent over the dining room table, which was now covered in turtle products and pages of directions. Jesse was hovering nearby. Every time he got too close, Todd would take him by the shoulders, walk him backward across the room, and leave him there. Within seconds, Jesse would reappear over his shoulder.

"Whatcha doin'?" Jesse would say for what I had no doubt was the thousandth time, trying to appear casual.

Thrilled as I was to see Jesse was getting exercise (and yes, that does count as exercise for Jesse), I could see that he was driving Todd crazy. I gave my son a stern talking-to about "bubble space" and asked him to remember some of the calming techniques his therapist taught him—we had literature on deep cleansing breaths and stuff, but I was pretty sure I'd thrown it out with the previous year's art projects. I went to press down on Jesse's head, like I've always done to help calm him, but he was getting taller and I couldn't get leverage. So, I just watched him make yet another break for Todd, which allowed me to make my own break for my mat and keys.

"I'm headed for yoga!" I announced. "Back soon!"

Todd understood that my yoga classes were a necessary way for me to blow off steam due to working so hard. So, I was stunned into almost silence when, rather than wish me namaste, my husband asked me to stay home and please keep Jesse occupied until he was done setting up the turtle tank. "Or I might put him through a wall," he said, almost completely serious.

Now there were two of us pacing and asking Todd if he was done yet. At one point, Todd looked up at me, his face red. He was sweating, his eyes were a little . . . crazy. A handy guy, especially for a Jew, he seemed to have met his match with this filtration system.

Phoebe, meanwhile, did not give one solitary shit about the turtles, having moved on to the soda-flavored Lip Smackers I'd ordered her from Amazon (another gift born of my working-mother guilt). Her disregard for these little beings, about whom she cared so much only the day before, was borderline chilling.

Jesse, on the other hand, was obsessed enough for them both. A raw nerve, my hyper-empathic son was growing more and more worried about the turtles' welfare by the minute, feverishly consulting the turtle care pages he'd downloaded from the Internet. He was worried that they still hadn't eaten their pellet. They were becoming "listless" and "lethargic."

"They're turtles." I tried to assure him. "They're supposed to be listless."

Jesse glared at me and informed me that was in fact a turtle misconception. Ask Google.

By then, Todd was done with the tank. My heart soared—I'd make the 9:15 class!

One hitch—we had nowhere to put the tank.

In full authoritarian mode, Todd announced that there was no surface big enough, deep enough, or strong enough to hold the tank. We needed a credenza. Until we had one, life was on hold.

Jesse fell to his knees and howled as if *credenza* were some form of torture. Before I could even log onto the Restoration Hardware website for something chic, Todd left to find a credenza—and left me to take care of the kids.

I started doing yoga in my mind as I fought to block the sound of Jesse rattling off red-ear slider turtle "red flags" from the literature he'd amassed.

"Mom? Do their eyelids look puffy?"

"They are not puffy. There is nothing puffy about them."

"Is that mouth discharge?"

"No. That's just a mouth."

Somewhere around his asking me to check their anuses for worms, I finally reminded Jesse it was spring break and he could use his electronics, which sent him joyfully off in search of dystopian worlds to destroy. I hoped.

Then Phoebe appeared, ordering me to close my eyes before shoving a Lip Smacker lip balm directly up my nostril and demanding I guess the flavor.

"Orange soda," I guessed.

Wrong. Grape. She shoved another at me. And another.

"Mom? Which one do you think is cuter?" Jesse had reappeared, his iPad spewing images of red-ear slider turtles.

"They're all cute," I offered lamely.

"Close your eyes!" Phoebe shouted. She's very loud.

Obediently, I closed my eyes again. It's no secret: Phoebe scares me a little.

"But which is the cutest?" Jesse asked again.

I opened one eye and pointed, randomly.

"You don't think this other one is cuter?"

"You're right. That one's cuter."

"But which is the cutest?"

A Lip Smacker shot up my nose.

"THEY ARE ALL CUTE!" I screamed. "PHOEBE, I ONLY SMELL ORANGE! YOU ARE MAKING ME VERY SICK!" Where were the kids from the Chinese food video? The ones I wanted to hold onto forever?

I wanted to go back to the day before.

No. I wanted to go back to my twenties.

I'd settle for yoga. And a house with a husband in it and turtles that weren't.

"Mom, did you know red-eared sliders get their name from the small red stripe around their ears? And the *slider* in their name comes from their ability to slide off rocks and logs and into the water quickly!"

I wanted to watch the little fuckers slide into a quart of wonton soup. Instead, I grabbed the iPad and told Jesse he couldn't use it to look up information, only for violent video games and inappropriate YouTube videos. He reminded me that we put parental controls on the iPad when his friend Carter's mom called about his bad language after a playdate at our house.

I promptly took the parental controls off his iPad and sent him on his way. Desperate times.

Finally, Todd returned with a hideous bright green, water-stained credenza he'd bought for $250 from a fish store that was going out of business. Behind him, dragging the other side of the credenza, was Warren, a bald man in his midfifties sporting a long white beard, faded arm tattoos, and cargo shorts with black socks— basically, a guy who looked like he worked at a fish store. For $80 an hour, Warren was going to help Todd put the filter together.

The $5 turtle total was now at $740. I half-jokingly asked Warren if it would be kind of us to return the turtles to nature via the LA River that runs right behind Jerry's Famous Deli. Neither Warren nor Jesse found this even half-funny. Jesse pounded hourly-compensated Warren with turtle questions, driving the turtle total up to $820.

Finally, Warren was gone, the filter was properly attached to the tank, and it was time to fill 'er up. Jesse went outside to turn the hose on, as I turned to my shell of a husband.

"How mad are you at Angela right now?" I asked conspiratorially.

"I'm not mad at Angela," Todd said.

"You're not?" He was clearly mad at someone.

"Angela asked," Todd said.

Oh, he was mad at me.

ME?!? "You're the one who said yes, Todd!" I shouted.

"I NEVER said yes!" he shouted back.

"Yes, you did . . .!" Grabbing my phone, I went back into the previous day's texts. There they were: the lunch video, the text from Angela asking if they could get the turtles, pictures of the turtles . . .

I continued to scroll, scroll, scroll, past my "Fine by me!," past Angela's article about illegal turtles . . . all the way to a picture of the kids in the kitchen with the turtles.

"I was in a meeting," Todd said. "I never responded. Remember? You called me six hundred times?"

I was getting a little nauseous, and not from my daughter's lip shit this time. "Well . . ." I stammered, "What kind of meeting were you in that you couldn't respond? Are you having an affair?!"

"I was in a meeting for work," Todd said quietly. "You forget I have a job sometimes."

"No, I don't!"

I do, though.

I do forget whenever I'm writing. And that somehow, he's always there for me, making it look easy as I bounce ideas off of him and ask him to read things over and over and over. He's always there when I'm in a ball on the bathroom floor because I can't think of a joke. Always ready to take care of the kids when I have to hole up in a hotel for the weekend to meet a deadline.

And of course, when I go to yoga every weekend, no matter what.

I forget—that's not his job.

I pay no attention to the fact that he might have somewhere else to be, mentally or physically, that isn't with me or our kids. I give him zero space for himself.

How could I ever think Todd would have an affair? He has no time for an affair. I don't even give him time to not answer a god-damned text. Or have a job all his own that gives him the same satisfaction that, for all its insanity, my work still gives me.

As if two kids, two dogs, a gecko, a gorgeous but vindictive nanny, and a slightly feral mommy weren't enough, now I'd added turtles that were going to outlive us to Todd's front-loaded life. And forgotten that my husband not only had a life—he deserved one.

I offered to help Jesse fill the tank. Todd told me to go to yoga. How could I go to yoga and leave him with this mess? Especially since it was my fault. Going to yoga would be selfish.

But also, necessary. For all our sakes. Obviously, I went.

LATER, WHEN I got home, Jesse and Phoebe met me at the door, excited to show me the turtles in their tank. Todd had gotten it all set up and functioning.

They led me to the playroom where two tiny baby turtles swam around, happily. I had to admit, they were pretty cute.

Jesse wrapped his arms around me and thanked me for letting them get the turtles. I told him to thank his dad. He's the one who did all the work.

"But I did say you could have them, so you're welcome." I kissed his head.

"We waited for you to get home," Phoebe squealed excitedly. "It's time for them to eat!"

As I looked around for the baggie of pellets, the kids rushed Todd, who stuck his hand into a plastic bag with reddish brown mushy stuff in the bottom. Pulling out a fistful, he held his hand over the tank and released it into the water. Instantly, the mush dissipated into dozens of opaque red threads, which started squirming as the turtles dove for them, sucking them up like spaghetti. Squirming and twisting up in knots, some fell to the bottom and others moved in place. The kids cheered, as I wondered what the hell I was looking at. "Is this, like, live seaweed, or someth—"

"They're bloodworms, Mom!" Jesse said, like he didn't know me at all. Like he didn't know about my revulsion toward insects. And my even bigger revulsion toward mushy things being eaten by slimy things.

My toes curled, my face made that deep frown all the beauty experts say is the most-aging facial expression and then, remembering this, I quickly smiled. But my smile was a lie. This was a scene from one of those nature shows Jesse plays on a loop. Whenever I enter the family room, I run the risk of glimpsing a fly's seven hundred eyeballs close up or a wildebeest being eaten by a hyena. I cover my eyes and shout at him to shut it off or else he'll be punished.

And now, live and in person, I watched as one of the turtles—one of our turtles—swam around an aquarium big as a small piano with a piece of disembodied worm hanging from his turtle lips. *National Geographic*, in my house. There was no changing the channel—to say nothing of turning off the lights.

"Their pale skin allows their hemoglobin to show through," Jesse announced, and pointed. "If you look closely you can see the antennae—the small fleshy projections running down their bodies—"

"Jesse, it's not nice to tell me that," I snapped, and turned to Todd, pointing at the mushy bag of nightmares. "Do we keep them in the garage?"

"The refrigerator," Todd said, sending more worms to their deaths. "They need to be kept cold."

That was the moment—the trifecta of Todd's anger, Jesse's mania, and my contemplating keeping those death-worms in the same fridge where I stored bottled water—when I started to realize the enormity of what I'd done.

For the first time in ages, I insisted that night on putting the kids to bed—their rooms were the farthest ones in the house from the ecosystem wriggling and munching downstairs. Once the kids were asleep, I walked past the "turtle room." The door was closed, a green glow from their lamps escaping the doorframe, like in a horror movie. One thin door separated me from live bloodworms and turtles that were growing bigger by the second.

What about when the turtles got bigger? What would they eat then—snakes? What if the worms got out? What if they ended up slithering all over the place? What if Crash ate them and shit them out on the carpet?

What if I ate them? What if, on one of my Ambien binges, I went into the fridge and grabbed the worms instead of the week-old ziti?!

No. No way. I could not take that risk. Bloodworms, it turns out, is where I draw the line.

I found Todd relaxing on the couch in the family room, drinking a beer.

"We need to get rid of those turtles," I said, frantic. "For all our sakes—we can't have them in the house."

"Liz—"

"Can you kill them? Make it look like an accident?"

"No."

"I'm serious, Todd . . . When does the 'territorial' thing happen? Can they eat each other? Is there a scenario where they both wind up dead?"

And with the most energy and excitement I'd seen in him since his precious Ohio State Buckeyes won the national championship, Todd sprang to his feet and told me the turtles weren't going anywhere. He had done too much work, busted his ass too hard to get everything set up. There was no way we were getting rid of them now.

"They are staying," said my beloved husband who didn't even have time for a measly affair. "For forty to seventy years."

"Then I'm going to kill myself," I said.

And with the most energy and excitement I'd seen in him since he told me the turtles were staying for forty to seventy years, he told me I was also staying. If he had to watch over me twenty-four hours a day to insure my safety, he would do that.

He would take care of us. All of us. Of me.

It was his job. He liked it.

But nowhere near as much as I loved him. And our crazy, wild life together.

I've offered the kids a kitten if they let me "find a new home" for the turtles.

They refused.

Todd doesn't know.

But I don't know how long I can keep it a secret that Phoebe really wants a kitten. And obviously I'm not going to say no.

Happy New Year

It's been years since the brother I knew was replaced by the religious doppelgänger bearing a strong resemblance to Jeff. I may not accept it, but I tolerate it—much as he no doubt tolerates some of my less pleasant quirks. And while I tend to avoid him when he's in the grips of—let's call it "religious behavior"—for the sake of maintaining a close relationship and fostering one between our children, once in a while Todd and I accept an invitation to spend a holiday with him and his family.

Like lunch at his house one recent Rosh Hashanah, which is the Jewish New Year. Rosh Hashanah is the first of the High Holy Days—the one where the Lord decides who will get to live another year and who won't—so I didn't think it would hurt for us to put in a little face time there. Another reason for us going was that my dad and Cathy had come up to visit and would also be there—no doubt trying to earn another turn around the sun themselves. I could kill two birds with one stone. That might even be a biblical slogan.

Even though in theory Dad and Cathy had recently moved from Long Island to Nevada to be closer to us, we rarely saw them. Which meant they were happy. So, I was happy. They were caught up in a very demanding social life in Las Vegas and, I suspected, some pretty weird shit as well. My suspicions were reinforced by Mitzy, their Maltipoo and favorite child, whom they had smothered into insanity with their artisanal cocktail of affection, control, and ambient terror.

Mitzy is about as unstable a dog as I've ever known, and Jeff, my sister-in-law Stephanie, Todd, and I were all of the same opinion that she was forever trying to kill herself. The countless times she ran directly into oncoming traffic despite rigorous training against the behavior was an early indicator. As was her constant picking fights with dogs large enough to swallow her whole. And her going out of her way to eat sharp objects and chocolate, which is notoriously poisonous to dogs. Mitzy had no doubt ridden up with Dad and Cathy from Vegas, strapped into her car seat—a legitimate car seat—and in two days they would depart as usual because according to Cathy, Mitzy didn't like to be away from home for longer than that.

Todd and I had been pretty lax in the religion department when it came to the kids and we'd recently begun thinking maybe we should start educating them on the faith they were born into before they started having really hard questions. One of the things Todd and I had bonded on early in our relationship was that we both hated Hebrew school to the point of faking our own near-deaths to get out of it (my thing was spontaneous coma, his was aneurism), and neither one of us wanted to put Jesse and Phoebe through that.

But Jesse was six and Phoebe was four, and it was time they

understood a little about their faith heritage. And at least they'll know where their neurosis comes from. And so, during our car ride over to lunch—an hour late to avoid the prayer portion of the festivities—it fell to me to deliver the bad news to our children that even though it was New Year's, it was the Jewish kind of new year, one that didn't come with confetti or ball dropping or staying up until midnight, but instead came with praying and bad food. "Because Jews like to be miserable," I explained.

Todd threw me that look that says he's wondering why I have to be me. I thought I was doing pretty well, myself.

"So, you're Jewish, guys," I continued. "Got it?"

"Not Christmas?" Phoebe asked.

"No. You're Hanukkah," I said.

"I think she was asking if we were Christians," Jesse said.

"You're not that, either," I told him.

"Can we ever celebrate Christmas?" my son asked, scared.

"No," I said. More bad news.

"Is there a Santa Claus?" Phoebe asked.

"Yes," I say only because I don't want my kids to tell the Catholic kids there's no Santa Claus and then we're *those* assholes. "There is Santa. He just hates Jews."

The talk had proven pretty easy. So easy, in fact, that I decided to broach another thorny subject.

"So, kids . . ." I started. "You need to know that Mommy and Daddy are gonna die someday."

That didn't go over quite as well. Todd shook his head as the kids started crying and said for my ears only, Don't worry, Mommy'll go first, which is why he was and remains the island of sanity in our family unit. And why I must go first.

After the kids stopped carrying on about our imminent deaths, we spent the rest of the ride discussing what the kids wanted for

Christmas that year. I'd fucked up. It had been a little premature of me to have the "death talk" with my kids, especially when they'd yet to experience death with anything beyond remote controls and the occasional fly.

Which got me wondering how I would have felt at their ages to have learned that I was a twin. Because I had been one.

I didn't learn about her until I was in high school and happened to take a good look at my birth certificate, where, in the space after "How Many Children Born," was the handwritten notation "Two Female." Which fucked me up a little back then, and I was eight years older than Jesse at the time.

Now here I was planting orphan nightmares in my kids' heads, though to be fair, they bounced back pretty quick when I told them Jewish Santa would probably get them another dog, and we got to Jeff's without further incident.

The moment we entered the house, we were hit with a burst of hot air that smelled of chicken, root vegetables, and if Jewishness has a smell, that. Before I could close the front door, sealing us in for the day, Mitzy sprinted over, a white cloud of carefully groomed fluff and neuroses, a pink bow tied tightly atop her bug-eyed little head.

"Mitzy!" I heard my dad yell frantically from somewhere. "Get the dog!"

I called that I had her and picked her up just as she was about to make a break for it. Through her open and panting mouth, I caught a flash of something metallic and, checking to make sure she wasn't chewing a razor, noticed the orthodonture and realized she was wearing braces to correct her underbite. Yes, doggy braces.

As Todd shut the door, I put Mitzy back down, and we went into the dining room, where Jeff was the picture of Orthodoxy in a black suit and hat with a beard, looking less like the comedy writer and dirty joke machine I knew and more like a Hasidic Abraham Lincoln.

Lunch had started, the dining table having been extended halfway across the living room to accommodate what looked like an entire road company of *Fiddler on the Roof*, who were all eating and talking.

"Mitzy made another run for it," I said to my brother lightly as a hello. Jeff just smirked and shook his head.

I found his wife Stephanie in the kitchen. More blond and blue-eyed than Cathy (I didn't think that was possible until I met her) and lovely in that naturally-thin, forgets-to-eat-sometimes, converted-to-Judaism-for-Jeff way. She was standing there, surrounded by women who were challenged in all of those physical departments to varying degrees and who I assumed, deep down, under their layers of skirts and pants, must have hated her.

I apologized to Stephanie for being late. I blamed traffic, but we both knew my strategy. This wasn't my first time at the High Holy rodeo. She pointed out that my favorite Orthodox friend of theirs was there, too. He had an uncanny resemblance to Tom Cruise, which tells you a lot about the scale I'm using for "normal."

I sat at the table next to Todd and across from my dad, who was handsome and fit, especially for his age, though he looked older than he had looked back east. His hair was a starker white, and his once strong features had softened like older men's do. Cathy, all blond and blue and sitting beside him in a red sundress, stood out like a primary-hued Irish Catholic sore thumb, fanning herself with a paper napkin. I asked her why it was so hot in the house. She told me the AC was broken, and because of "Jewish rules," they couldn't call the guy to come because no one was allowed to touch the phone on the New Year. Not the fun one, but still.

"Wouldn't God want us to be cool?" I asked her. We were in a desert after all.

My dad shushed me sharply, glancing at my brother, his pride and joy. I thought I'd been whispering. My old man kept playing with his napkin, whittling it down obsessively to a tiny spear with his thumb and forefinger. Personally, I would have been more than happy to nominate myself and risk not getting that extra year by offering to call the AC guy. Not fix the AC, mind you—just fucking call someone who could. But my brother had chosen this life of excessive suffering—this was their house, their rules. So instead, I sat there in an ever-growing pool of my own sweat.

After lunch, we all dipped apples in honey and asked the almighty for a sweet new year, Amen, and the kids ran off to play. I think there were a hundred children in that house. Like for Catholics, one of the mandates of being Orthodox is to make more Jews, and this gang was killing it in that department. Jesse and Phoebe went to join them, but not before stopping to pet Mitzy, whom they made the mistake of treating like, oh, a dog. Cathy, obviously rattled, gently extracted their hands from the coat fresh from the groomer blowout.

"Let's not pet her too hard," she instructed them, in a singsong tone that bordered on hysterics. "We don't want her to get over-tired."

The Orthodox wives moved into the kitchen to discuss their nation of children, leaving the menfolk to sit around the table and discuss the state of Israel. I decided to Getanyahu the hell out of the line of fire and retreated to the living room with Todd and the other non-Zionists.

Orthodox Tom Cruise was already there, sitting on the couch and looking for a rock in his shoe. My dad was there, too, cross-legged in a sofa chair, staring into space, still honing his napkin-spear from before. I plopped down on the sofa between Orthodox Tom Cruise and Todd, who flipped through a copy of *Jewish Journal*—there was literally nothing else on the coffee table.

When it comes to our family, as I'm sure it does with others, this is when the TV usually came on. Ah, TV, that warm box of inoculation against conversation, which always runs the risk of escalating into argument. But in this kosher house, where we couldn't operate anything more mechanical than the doorknob on the way out, we were trapped for the duration and would now be forced to talk to each other. Which we did, gamely (and quickly) exhausting all the small-talk topics—kids, school, work, Las Vegas, Mitzy's latest squirrel encounter.

The afternoon heat made the absence of AC even more unbearable. Still we persevered, until we all—or at least I—started to get a little woozy and lightheaded. While I pondered just how much carbon monoxide it would take to kill a party our size, in the other sofa chair Cathy was fanning herself and Mitzy, who panted on her lap. The *Glamour* magazine from 2009 moved from Cathy to Mitzy at intervals, Jennifer Aniston's face flipping back and forth at me as Cathy cooed her beloved's name in an attempt to soothe discomforts both real and imaginary.

Had there ever been doubt as to the hierarchy in our family, it was pretty clear at that point that Mitzy was Cathy's favorite child. Which made that crazy dog the sister I never had—or rather the sister I actually did have who never lived. And since I'd already read all the literature the coffee table had to offer, I decided to broach the subject and turned to my father.

"Hey—did my twin sister have a name before she died?" I asked him.

Orthodox Tom Cruise looked up from his shoe. Todd put down the *Jewish Journal* he was pretending to read. Cathy fanned faster.

My dad stared straight ahead and didn't answer. I thought he hadn't heard me, and I started to ask him again, until he cut me off.

"Elizabeth," he warned, "why ask something like that now?"

I wanted to tell him I was just curious, that I figured it might have been a conversation springboard since we couldn't watch TV. Instead I just said, "Forget it." Ours was never the sort of relationship where real talk about life shit or feelings about life shit had ever taken place, and clearly this was neither the topic nor the temperature to change our routine.

I started steering the conversation back to Vegas when Orthodox Tom Cruise interrupted me. Tom Cruises can be so persistent.

"Wait," he said. "You and Jeff had a sister? Did she have a name?"

I just scrunched up my nose and shook my head in a code that implied that it didn't matter and we should just drop the subject and stare into space.

"No, she didn't," my father suddenly boomed. "She was dead on arrival. Where's the dog?"

Stunned—like pretty much everyone else—I pointed to Mitzy across from his chair, now lying on the floor next to Cathy (heat rises). Cathy laughed nervously, a hehehehe chuckle as a reaction to my dad talking about his dead child like a coroner on *Law and Order*.

It was entirely possible that this could be the last conversation my father would ever have with me, I knew. So, I forged ahead.

"So . . . was she complete?" I asked. "I mean—did she have all of her . . . parts?"

My dad had been focused on Mitzy, but now he looked at me. "What?" he asked.

"My sister," I pressed him, "was she, like, formed?" I really wanted to picture her now.

He picked up his napkin spear, examining it like it was something much more interesting than a napkin spear.

"She'd been dead a while," he said. "She was a little smaller than you—but she was formed, yes."

"She was a baby," I said faux-casually, mostly to myself. Until now, I'd thought she was like a blob of cells or one of those cysts with teeth and hair that might even pop out of my neck if I lost enough weight. Not an actual baby . . . person.

Todd put his arm around me reassuringly and squeezed my shoulder kind of hard—almost aggressively, which I appreciated because he knows I hate soft touching. If you want to show me affection, give me a noogie or punch me in the arm. Or, like Todd was doing at the moment, dig your knuckles into my flesh, which I was pretty sure was bruising as I imagined my wet little baby sister. Kind of blue, I guessed, due to deadness, with little baby arms and legs and shoulders and feet. An intricate system of veins and arteries that led to a still baby heart that once had a beat.

"Bummer," I said. Which was a deliberate understatement—I'd had a full-sized sister.

But for some reason—maybe because I couldn't disappear into a Facebook wormhole on my phone—I was determined to know more. And now that I'd broached it, I treated the topic like I was taking on a quart of ice cream that's begun to melt: I might regret it afterward, but I needed to get to the bottom of it.

"So, what did they do with her?" I asked. Was there a plot somewhere? A mosque? A morgue? Was she in a drawer? A jar on a mantel?

"I don't know!" My father was becoming exasperated. "Stop it—it was a long time ago, no one remembers."

He laid down his napkin spear and straightened his pant creases, looking on proudly as Mitzy uncrossed and then recrossed her paws. He knew every move his dog made, yet he had no idea what doctors did with his dead human fully formed daughter who had been my two-legged, two-armed sister.

In between giggles, Cathy said, "Why ask now?" And offered Mitzy her bare foot to lick, and the conversation fizzled into humid silence.

Since it was up to me to concoct an end to my curiosity, I conjured a fantasy of my sister's funeral—a sendoff complete with her little body enshrouded in a pink blanket. Maybe a doll dress. A burial in a place where babies like her went, where the doctors and nurses cried and held our sobbing parents' hands . . .

"They threw her out!" my dad suddenly remembered triumphantly, jolting me back into reality.

Threw her out.

I could almost hear Orthodox Tom Cruise's jaw drop. Or maybe it was my jaw dropping. Or Todd's knuckles grinding harder into my shoulder bones.

"Like in the garbage?!" I asked, when I found my voice. Actually, I must've shouted it because all of Anatevka at the long table stopped talking for a moment before resuming their heated debate. Legs crossed, arms crossed, I tightened my grip on myself and swallowed hard.

"So . . ." I spoke slowly, "was the doctor just like, 'Are you done with this baby?' And you guys were just like, 'Sure, chuck her'?"

"What did you expect?" my father snapped, suddenly hurt and on the defensive. "It was the seventies, Liz." As if it being the '70s was an excuse for discarding a baby in a garbage can.

I laughed my giant guttural laugh to deflect the horror of it all. Cathy joined in with her nervous laugh.

"Hahahahhahahah!"

"Heheheheheheh."

"Hahaha!"

"Heheheh!"

I heard Orthodox Tom Cruise ask Todd if this was all for real.

Todd, who at this point had pulled his phone out and was openly playing Words with Friends, assured him it was.

But it wasn't for real. It was surreal. I was starting to feel a vague panic I couldn't quite identify.

I asked my father how long she'd been dead before they took her out. I dreaded the answer but figured if my dad barely remembered they'd chucked his baby, he couldn't possibly know how long I'd floated around my mother's womb with a dead body.

I watched him actually start to do the math.

"You were born two months early. . . ." He calculated. "And they said they thought she died two weeks before that."

"Fuuuck," Todd said. Fuck, indeed.

"Shit," Orthodox Tom Cruise said. Shit, exactly.

"How'd they know she was dead? Did the smell start to float into the hallway?" I asked, wincing at my own impulse to make a joke, even through my horror at living with a dead body.

"Her body started filling up with toxins, poison, and she got sick."

My father nodded enthusiastically, the details coming back to him. He sat upright, pointing to his middle.

"Her umbilical cord was wrapped around her here . . ." he continued. "And it was in a way that kept her from growing anymore, so . . . she died." He threw his hands up. It was the first show of emotion he'd demonstrated.

Cathy was folding a Soy Delicious wrapper into a neat little square. "That's common," she said. (How would she know? And where the hell did she get ice cream?)

My father nodded sadly. I immediately regretted bringing it up. I opened a can of (kosher) worms, on the New Year. Not the fun one, but still a New Year.

Orthodox Tom Cruise looked at me. "Do they know if you were

fraternal or identical?" he asked. He knew I couldn't possibly know the answer, but he was so personally thrown by the morbid turn the story had taken that he wanted to get the question out there.

"I don't think you can know," I answered.

"Oh no," Cathy chirped. "They know."

My dad had settled back in his chair. A yawn escaped him, and he closed his eyes.

"One sac means identical, and two means fraternal," he said, and without opening his eyes, he gestured in my general direction. "They were in one sac," he mumbled sleepily.

"Sac," Todd said quietly and smiled a little, then contritely dug his knuckles deeper into my shoulder. And then, my other shoulder—to even me out of course. I wondered if my twin had the same need for symmetry before she dropped dead.

So, I had been a they. As they as they come. Identical. Another me. It seemed fun, like looking in a mirror. And terrible, like looking in a mirror. Identical meant she would've also had my "tragically short" legs, as my friend Julie once described them, even though I didn't ask for her opinion. Maybe I wouldn't have needed a friend as brutally honest as Julie at all, because I'd have had my twin sister, who would have also had baby-fine hair that refused to stay feathered or stand up on its own without a full can of hairspray. She'd also have been allergic to hairspray. And eye shadow. Like me. She'd also have been tested by the school nurse every year for scoliosis because her ass stuck out so much. She'd also not have had scoliosis but just a big ass.

We would have been inseparable. My younger twin cousins Emily and Jackie were. I'd always been jealous of the way they finished each other's sentences and felt each other's pain—from far away even. They always had each other to play with and talk to. They fought like crazy growing up, and still did—one time Emily threw a card table at Jackie's head over a stretched-out bathing suit—but then five minutes later they always acted like nothing had happened because they were twins.

And Emily and Jackie were only fraternal (though just by virtue of being twins, none of us could ever tell them apart). My sister and I were identical; we had shared the same space for two weeks after she died.

Maybe I held her as she died. Maybe I'd held my dead sister for two weeks, until we both emerged—one alive, one dead—from our mother.

Our mother.

The intense but vague panic I'd been feeling suddenly homed in on its source. The thought of carrying a child almost to term only to have it die in the last few weeks was unbearable to me.

That hateful, filthy, horrible witch of a woman had experienced something I would wish on no mother, not even my own. In that moment I found myself sympathizing with her—maybe I would be the same way if I lost a child?

No wonder she kidnapped me and made me look at that cesarean scar—a crime scene, literally and figuratively. I was pulled out of there, alive. And then she didn't get to even keep me.

It was the stuff of nightmares, of opera. Of my family. Of my mother, who was warped as they came, thanks to the two of us. Only I was the one who survived to experience the fallout.

As was my habit, and as my profession mandated, I obviously had to make a joke of the forensic nightmare I'd exhumed.

"It's not like it was anyone's fault, then," I said a little too brightly. "I mean, if the cord was wrapped around her, that was just bad luck. It's not like it was my fault. And at least mom had me!"

My father laughed, but not the kind of laugh I was going for. A bad laugh.

"Well, your mother sure as hell didn't want anything to do with you when you were born," he said, shaking his head, chuckling at the memory of the woman he hated so much.

"So, she hated me because my sister died? She blamed me? Like maybe I had something to do with it?" I asked him.

His bitter cackle was loud enough to rouse Mitzy, who had fallen asleep. Cathy shushed her husband. He continued in a softer, condescending voice, as if he were addressing the village idiot.

"Your mother's problem wasn't that your sister died," he said matter-of-factly. "Her problem was that you lived."

The words hung there for a bit, the silence broken only by a beardless Orthodox dude who came over and asked Orthodox Tom Cruise if he wanted to join in the Taschlich prayers—these are the prayers where you throw your sins (in the form of bread) into water (in the form of the LA River). My sofa buddy leapt to his feet, which to me was the most shocking moment yet—who would willingly leave a story about a dead twin to drown their sins in anything but alcohol?

"So, she didn't go crazy out of . . . grief?" I asked, just to be sure.

My father shook his head dismissively.

"Your mother didn't want children." He liked to say *your mother* as if he had never been her husband. Like I had somehow conjured her just to torture him.

"You already had Jeff," I reminded him. It wasn't like my arrival changed everything—though to be fair, Mom was clearly no fan of my brother.

"My mother took care of Jeff," Dad said, as if it was the most obvious thing in the world. He tossed the napkin spear on the coffee table. "Your mother would park him at her house and take off. But Grandma couldn't take care of both of you—they didn't have double strollers back then, you know, and she was older. Your arrival made it a hassle."

Maybe my sister had somehow sensed what we were in for and offed herself, just got up on a little amniotic stool, wrapped the cord around herself, and took off in search of a less poisonous womb, a better future, leaving me to hold the family bag.

Suddenly Caleb, my nephew, who'd inherited my brother's sarcasm and comedic timing, appeared at the sliding glass doors to the backyard.

"Jesse fell in the pool!" he yelled, smirking.

As Todd and I bolted outside, Cathy called after us to make sure we closed the door behind us so Mitzy wouldn't get out.

My father wondered aloud what the big deal was—the subtext being that it wasn't like the dog had fallen in the pool.

And it wasn't that Jesse couldn't swim. He was actually a great swimmer. He'd even inherited the ability to cry and swim at the same time from me—which he was doing as he made his way to the side of the cold, leaf-filled pool. The trouble was that Jesse didn't like surprises; they made him anxious. There was no going with the flow for Jesse—in the words of his school principal, he required "a lot of emotional unpacking."

I could relate. Could I ever.

Todd pulled him out and ran inside to get a towel. Jesse stood there, his glasses crooked and dripping, the holiday outfit he'd assembled for himself—from the dressy plaid shorts and collared white polo shirt down to the white socks and loafers; he'd wanted to look "sharp"—all soaking wet.

He balled up his fists tightly—in addition to anxiety, he had sensory issues, and I knew he needed deep pressure if we were going to stop this forty-nine-pound potential volcano from erupting. Deep pressure helped at times like this—like from the large foam rolling pin we rolled him with before birthday parties. Or by my holding his legs in the air while making him walk on his hands, the blood rushing to his head, and which was actually a great ab workout for me.

Sometimes all I needed to do, all I could do, though, was just press down on his head.

I knelt down and bowed my head, like I'd learned to do to soothe my son. He leaned in and pressed his head against mine, like he'd learned to do to be soothed. And we silently pressed our heads against each other's, shutting everyone else out.

"It's okay, you're okay," I said, softly, over and over.

I felt the tension leaving my son's body, his fists starting to open. Relief.

Your mother's problem wasn't that your sister died. It was that you lived.

If ever I feared I was anything like my mother—which I did, every moment of every day—it was moments like this, moments of knowing what to do for my child and wanting to do it, that proved to me that I wasn't anything like her.

"Elizabeth, you pamper him too much."

My father had come outside.

"You're gonna make him weird," he scolded, and turned to go back into the house. He stopped when he saw Cathy standing in the doorway.

"Where's the dog?" he asked her.

"I thought you had her," Cathy said in a sudden panic.

"She's in the pool?!"

My niece Sasha was pointing at Mitzy, who was swimming—or possibly trying to drown, Ophelia-like, her pink bow floating toward the drain.

"Goddamnit!! Jesus Christ Almighty!" my dad yelled, alienating at least two-thirds of those gathered around the dining room table.

Jesse's mood lightened, and soon he was cracking up along with his cousins as Dad and Cathy melted down and the dog continued to elude them.

I thought, *Too bad my sister isn't here to see this.* And then, *Well, fuck her anyway, she left.*

Jeff came over. "Thanks for coming over today," he said, and he meant it. He put his arm around me and wished me a Happy New Year.

Squeezing him tight, I wished him the same.

And I meant it.

Out of the Basement,
Into the Fire

On an early summer Saturday afternoon in Seaford, Long Island, something happened to me. The type of thing therapists dream about. It's actually the first story I tell therapists upon meeting them, just so they know what they're dealing with going in. Real first-appointment material. They listen attentively and nod empathetically, visions of new waiting room furniture and the trip to Nepal they wanted to take or a cruise (on one of the fancier cruise lines—the ones that make you forget you're on a cruise) they couldn't afford filling their heads. I'm pay dirt.

What I tell them is this:

I was twelve, and from deep in the cool, shag-carpeted basement of our split-level house I could smell the lilacs and the freshly cut grass outside, and could hear our neighbors Rubin and Anna screaming at each other on their porch.

Everyone was enjoying the beautiful weather in their own ways. I was drawing my warmth from the staticky heat that rose off of the TV set downstairs, lying on the tiny brown suede couch, legs dangling over the side, occasionally making my way to the fold-out wet bar that was home to one of my many secret junk food stashes. It was the only room in the house that bore any semblance of life Before Cathy, who was no longer quite the fairy princess she seemed when she first moved in. Beautiful Kind Clean Cathy had certainly brought normalcy to our lives, but slowly her preferences began to take over both the house and my father. Everything got "nicer," "neater," and more "presentable"—shorthand for "less comfortable."

Our living room, once for "living" in, now had pristine matching twill couches, a glass coffee table, and a sculpture of a ballerina no one could walk within fifty feet of because it was something called a Lladró. It was one of those things that was so valuable, it needed to be separated from the rest of the words in a sentence.

"Keep your sticky hands away from my . . . Lladró."

"Don't let that dog near my . . . Lladró."

"Who cracked the . . . Lladró?!"

A broken-off piece of a ballerina's pinky with a tiny red painted nail remained hidden in the deepest pocket of the Smith's carpenter pants I was wearing when I just wanted to see if the ballerina's fingers bent. They didn't.

This is why it was best I stayed downstairs. The basement, my own little refuge. I considered it to be like Jeannie's bottle or Fonzie's apartment above the Cunninghams' garage. When my best friend Rachel Schein would come over, we'd play *Love Boat* down there, turning the room into the ship's bar or the Pirate's Cove (did Isaac ever get time off?). I'd be Julie McCoy, and Rachel liked being a glamorous guest star, and together we'd pretend to slow-dance with our dates, arms wrapped around the air, to France Jolie's "Come to

Me" until, exhausted from the exertion, we'd call it a day, dip into the snack stash, and laugh hysterically, to the point of almost choking on our Razzles or Twinkies, at some silly private joke, like best friends do.

On this particular day, however, I'd been on my own, watching sitcoms, willing myself into happy lives and madcap scenarios where even the worst of conflicts were resolved in twenty-five minutes or at most teased out into cliffhangers. In that basement, I was no longer the tubby daughter who was the cause of Dad and Cathy's endless displeasure, expressed full volume and at all hours through closed doors. I was no longer the not-so-anonymous culprit behind the crumbs that made Cathy passively-aggressively Dustbust the kitchen overhead. Downstairs, the "presentable" upstairs receded, leaving me free to move into Jack and Janet and Chrissy's wicker-chic place, or Felix and Oscar's bachelor pad, or the Jeffersons' Deluxe Apartment in the Sky. I could be Julie McCoy or Rhoda Morgenstern, or Laverne DeFazio, mainlining wisecracks as I simultaneously fed off the pile of Cheez Doodles that rested on my stomach.

I don't remember what I was watching. Nor do I remember what it was that actually got me off the couch. My guess is that I couldn't get the foil-covered rabbit ears into the right position to get good TV reception—a skill unrecognized by my dad and Cathy. Or maybe the Dustbuster had pierced through the theme songs to the part of me that knew just how much my sloppiness and inability to be motivated by physical movement was letting everyone down.

After all, it had only been a few months earlier on Hanukkah that my father had asked me to go down to the garage fridge and get a cake he said we were having for dessert. I'd run to the garage, where a brand-new 10-speed bike with a giant ribbon and my name on it was blocking the fridge. I'd swiftly moved the bicycle out of the way to get to the cake, only to discover that the only item in the fridge was an orange box of Arm & Hammer baking soda in the door. Left to only wonder what sort of person lied about cake—and on a holiday, no less—I had no recourse but to cry while my dad made me ride the bike around the block, both of us equally baffled by each other.

But today was going to be different than that cold December night, for today I'd ventured outside of my own volition. Standing in the driveway, in my faded, light-blue, baggy Jordache sweatshirt and Smith's carpenter pants (the very ones that held the Lladro pinky), which squeezed tight at the waist and stretched to capacity around my crotchal area, pulling terribly at my inner thighs, I decided to take a stab at exercising. I got a red, half-deflated kickball from the garage and attempted to bounce, toss, and catch it, exerting as little energy as possible, of course. I wasn't trying to be a hero.

Foreigner's "Hot Blooded" blasted from Jeff's open window. No doubt, I thought, he was parading back and forth in front of his mirror, blowing kisses at his own reflection. And I was glad. As long as he was preening over himself, he couldn't hurl abuse down on me in the form of pig noises that bounced off the windows of the high school across the street, surrounding me in a wall of echoing oinks.

Gone were the days when Jeff and I, united against our mother, huddled together like penguins against an Antarctic wind. We now pretty much hated each other. This was largely due to old-fashioned sibling rivalry and the fact that we were a teen and a tween and shared a bathroom. But added to that was the fact that Jeff was my father's favorite child, his golden boy. He could do no wrong. Even when he was teasing me, relentlessly. A mere line into one of Jeff's cruel—albeit brilliant—limericks about my weight, I would lose my shit, which would send my father into a rage. Against me. It was my father, Cathy, and Jeff against me.

Jeff's music was loud, but not loud enough to drown out Rubin and Anna, who had moved their fight to the sidewalk, where Rubin asked Anna if she'd like dirt in the steak he was grilling for dinner as Mr. Andretta, our neighbor on the other side, waxed his new red Corvette in his pitted-out undershirt and grease-stained Dickies pants. Finally, after about five hours' (four minutes') exertion, my dad's light-brown Cadillac Seville came up the street and pulled into the driveway, setting off Mr. Andretta's car alarm. I didn't realize until that moment that I'd actually been waiting for him to show up and see me, his daughter, exercising by choice.

My father stayed in the car—floored, I suspected, by my activity level. I decided to show off for him a little bit. I tried bouncing the ball extra high, but since it wasn't fully inflated, it instead just landed with a thump. It didn't matter; my father, who I assumed was completely bowled over, had still not emerged from the car.

I scooped up the ball with a flourish, tripping over the leg of my pants, but recovering and even breaking a sweat. I pushed up the sleeve of my sweatshirt and pulled my pants away from my thighs. I was Joanie with her baton, Greg on his surfboard (before the wipeout). I was the shit—as my father, still inside his car, was clearly witnessing.

He finally got out of the car. He'd been in Manhattan, where he'd gone to get his fancier toupee tended to. I pretended to be too focused on the bouncing sport I was doing to notice him standing in the driveway. In his fitted maroon velour-collared shirt and slacks, his good rug permed tight, the same sandy blond color as his pants, he was as hip and trim as he would ever get.

Barely glancing at me, his briefcase in one hand, a small white box containing his spare toupee in the other, he waved to

Mr. Andretta, who was struggling to stop his car alarm, before entering the house.

I was now exhausted and smelled surreally like outside. Ready to call it a day and go back down to the couch, I heard the music in my brother's room stop. Turning toward the house to see if Jeff was going to start teasing me after all, I saw that my dad was back outside, standing on the stoop. I decided to go for a quick, spur-of-the-moment ball toss and was exhilarated when I actually caught it.

"Elizabeth, please come inside," my father said.

Elizabeth was my name when I was in trouble. How could I be in trouble? I was outside. With a ball.

I dropped the now officially flat kickball and nervously headed past him and inside. Without looking at me, my father told me to go into the kitchen, where Jeff sat at the head of our new butcher block kitchen table, wearing his favorite T-shirt—black with a neon green frog saying, "I'm so Happy, I Could Just Shit." Cathy hovered nearby, Dustbuster still in hand—I swear she wanted to vacuum me right up so she'd never have to deal with my crumbs again.

They said nothing. Jeff fiddled with his braces, looking kind of nervous. He didn't make fun of me at all, not one oink or moo regarding my outside exertions, which he'd no doubt seen. Cathy, clad in the Long Island trophy wife uniform—metallic electric-blue Sergio Tacchini warm-up suit with splashes of raspberry pink on the collar, white tennis sneakers, diamond tennis bracelet, and fuchsia acrylic nails—focused her attention on putting the Dustbuster back in its cradle on the wall, which seemed trickier than usual.

My father walked in.

"Go stand in the corner and smile," he said to me, picking up a Polaroid camera.

I obediently went and stood, my back against the black-and-white-flowered wallpaper.

"Smile!" he said brightly, and for a moment I almost recognized him as his old self, the balding man in loose sweatpants and wrinkled T-shirts stretched over a big belly. The man he had been before Aruba, where he'd eloped with Cathy and, as legend had it, killed a fly between his stomach rolls. He'd set about losing sixty pounds after that and succeeded by eating only one big salad a night and by jogging or, in the winter, running in place against the resistance of a bungie cord attached to my brother's doorknob. As the pounds melted away, he became less and less recognizable as the man who once loved me enough to rescue me from my mother, morphing into the man who hated that I was turning into a younger version of his first wife.

But now he was taking my picture, seeing me not as hatred incarnate, but as me—and maybe even a little as him or even better, as Cathy.

I smiled as he took the picture and asked what the occasion was, though I could pretty much guess. I'd gone outside. I had done a sport. I secretly began to suspect this photo op would be followed by a pizza and ice cream celebration.

My father pulled the wet photo out of the bottom of the camera. "We wanted something to remember you by," he said.

"Why do you have to remember me?" I asked.

"We're sending you away," my father said, looking at me at last. "You aren't going to live here. You're fat, and we can't look at you anymore." He shook the picture and set it on the counter to dry.

I wasn't expecting that. I wasn't prepared to be kicked out of my house for being fat. This wasn't the sort of thing that happened in sitcoms. Not even the "very special" episodes.

Survival instincts kicking in, I asked them where I was going to live, suddenly hopeful that I'd get to live with Rachel and her family, where I slept over as often as I could. I loved their house, even though it was half the size of mine and smelled like guinea pigs (and they didn't have guinea pigs). They may have had one bathroom instead of three like we did, but they didn't find me hard to look at, and Rachel could eat junk food and drink soda out in the open, in broad daylight, instead of late at night after everyone else went to bed, like me. It was at Rachel Schein's house where I'd had my first bucket of fried chicken.

The Scheins had fun with each other. They made each other laugh. And they made grilled cheese in a frying pan with butter, instead of . . . dry in a toaster oven on wheat bread—nothing "grilled" about it. Rachel looked just like her mother, too, but it was okay. It was great actually. "You guys should be a sitcom," I would say to them—the highest compliment I could bestow. The Scheins lived in a *Good Times* world, and if I lived there, I would be their J.J. It was going to be dy-no-mite, seven days a week. What's more, they were one of the other four Jewish families in our town, so I would even know all the holidays they celebrated . . .

"You're going to live with your mother," my father said, unable to look me in the eye because he knew that was the worst answer he could give.

The most important, influential person in my life, the man who rescued me from Philadelphia, was now sending me back. It was the ultimate punishment for the ultimate crime—looking the way I did.

You're fat and we can't look at you anymore. I made him sick. I made them all sick. I was unsafe, disgusting, too fat to live with normal people.

I skipped the beginning part of crying and went straight to the part where you can't breathe. I slid down the wall and sat on the floor, sobbing. In between heaves, I asked when my mother was coming to get me.

My father said he had to call her to make all the arrangements.

"But she lives five hours away," I cried. "What about my friends?" Unpopular as I was in my home, I was popular at school. Being "blessed" with an awareness of my weight from the time I was four—my mother made sure of it before she took off—I'd learned early that if I could make people laugh, entering a room on a joke, like the characters in my favorite sitcoms, they wouldn't notice my body so quickly. And if I could also exit a room on a joke, they'd be left thinking, "she's funny" and not "she's fat." For the most part, my strategy worked. By eleven, I was never the girl the boys liked, and I was always picked last for kickball at recess, but I was funny, so I was popular. The thought of leaving behind all the hard work I'd done to distract and amuse my classmates was a tragedy of cliffhanger proportions.

My father simply repeated what he'd said before—I couldn't stay where I was. They didn't want me anymore.

I crawled to the counter where my father had left the Polaroid. My image from five minutes before was now clear, smiling brightly, proudly, thinking a whole other kind of night was in store. "But I was just outside . . ." I said.

My protest seemed to set my father off.

"Outside—in a sweatshirt in June!" he bellowed. "You don't even fit into shorts! Look at you!"

I didn't want to look at me anymore. I didn't want to be me anymore.

Cathy, who had been standing behind my father watching, finally intervened. "Liz . . ." she said, "calm down. Come on. It's enough."

I wondered suddenly if she had found my candy stash, or Cheez Doodle stash, or Twinkie stash. I wondered if I was being sent away because I ate the last of her Pecan Sandies and hadn't buried the empty box in the bottom of the bathroom garbage well enough. Whether a simple paper towel on top of the trash could have saved me from the fate that now awaited me: my mother.

Frantic, I started begging them to let me stay. I couldn't live with my mother. The weeks I'd spent there when I was six had left me with a deluxe set of scars. In full crisis mode, I promised to diet, to eat only chicken breast with no skin even though the skin was the best part. To run every day. To run to running. Anything. Please don't make me live with my mother. Please let me stay with you, you terrible people.

My father stood his ground. "We've tried everything," he said. "You're out of control. You don't want to change."

"I do!" I shout-cried.

"All the other girls have adorable figures," he said, which, even then, was creepy. "You can't be happy looking like this."

And I had to admit, he was right—I was anything but happy. I would have loved to have stopped eating and been like all the adorable girls. But food was my drug. It numbed me. Food released me from having to make sense of why my parents beat the shit out of each other and why my mother had the energy to steal stuff from our neighbors but couldn't get out of bed to take care of me and my brother. I was a bottomless pit of memories buried under the Cheez Doodles that kept me calm but made my father hate me.

I could hear my father tallying off a list of my crimes, starting with how Jeff couldn't put a cheeseburger in the refrigerator for later without me eating it. He was right. I couldn't resist bait like that—always starting with a bite, which would lead to another to "even it out" until the best option was to destroy the evidence altogether. He laid into me about the indignity Cathy had suffered in taking me to women's departments to buy clothes, the trauma she'd endured watching me and my third-grade teacher Mrs. Galvin in our underwear trying on the same pants in the open dressing room at May's department store.

With every indictment, his rage grew. He accused me of living on the basement couch, and there was no point reminding him that I'd just been outside. It was too little, too late for that. The skinny man I didn't recognize as my dad was getting angrier and angrier.

"You're sloppy and lazy and—"

Here it comes, I thought.

"—just like your mother!"

Cathy told my father to calm down. She had to open the back door to let the dog outside, and the whole neighborhood didn't need to hear what was going on. We had to be "presentable." Which I was not.

My father calmed down. Cathy opened the door, and the smell of summer cooking wafted inside. Hamburgers, it smelled like. It dawned on me that other people were going about their evenings making dinner, like everything was normal. Nothing like the shit show that was going on here. I wanted to be them. All the other families with their "adorable" daughters were eating dinner and getting along and not kicking their child out for being fat and just like her mother.

"Okay . . ." my father said at last. I wasn't sure who he was talking to. "Okay. There's one way you can stay . . ." He was pulling something out of the junk drawer.

I couldn't believe his words. A leftover sob left me like the last breath of a corpse.

"What are you crying about?" He was exasperated. "I said you might be able to stay." He handed me a glossy brochure. "It's a weight-loss camp. If you go there, and you lose weight, you don't have to go live with your mother."

On the cover was a collage of fat kids engaging in all kinds of sports. Most shots taken from behind so you couldn't see their miserable, suffering faces.

"Camp Shame?" I asked.

"Camp *Shane*," my father corrected me.

The inside of the brochure was a picture of the camp owners— Selma and her son, David. Of course, they were smiling—they didn't have to do any of this shit.

"The Camp Shane Experience" offered registered dietitians, exercise programs, restricted calorie intakes, and FUN. Plus off-site day trips. To illustrate this, there was a photo of a morbidly obese boy, stuffed into an inner tube floating down a river, having anything but fun. I wonder what torture he endured. What hell. What horror. What . . . FUN.

I was staring down the barrel of a summer in a Twinkie-and-TV-deprived prison.

But better than staring down the barrel of my mother.

"I'll go to Camp Shame," I said, and just like that my father swept me into his arms.

"You know we love you," he said as he hugged me.

I did not know that.

The tension now broken, Jeff made nine or ten requisite fat jokes about the kids in the brochure, and Cathy, in a show of major emotion, awkwardly hugged me. I worried absently that she'd feel the sweat on my back and tell my dad to decide I should go live with my mother after all. I was on thin ice. I could be sent to my mother at any time. One false move, and I was out.

But in that moment, I was relieved. Sickeningly relieved.

The weeks leading up to my departure were a blur, with my devouring every morsel of food I could lay my hands on. If they didn't have an overweight child in that Polaroid, they certainly had a child that had increased a size by The Night Before Fat Camp, when they took me to Friendly's for my last meal, complete with not one but two Fribbles and a Reese's Pieces sundae.

The next day I was in a parking lot, being all but cavity-searched for food of any kind by a masculine woman named Terri who introduced herself as "your worst nightmare for the next nine weeks" before getting on the bus for Camp Sha(m)e.

Boarding the prison bus, I heard my father calling my name. I turned and scanned the sea of mostly overweight parents waving to their poor, sad, scared kids. My heart leapt—maybe this had all been a trick, maybe my father was testing me to find out the lengths I'd go to to avoid living with the woman we both hated, and he was now calling for me to get off the bus. That all was forgiven. Please, let him be that fucked up, let this be a scared-straight situation, I remember praying. Please let us stop at McDonald's on the way home.

I found my father, screaming through cupped hands, "If anyone asks, you're obese!"

"Am I obese?" I shouted back.

"No!" he hollered. "But Doctor Berman wrote 'obese' on your record to get me a tax break on camp—see you when you're thinner!"

He, Cathy, and Jeff went back to their car. I got on the bus with my new identity, a revised permanent record, and the kind of ruining of a future that therapists can retire on.

The Kids in
the Orange Shirts

I loved it when my kids were at that fun age where they were old enough to hold a conversation and wipe themselves pretty well, but still young and innocent enough where I could lie to them and they'd believe me.

"If you don't go to bed, night monsters will eat you!"

And:

"People who whine don't go to heaven!"

And:

"Mommy will always be thirty-three!"

The most egregious of all the lies, however—the one I was about a year from getting caught in—was the first one I told them, from the time when they first came out and their brains were still soft and most impressionable:

"Get over Disneyland, because we live too far away to ever go there. We're never going. Ever."

We live in Southern California, and Disneyland is a breezy forty-minute car ride, with traffic, at most. I'm pretty sure my street name means "Not too far from Disney" in Spanish.

But I will never go to an amusement park. Not to be confused with a waterpark. They are completely different in my mind. Because of Wonderland in upstate New York. Where I sustained permanent injury. On an emotional roller coaster.

IT WAS DAY 42 of fat camp, and my whole bunk at Camp Sha(m)e woke before reveille, which had never happened in the history of any fat camp ever. But today was the day we were going on an off-site trip to Wonderland, a Westchester County amusement park with five roller coasters, six water rides, go-carts, live entertainment, and both haunted and fun houses.

Of course, the inmates of Camp Sha(m)e didn't give a shit about any of that. We'd woken up before dawn because Wonderland also boasted fried dough, pizza, fudge, popcorn, cotton candy, pretzels, donuts, hot dogs, hamburgers, French fries, and ice cream, and at this point I would have done pretty much fucking anything for a Klondike Bar.

It had been forty-one days of living on a diet of steamed vegetables, skinless chicken breasts, water, and the occasional half-banana.

Forty-one days of running the length of the soccer field six times in 90-degree heat before playing an actual soccer game. And doing wind sprints on the tennis court before playing an actual match.

Forty-one days of countless laps in an Olympic-size pool where, after each lap, they would make us get out of the pool without using the ladder, our wet bodies slapping the ground, knees scraping on concrete, and heave ourselves up before running to the other end of the pool to do it again.

Forty-one hungry days of step aerobics, calisthenics, and power walks. Of sweating, chafing, bleeding, crying, and starving.

TIME BEHIND BARS had hardened me. I may have been into food back home, but deprivation of my only source of comfort had turned me into a steely-eyed, opportunistic addict who thought of nothing but her next fix and how to get it.

And today—day 42—was the day of my next fix.

With money we kept rolled up in socks, in the soles of our shoes, and in our asses—not really, but a little really—my compatriots and I were going to take Wonderland for every last crumb. But we didn't talk about it openly. That was too risky. The consequences of getting caught for what we had planned were horrifying. Terry, our large and androgynous head counselor with forearms like calves and calves like tree trunks, had proved as stealth and cunning an adversary as I would ever encounter—and I work in television. At the first sign of so much as an unaccounted-for ketchup packet (did you know that in the right stage of deprivation, it tastes like maple syrup?), Terry's full wrath would surface until, like the victim of a psycho camp counselor in urban legends, the culprit would be found the next day . . . on a hike.

The energy in the air as our coach bus struggled down I-90 that morning was . . . different—primal subtext churning beneath the almost humane, and oddly sad, surface. We talked and laughed and sang happy camp songs like normal kids. Our counselors had morphed from prison wardens into real people, and we went from being prisoners to being free. Or nearly free, with the exception of the bright orange T-shirts we were sporting for identification. We were still "camp kids," but we were "normal camp kids," if only for one day.

It felt fantastic.

We were allowed to walk around the park with a buddy without adult supervision because it was a simpler time, when people didn't worry about kidnappings, pedophiles, and mass shootings. My friend-cellmate Marni Shapiro and I had decided to be buddies and pooled our money together the night before. We had sat on her top bunk under her Holly Hobbie blanket by the fading glow of a flashlight, snacking on toothpaste, whisper-counting out our twenty-seven dollars and eighty-seven cents.

As we pulled into the parking lot, Marni bent down to tie her shoe and snuck a five-dollar bill into my sock.

"Just in case we get separated," she whispered. Marni had her shit together. I think she might be a senator now.

The bus doors opened, and a sea of kids poured out. From above, in our two hundred bright-orange "Camp Sha(m)e" T-shirts, we must've looked like a giant orange ball pit.

Right away, we were slammed with the smell of fried dough. At once, all two hundred double chins pointed skyward to get a whiff, pulling in what we'd been missing.

The counselors passed out money to be used "for diet sodas." The fact that they trusted us was very flattering. Almost touching. And stupid. This money went straight into the cheating kitty.

Before letting us loose, Terry announced that in two hours, a boxed lunch would be available in some designated picnic table area. No doubt a mayonnaise-free lettuce-wrapped turkey sandwich. Even the counselors didn't look like they meant it. I imagined that deep down, they knew we were going to treat ourselves to something verboten and they could look the other way, because this was practice of being fat people in the real world.

Once inside the gates, I saw in the distance a small white cement structure, covered on the front with vibrantly painted pictures of delicious junk food. On top was a giant slushy spinning on its axis like a magical, colorful cross, tolling its intent to all who worshipped there. Oh, Concession Stand, I thought, how I missed thee.

Light-headed, I walked closer to get a better look. From ten feet away, I could see a box of individually wrapped candy and a plastic case holding soft baked pretzels. Through the window, I could faintly make out a grill roasting the hot dogs and hamburgers, a fryer filled with greasy French fries as comforting as my blanket back home. A cotton candy machine spun blue and pink sugar into fluffy swirls of delight.

I had forgotten how beautiful life was on the outside. I decided then and there to be a concession stand operator when I grew up.

I was almost there when Marni yanked my arm.

"Zimbo," she snapped.

It was the code word we came up with for when we saw a counselor. Her idea. I told you she was a genius.

I followed Marni's alarmed gaze to see Terry striding toward us, hands on hips, taking in the park. Oh noooo. I froze. I hadn't done anything wrong, yet. But still, I felt like I had the words "I'm about to go off my diet" written all over my face.

Marni and I found temporary asylum in the funhouse, where we planned to wait until the coast was clear. We paced back and forth at the entrance. The smell of the grill was killing me, and I left Marni to hide farther inside.

Wandering through the cheesy corridors, I spotted a lanky girl out of the corner of my eye, a girl with light brown hair wearing a bright orange shirt looking at me. What the fuck was she staring at? Hadn't she ever seen a fat kid waiting for her androgynous head counselor to wander off, so she could eat real food for the first time in forty-two days? Of course, that agony would be foreign to her, because she was skinny. Lucky, skinny bitch. I haaaated her.

But when I finally stared back at her in defiance, I realized I had been looking at my own reflection in one of the skinny mirrors, my body stretched from head to toe.

I stepped closer. She got taller and thinner. I got taller and thinner. *I look like the popular girls in school*, I thought, forgetting that I already was popular. I looked like what my father and Cathy thought a popular girl looked like. What everyone thought a popular girl was supposed to look like.

I looked like I didn't have a care in the world. Like I could wear designer jeans and short sweaters and my ballet costume wouldn't have to come from a separate company in a slightly different shade of pink because they didn't make my size in children's. Like I wouldn't be embarrassed to change in front of the other kids in the locker room, expertly hiding my stomach rolls with one arm and my upper thighs with the other. Like I could walk by a group of boys without bracing myself for pig noises and name calling. Like I wouldn't have to make people laugh so I could distract them from my weight or thank God for the days the boys in my class forgot the nicknames Liz Fatstrof and Liz Fat-ass-strof.

I looked like a girl who didn't need a special camp.

I looked like a girl whose father would say was "adorable."

In the mirror, I was "normal."

The weight of the world literally lifted off my shoulders.

Marni popped her head out from around the corner. "We need to make a move."

The moment I'd been waiting forty-one days for had come. Everything I had been dreaming about was just outside that funhouse. Yet I stood there, captivated. Because at that moment, even more than food, I wanted to be that girl in the mirror. I could be that girl. I just needed to be "good."

I'd lost 8 pounds. I'd taken 2 inches off my thighs and 3 from my waist. I was feeling proud of myself after the weigh-ins, and my shorts weren't cutting off my circulation quite as much. I needed less and less baby powder between my legs before and after running.

I felt the beginnings of a collarbone. A rib had started to make itself clear. On my body. It had been alarming at first, because I thought it was a tumor, but it was ultimately exciting.

Did I really want to throw all of that away on food?

Of course I did.

But did I *really*?

Yes.

I tilted my head to each side, as if to shake the desire to be "good" out of my ears like water. I didn't want to hear it. I didn't want to have doubts.

Marni was shouting for me to snap out of it and move my ass. "What are you waiting for?" she asked desperately.

"Maybe we should go on one ride first," I suggested.

"Liz!" Marni snapped. "If you're not going to eat with me, then fuck you. And give me my five dollars back. I'll walk around with Heather Gelfand."

I jumped back like she was hot-wired and apologized, the smells from the concession stand entering the funhouse from the back entrance right behind me ending my inner conflict.

We bolted for the concession stand, on high alert for counselor traffic. The line was short. I watched the rides while Marni covered the bathrooms.

With one person ahead of us, I looked at the menu, poring over the food listings like the Torah. We didn't want to spend all of our money in one go, so we had some big decisions to make.

We had tentatively decided that the first course would be cheeseburgers, French fries, and pizza. That would leave us money for dessert on the other side of the park. In between, of course, would be our boxed lunches—we weren't going to not eat them.

"I'm getting nachos," Marni said once we got close, throwing our plan out the window.

Nachos were two-fifty. I suggested we split them. "I'm not splitting," Marni said firmly, her head on a swivel. An only child whose birth was a "miracle," as her mom had one ovary, Marni was used to calling the shots.

"I'll get a pretzel then," I relented.

The midday sun was beating down on me; my mouth started watering at the sight of that giant cherry slushy spinning in the air above the concession stand. I couldn't believe I ever doubted my original plan to stuff my goddamn face.

The people in front of us paid for their shit and moved off. We were up.

The stoned, greasy-haired, and acne-covered teenager behind the counter stubbed a cigarette out in a plastic soda lid and said the words I'd been waiting to hear for forty-two days: "Whattya want?"

"I'd like a pretzel," I said the words, out loud. Smiling, I closed my eyes, overwhelmed with a feeling of freedom. The freedom to ask for what I wanted, out loud, and not be punished for it. I was entitled to a pretzel.

The kid shrugged. "Sorry—can't."

"Hot dog, then," Marni chimed in.

"Can't sell you food," the kid said, nodding toward a flyer on the inside wall of the concession stand. We followed his eyes to a crude drawing of a fat kid with a giant orange triangle for its middle, an X marked through the figure.

Beneath it the flyer said:

DO NOT FEED THE KIDS IN THE ORANGE SHIRTS.
So much for freedom.

"We'll just go to another stand," Marni said to me.

"Don't bother," the kid told us, handing us two diet sodas. "Everyone knows. We can sell you the soda, though."

We walked off, reeling, in shock. And livid—how could they not trust us? Even though, clearly, they couldn't?

But that wasn't what stunned me most.

It was the sign. Like the signs at the zoo telling you not to feed the elephants. Or the signs at the circus telling you not to take pictures of the side-show attractions. Our orange shirts didn't just distinguish us from other kids or even other campers—they separated us from our species.

We were both too embarrassed to even look at each other, never mind talk about the fact that we were basically zoo animals. We'd been at the park for two hours, so Marni decided we may as well eat our boxed lunches and stormed toward the designated picnic area.

Halfway there, we saw about twenty campers in orange shirts huddled behind the haunted house. We went to see what was up.

I saw Heather Skovall. She was two years older than us, and even though she was a good forty pounds overweight, she went around telling people that she was allowed to go to "regular" camp but decided to come back anyway. It was a thing. She was standing with Tara Bernett, who was camp-famous, because she claimed to be a slut back at home. She even brought a picture of a boy she claimed she'd done it with. But the picture was taken from a far enough distance that convinced me she was lying. I asked Tara what was going on here.

"Robert Buffa's getting us food," she said breathlessly.

In the middle of the cluster of orange shirts, thirteen-year-old Robert—shirtless and glistening with sweat—was collecting balled-up wads of cash. Our fearless leader, athletic despite his unfortunate pecs and drooping stomach, radiated leadership, determination, and something very close to sexiness as he took up the cause of his fellow campers.

Our hero. To this day, my offer of writing a starring role for him stands. Robert Buffa, call me.

Eventually, three other boys and one girl went topless that day in a quest for amusement park food for all of us. I wish I could say I was one of them. I wasn't. But I cheered them on and in that moment, I felt more a part of a community than ever before. Part of a movement. A slow movement, but a movement. I wouldn't feel even close to this way again until the Women's March in Los Angeles in 2017, and still the camaraderie would pale in comparison to those five kids taking one, shirtless, for the team.

The camp thought they had us fatsos figured out. They thought they were ahead of the game. They thought we were predictable. They thought their flabby charges were incapable of thinking as a united collective.

But we didn't get fat by giving up. Not at getting food, anyway.

We gave our money to the shirtless warriors and waved them off, then sat down with our boxed lunches and awaited their return.

Waiting for whatever melty square of fudge my five dollars would buy me, I thought about my funhouse reflection and how badly I wanted to be her. And eventually I would—not by the Camp Sha(m)e playbook, but by the way normal, non-orange girls kept their "adorable figures": I'd like a boy and stop eating. I'd take up smoking and sugar-free gum, I'd start jogging obsessively at my own will and watch the pounds drop off.

I'd be her. Briefly. And then, food would win, I'd lose control and gain weight again. With fasts, fad diets, five days on a holistic retreat where I drank tea that tasted like dirt and got colonics, I'd make my way back to her. I'd go up and down like a yo-yo. A seemingly fleeting image in a funhouse mirror stayed with me forever.

On day 42 of Camp Sha(m)e, I met the person I wanted to be. But I wasn't at Camp Sha(m)e because I had willpower. So, with the rest of the kids in the orange shirts, we fought our oppressors, and we fulfilled our plan to take Wonderland for every last crumb. And then we ate our boxed lunches. We weren't going to not eat them.

Little Royalty

I stayed on the straight and narrow for a while after I was paroled from fat camp. Choosing fruits and vegetables, with proteins no bigger than a deck of cards, all washed down with water instead of an entire gallon of milk, I'd talk myself off a chocolate fudge cake ledge over and over, armed with my "Nothing tastes as good as being thin feels" mantra.

But like any junkie, I could avoid the siren song of junk food for only so long. Soon I was once again making my way on my Hanuk-kah bike to 7-Eleven, my pockets full of change I'd lifted from the tennis ball can on my dad's dresser, always making sure to leave a layer of quarters on top so he wouldn't become suspicious. I'd learned to appreciate the bike—it served as a sort of equalizer for the copious amount of snacks I was consuming. Also, riding a bike was easier than walking, especially since I found a way to coast downhill both ways.

Whatever I couldn't eat before I got home I'd save for later, although since my dad and Cathy had taken the dust ruffle off my bed in an effort to keep me honest, I could no longer keep food in my room.

But Camp Sha(m)e had honed my inner savvy, and I'd taken to hiding my stash along the side of the house behind the garbage cans. As long as I moved it before garbage day, I was golden as a classic Twinkie.

One morning on my way to school, I went to grab a piece of candy for the four-minute walk. I remember pondering if it was a Starburst Fruit Chew or Twix kind of morning. Maybe both? Both.

I reached behind the garbage can and unrolled the brown paper bag—only to find that one Twinkie was missing from a package of two.

I knew this wasn't the work of an animal, because an animal would have eaten all of it and torn the bag to pieces. It wasn't my parents either, because if it were, I'd be standing there dead. It couldn't have been my brother, because Jeff would have finked on me immediately.

So, who stole my Twinkie?

I circled back to Jeff. Maybe he was working on how he would "out" me—he was super smart and did shit like that. Maybe he was advancing the assault on our thorny relationship up to extortion levels. I was wondering what I might be forced to pay, what indentured servitude he could exact from me. I figured he'd turn me in via one of his award-winning essays and was imagining a story being published in the school paper about what a fucking pig I was when, out of the corner of my eye, I noticed my neighbor Rubin standing frozen in his driveway.

We locked eyes, and, in that moment, I knew he was the culprit. He had that telltale look of shame—the same one I had when my hand was caught in the cookie jar. He scurried away, busted and embarrassed. We both were.

The whole neighborhood knew Rubin's story—the saga of the world's most miserable couple (my parents now being divorced). While I'd been at fat camp, Rubin's "hateful" wife Anna (his word) had put him on a diet because he was "a fat piece of shit" (her words), and she didn't want him to have a heart attack and leave her with their "asshole kids" (their words). My family and I often saw Rubin's brown Oldsmobile Cutlass Ciera sitting in fast-food parking lots, Rubin hunched over the wheel, stuffing his face. Poor bastard, my dad would say.

Now here he was. Stealing candy from a baby. Well, a thirteen-year-old.

And all I could think was, *That poor bastard*.

I figured now that I had caught this poor bastard and even shook my head a little in a public-shaming way and gave him a wide-eyed look that said, "How could you?," he would keep his hands to himself. Quite the contrary—the very next day I unrolled my brown bag to see the addition of not one but two more Twinkies and a pack of Twizzlers. All thanks to my neighbor/food-thief/partner in crime. He had taketh away, but he had also giveth.

I bought more candy and snacks that day than usual, and that night I left the top of the bag unrolled. An invitation.

And it began. Without a word ever spoken, Rubin and I would go back and forth. He would eat, he would add. I would eat, I would add.

We started to mix things up to surprise each other. A Whatchamacallit bar here, a Hostess Blueberry Pie there. I found out he was a "sweet" guy and not "sour" when he passed on the roll of tart Spree Wafers. He learned I didn't like spicy when I left the Chili Lime chips untouched.

This went on for months. Was it sexual? No. Sensual? Absolutely. And secret—so long as we didn't get sloppy, like leaving the bag in plain sight or trying to stuff something that clearly didn't fit into it, we were safe.

Until just before my Bat Mitzvah.

The big event was at the end of the month. Cathy had spent an entire year planning the black-tie affair, which was to be held at our temple two towns away in Massapequa. The ballroom at Temple Judea, intended for High Holiday overflow and bingo, was being transformed into an ethereal garden. Ficus trees with twinkly lights, custom pastel linens, matching china, and white satin-backed chairs were being brought in. Cathy and my dad had eloped on a tiny boat in Aruba seven years earlier, so this was going to be the wedding she never had. She was even wearing a white gown. Cathy was not fucking around.

I was wearing a pink, custom-made, signature Little Royalty dress that Cathy had picked out at the local fancy dress store on Long Island's North Shore, and on the day in question, Cathy and I were headed to my final fitting at Little Royalty. The plan was to pick my dad up at his real estate office in Mineola and go to the fitting, after which we would all have lunch at the Delta Diner on Old Country Road where, as a reward for keeping my weight off since fat camp, I was going to be allowed to order whatever I wanted for lunch.

I was pretty sure I was going to have the cheeseburger deluxe with French fries and onion rings. The fries at the Delta Diner were something between steak fries and shoestring and soaked up a lot of grease, so they were almost uniformly crispy on the tips. The burgers were giant and juicy, and the onion rings were good, if not a little too batter-crusted. If an onion ring can be too batter-crusted.

Cathy drove us in her lipstick-red Cadillac Eldorado, her Gucci tote on the seat between us. The car had been a gift from my dad to replace the beat-up Pontiac Grand Am she'd driven when she was his assistant. He was doing well and clearly wanted her to look the part of Long Island trophy wife. Also, if she was going to have to shuttle my brother and me around, she may as well ride in style.

She was wearing wearing one of her many designer tennis warm-up suits. This one was raspberry with splashes of turquoise on the shoulders. It was loose on her like everything else and I wondered if she EVER had to lie down to zip up a pair of pants. Cathy's blond hair was blown out with perfect wings that clung to the sides of her map-of-Ireland face as we headed to her Jewish stepdaughter's fitting for the biggest Bat Mitzvah/wedding reception this side of What the Fuck. The car smelled like spearmint gum masking cigarette smoke because although Cathy and my dad had quit smoking together a few years before—they sat at the kitchen table and stubbed out their last Vantage menthols together—I'd gotten word from a friend who saw her on Sunrise Highway that Cathy was still sneaking butts. I so totally had her number.

My dad was waiting outside his office for us and climbed into the backseat for the short drive over to Nassau County's "It" destination for children's formal wear. I debated with myself whether to have cheesecake or a sundae for dessert.

Little Royalty was floor to ceiling in 1984's hottest taffeta and satin—from the walls to the curtains to the giant poufy dresses hanging everywhere like frilly pastel wasp nests. "Always Something There to Remind Me" pumped through the speakers. A song that would always and forever remind me of taffeta. And one of the most humiliating days of my life.

It was a weekday, so the store was empty except for a mother and daughter at the register. The daughter was my age, a little chubby with greasy hair, and I was surprised she didn't appear to be in trouble for looking that way. To keep the peace and in spite of the unseasonably warm weather, to look presentable, I had dressed up in my fancy blue corduroy pants with a heavy gold sweater that didn't go at all, but fit.

Sensing the one-up(wo)man-ship potential, Cathy got the girl's mom to chatting. Her daughter Shari's Bat Mitzvah was in two weeks, her mom said. Her theme was disco, and she was giving out Lucite monogrammed microphones. To her credit, Cathy didn't burst the woman's bush-league bubble by revealing the high-end visors with battery-free blinking lights she'd be sending my/her guests home with. She was nothing if not polite, but I could sense her pride swelling.

Beaming at her daughter, Shari's mom said she'd been studying very hard and was ready to read in Hebrew. I happened to be pretty fucked, Torah-wise. I hadn't studied at all and had just planned on making up the words once I got up on stage. The only person who would know would be my great uncle Sy, who was mercifully in the hospital and with any luck wouldn't make a miraculous recovery in time to come to the affair.

Shari's mom paid for her shit and they left. As Cathy went to settle my dad in the "dad's section" of the store with the chairs and magazines, I watched Shari and her mom walk to their car, happily chatting. Her hand on her daughter's back, the mother wrapped her arm around Shari's waist and gently pulled her closer. Instinctively, I held my breath, waiting for the explosion. For Shari to pull away. But Shari, to my surprise, leaned into her mother's squeeze, clearly comfortable with the affection.

I wondered what that was like. I put my own hand on my waist, gently, and leaned into it to feel what that might feel like. To not be afraid of your mother. To be loved by her, unconditionally. To feel like a part of her: your skin, your hair, your smell. To begin where your mother ended. For that to be a good thing. I wondered what it was like to not question your mother's love because it was constant and unwavering. And for that to be a good thing.

I turned from the window to look at my maternal figure, politely oohing and ahhing at the children's dress selection. The week before my first Mother's Day after Cathy moved in (the Mother's Day Kidnapping, as I thought of it), we'd made cards in my first-grade class, and I told Mrs. Breen that I needed yellow construction paper for my mommy's hair.

"Doesn't your mom have black hair?" Sandy Noonan asked.

"And didn't she get caught stealing lunch meat at ShopRite?" asked Dana Cook.

"Different mommy," I told them, cutting the yellow paper into a neat crescent shape. I'd gotten a new one. I loved Beautiful Kind Clean Cathy that much. And she loved me, too.

The love affair didn't last, though. Cathy tried, I know she did. She took me to doctors' appointments and haircuts and slathered aloe on me after I burned myself to a crisp in the sun. She stayed up with me for an entire year when I was having nightmares about fire and helped throw together a book report when I realized at nine o'clock one night that it was due the next day. She left her job and stayed home to take care of Jeff and me. Best of all, when I couldn't fit into Sassoon jeans like my friends, she cut the label from hers and sewed it on the back pocket of my Huskies.

But we didn't have the kind of bond you could spot across a parking lot. I hated her for it. But more, I hated myself for it. There had to be something wrong with me. I wasn't good enough. Try as I might—and try as Cathy might—I was my mother's daughter. I was just like her.

I watched Shari and her mom drive away, my forehead pressed against the glass door, before going over to Cathy and my dad, who were talking with Sheila, the owner of the store. Sheila was a classically pushy woman in her late fifties, her arms and neck dripping with chunky gold jewelry, her hair sprayed into a brown helmet. She told my parents that they were going to be thrilled with the way the dress came out before disappearing into the back. I decided I'd order my burger medium rare—more juice for the French fries to soak up.

Sheila returned carrying a giant plastic bag containing my dress, two seamstresses at her heels. Berta was old, short, and disheveled, wearing a housecoat and apron filled with sewing tools—Bat Mitzvah season had clearly kicked her ass. Alina was younger and taller, and reeked of perfume. Something with . . . citrus and woodsy notes. Both women spoke with heavy Russian accents.

Cathy ceremoniously lifted the dress out of the plastic like a frilly C-section. All flowing pink chiffon, a much larger version of the sample we'd seen on the rack months before. My father nodded and found the one armchair in the store to sit in. I looked at the dress and thought I'd maybe prefer a bacon grilled cheese for lunch; Delta Diner had great bread—it had a heavy, challah-like consistency. When I think about it, it may have been actual challah. They also used real butter when frying their grilled cheese.

I followed the seamstresses to a tiny, carpeted dressing room in the back of the store next to a bathroom. A cheap, narrow, full-length mirror was propped against the far wall and a tiny window was held open by a broken-off broom handle. Clearly, Sheila was a front-of-store proprietress.

Alina closed the curtain, which didn't go all the way across the opening—more of a suggestion than an actual barrier from the outside—and told me to take my clothes off, while Berta removed the dress from its hanger.

I stood in my training bra, worn-out unicorn underwear with a faded rainbow waistband, and mismatched tube socks. I was cold. I wanted this over with.

Berta firmly put her hands inside the bottom of the dress, swiftly gathered it around her arms like a pro and moved toward me, reached up, and put the dress over my head. Instantly blinded by pink material and searching for openings, I swam toward the light parts. I found the neck first, then the arms. They all seemed . . . small. Frantic, my mind escaped to the idea of going rogue and getting a tuna melt at the diner.

I held my breath, as if that would make my head smaller and my arms thinner while simultaneously pushing through each hole. My head was the only thing that made it to the other side, though not without tearing out a chunk of my hair on the collar button.

Berta frowned. She dove to the bottom of the dress and started pulling down. Alina also frowned and stepped back to assess the situation. In defiance, I forced my arms through the holes and, though they technically made it through, the sleeves were cutting off my circulation.

Alina said something in Russian to Berta in a cautioning, defeated tone. Berta spat something back at her, also in Russian, something that took no translator to understand meant "We must make it work." Dropping to the floor beside Berta, Alina grabbed half the skirts and began tugging hard to move the dress past my gut.

That was when I heard a rip. Followed by a collective gasp. And I decided on the grilled cheese.

It was getting hot in the tiny room, like we were running out of air. Berta had broken a sweat. Alina's makeup was starting to cake near her ears and she was so close to my face that her perfume was making my nose itch, which I couldn't scratch because my arms were trapped at my sides. Alina rose to her feet and started circling me like a shark would its prey. She poked the roll of back fat right above the band of my underwear. I flinched.

"How does it look?" Cathy chirped from outside the dressing room.

The Russians and I exchanged terrified looks. I checked my

reflection in the mirror. I was a giant pile of tumorous chiffon from my neck to right under my training bra, my stomach even bigger under the pressure of the dress, which had flattened out my chest.

"Liz . . .??" Cathy called again, in her polite "company" voice. "Let's see—come on out."

I heard the fabric of Cathy's warm-up suit swishing toward us and, before I could do anything to stop her, she had pulled the curtain open to see me stuck in my custom-made pink gown.

She gasped. Which made me gasp. Which hurt, because the dress was constricting my lungs.

"Eet doesn't feet," Alina said, throwing her hands up in my direction.

Cathy took it all in, in complete disbelief, then aggressively grabbed the dress and pulled at it as if we were too stupid to have not tried that without her.

Berta snorted. "Eet won't move," she replied. In response to Cathy's ensuing glare, Berta reached into her apron and pulled out a comically giant pair of scissors—what the fuck was she planning on doing with those?

She wedged the scissors between my arm and the dress fabric. I felt the cold metal against my skin, the point of the scissors poking under my arm, as she started cutting.

That was when Cathy lost her shit.

"It's less than two weeks before the affair and you're hacking the dress apart!" Cathy literally screamed. "What is she supposed to wear?!? Are we supposed to cancel the whole fucking Bat Mitzvah?!? We'll lose our deposit. Your father will have to eat the cost of the ficus trees!"

A fresh layer of sweat covered my body as Cathy turned her eyes to me, two disgusted klieg lights boring holes into my conscience. Any charitable feeling I'd been entertaining about Cathy went into deep freeze when those icy eyes met mine. I'd ruined her big day. I was going to be the naked, bad-Torah-reading fatso at what was supposed to be her dream wedding reception.

"We'll talk about this when we get home," she said, before storming out of the dressing room.

I looked at the two sweaty Russians. "I don't know how this happened," I said, giving my lie a test-run on two people who barely spoke English. "I've been good . . ."

Of course, I hadn't been good. I did know how this happened, and Rubin's and my secret was being cut out of this taffeta nightmare along with my fat-assed self.

I could hear my dad bellowing in the fancy front room. "What do you mean, they're cutting her out of the dress?!"

"They are cutting. Her. Out. Of the dress. Les, it doesn't fit."

"Jesus Christ almighty, how could she have ballooned since diet camp?! She doesn't look any bigger!"

Just like your mother, I thought into the mirror, which captured the scene of Berta and those giant scissors, cutting me to freedom. I prayed she would hit an artery and end it all for me right then and there.

She finished cutting and mercifully pulled the remains of the dress off of me, now with ease. The women left the room so that I could get dressed. I turned and looked into the mirror one more time and, while I kept eye contact with myself, with my thumb and forefinger I pinched my love handle as hard as I possibly could. It hurt. I wanted it to. I deserved it. I hated myself as much as they did. When I let go, two pink crescents formed on my skin where my nails had dug in.

I got dressed slowly. I knew that what awaited me on the other side of that curtain was the punishment of a lifetime. Because of the nature of my crime, there would also be forced exercise. Which would most likely involve a humiliating jog around the neighborhood alongside our car, a room-ransacking for contraband, and a verbal whipping like no other. I glanced at the tiny broken window in the dressing room. I thought of making an escape, but it looked even smaller than the dress, and I didn't want to be cut out of a dress and a window in one day.

I knew what I had to do. I had no choice. I needed to take the spotlight off of me. It was time to play my only card.

I stepped over the pink chiffon carcass on the floor and left the dressing room. Back in the store I took a deep breath.

"Cathy still smokes!" I yelled at the top of my lungs.

Silence followed. I looked around. No one was there. Had they driven off without me? Could I just grow up in this store with Berta? I'd take it. Sheila kept a candy dish by the register.

I heard my dad's condescending singsong tone coming from somewhere. "The question is—what now?"

"Okay, just a moment, Mr. Astrof—"

I followed the voices to a back room and poked my head in quietly. Sheila's office was cluttered with more dresses. She was at her desk, hunched over some book, her glasses on the end of her nose, the gold chain keeping them around her neck, draped over her ears, the long red nail of her pointer finger moving along the margins. My father stood behind her, watching over her shoulder, rocking back and forth in his designer loafers. Cathy paced in the few feet of clear floor space, nervously spinning her giant engagement ring around on her bony finger with her thumb. She was having a hard time keeping weight on with the stress of the Bat Mitzvah. Oh, to have been her biological daughter!

Sheila put her hand over her mouth, let out a closed-mouth squeal and shook her head, she couldn't believe what she was seeing, but then she nodded. She took her hand away and put it on her hip; she stood up straight and scrunched up her face, her lips disappearing.

She sharply inhaled; this was difficult for her. "Actually, it was our mistake," she said. "We made a children's size twelve, but really she's a teen size twelve." Another squeal.

They'd made the wrong size. It wasn't my fault. Something wasn't my fault.

OH, THE RELIEF!

I wanted to kiss Sheila right on the lips. Wherever they were.

Only now, I entered the office tentatively. Cathy and my dad, still taking this in, turned and looked at me. Based on their faces, I was pretty certain "Cathy still smokes" hadn't gotten through, so my hold card was still deep in my deck.

Sheila looked at me apologetically, though not apologetically enough for that nightmare bestowed on a thirteen-year-old, and promised they'd have a new dress to us by Thursday.

We left the store, Dad and Cathy discussing how deeply disappointed they were in Little Royalty. Unlike Shari and her mother, the three of us walked far apart from each other, but I was striding to Cathy's car—almost weightless. Almost light.

In the end, I stuck with the cheeseburger deluxe, which did not disappoint. And as we left Delta Diner, while no one was looking, I pocketed a black and white cookie with a stealth that would have impressed my mother.

Rubin liked black and white cookies.

The Typhoid Mary
of Playa Blanca

My father called it "a new beginning."

We were in his Cadillac on the way to JFK, and I was hopeful he was right—after all, Club Med's slogan was "The Way Life Should Be," wasn't it? With my suitcase loaded up with a new J.Crew wardrobe on which I'd maxed out my credit cards, a month's back issues of *People*, and a week's supply of Circus Peanuts and Jujyfruits, I set out for Mexico and my "new beginning."

I was going with my friend Kara, whom I'd first met working at a stock photography company. We sat side by side hunched over a light box, sifting through slides of toned happy couples frolicking on the beach, trying to find the perfect one for an STD medication or life insurance ad.

"I want to be a couple on the beach," I'd say wistfully, my eye way too close to the light box. "Even one with Chlamydia."

Kara would scoff and point to the visible sweat stains on the models' bathing suits, the yellow teeth, strained smiles, and obviously fake sunsets. Kara obviously had a great eye for flaws and eventually moved on to a prestigious editorial photo agency as a result, while I stayed on at the generic stock shop, mining for pictures of everything from broccoli to Mt. Kilimanjaro to couples on the beach.

But we remained close. She was the one who suggested the trip after my longtime relationship with my ex, Andy, came to a crashing end. After years of on-again-off-again mind fuckery on his part, a breakup on my part, and, after a brief stalking period that resulted in his realization that he was gay, I'd concluded I was, in fact, unlovable.

At that point, Kara had swooped in and decided that what we both needed was a trip to Club Med Playa Blanca, The Way Life Should Be.

Since I was living in Manhattan, Dad and Cathy had sold my car, a 1988 Buick Skyhawk. They got $2,000 for it, which was a lot given that the engine blew up on the Long Island Expressway a week later. (Admittedly, I probably should have disclosed the fact that the car tended to "smoke" and . . . weave a lot on long drives.) Dad and Cathy generously gave me that money for my trip in the hopes that it would get me over Andy—in other words, that I would meet a (straight) guy who would take care of my loser ass. My father—possibly the only person more surprised than I had been about my former future-husband—even offered to drive me to the airport.

"You can do better," he said, pulling up to the terminal.

"Thanks, Dad."

"Actually, Liz . . . I don't think you can."

"Thanks, Dad," I said, as he pulled away, calling into the swarms of travelers and the entire taxi line, "Don't be picky! And SMILE!"

Almost immediately, I had the feeling my father was right—at least in the short term. There were pretty slim pickins on the guy side of the flight from New York. The men were all either eighteen or sixty and mostly shorter than me—and I'm not tall. I was at the gate only five minutes before two particularly hirsute gentlemen gave me the once over and made a mutual no, thanks noise to each other—the same kind of noise that would eventually lead to my refusing to attend any more JDate events.

We all boarded the plane. Kara took the window seat, leaving me to get whacked by the Louis Vuitton carry-on of a bottle-blond woman in her late forties clad in a teeny tube top that revealed a way-too-tan chest for the start rather than the end of a beach vacation.

"Oh my gawd—I'm sawrry!" she said, her Long Island accent so thick that the uninitiated would need a phrase book. I was relieved when she ended up sitting diagonally behind me.

Alysse had all the hallmarks of a seasoned Club Med goer. As I looked at the other hopeful New Yorkers filing past our seats, I asked her if maybe there was a Club Med plane taking off from LaGuardia with all the "good" New Yorkers on it.

"Nah, these're allda New Yawk guys," she said. "I assed the Club Med represennive guy—who'd be cute by the way, but he's like twelve."

"Whatevah." Dale was Alysse's friend—also in her forties, also from Long Island, but sporting dark, very curly (temperamental) hair. She was wearing a modest black sundress and carrying a book. "We're going there to relax."

Hearing that, Kara looked up from her camera's instruction manual. "Amen," she said.

Alysse gasped, standing up. "Oh, my gawd—you look exactly like Julia Robbits!! Dale—look! Ammiright?"

Julia Roberts?! Kara?! Was I missing something?!

"Ya totally do," Dale agreed.

"Stop, stop." Kara waved them off modestly but was also trying desperately to catch her reflection in the in-flight magazine to confirm.

Alysse then looked at me, a little critical. "Ya know who you look like?" she asked.

"No," I said. "Who?" I asked, hopeful that it was someone who hangs out with Julia Roberts . . . on the cover of *Vanity Fair*.

There was a long silence.

"Nah," Alysse said, sitting back down. "Nevah moind—I'm not gonna say it."

So began my week at Club Med, the Way Life Should Be, on a withholding note. I settled back into my seat next to Julia Roberts and closed my eyes.

Up until our third or maybe even fourth breakup, I'd held out hope that my first resort vacation would be with Andy. He thought I was pretty—or at least my looks had grown on him. And I thought he was handsome—or at least pretty.

He was Italian with thick black hair, brown eyes, and he definitely had a look. He was fit, but with a slight build that weirdly seemed to accentuate his high-pitched voice. We'd started to date the summer after he graduated law school when we were both waiting tables at the Jones Beach Boardwalk Restaurant. We were just friends, but then one day I showed up for my shift with my hair cut in a short bob. Apparently, it was a major transformation because it wasn't until I set my plastic fingernail on fire lighting the votive on a table that Andy recognized me.

"Liz!" he'd said, surprised. "I saw you from behind and actually had the thought, 'That girl is attractive.'"

My heart melted at his words, as did the silicone manicure wrap on my finger. That night, both smelling faintly of coleslaw and mozzarella sticks, we had our first kiss under the flickering sodium lights of the Jones Beach parking lot.

It wasn't until he asked me for fifty dollars, though, that I considered us an actual couple. Which says a lot. I gave him the money—despite my really not being able to spare it—and our relationship grew. Like a weed.

He loved all the things I loved—reading, long conversations about other people, reading. He loved to work out—which we did together often because he was intensely competitive with me about weight. He made me a better person. Well, he tried to. He would criticize everything about me—which at least felt familiar. From my not drinking enough water to my driving too fast, to the way I ordered salad dressing, all were cause for derision.

Our shared world mostly centered around his migraines. They were a misery for him and, by association, me. We were constantly having to leave movies and parties and dinners only to spend hours in ERs, where doctors would present his cluster symptoms to residents, who would *oooh* and *ahhh* and run fingers over Andy's drooping eye and the pulsating vein popping out of his forehead while he writhed in pain. And while the migraines weren't his fault, they ruined a lot of Saturday nights.

Not that our Saturday nights were filled with passion the rest of the time. Far from it. He never wanted to have sex, even when he woke up with a boner. He'd just hop out of bed and get the day started, including those days when we'd go away on what were (at least in theory) "romantic" weekends at bed-and-breakfasts—another passion of his that I didn't share. Sorry, but I've never understood the quaintness people feel about sleeping where some kid died of polio in the 1800s and now lives in an attic as an angry ghost. But Andy loved B&Bs, so we went.

Over two and a half years, he dumped me five times. There was never any really good reason to set the ball rolling; it was always something trivial. But his final indictment against me was always the same: "I can't be with you, and no man ever could."

That's what he would say, but before he did, he would always hand me a check for the money he'd owed me. That's how I knew we were breaking up—he'd break out his checkbook. He'd casually, even cavalierly, sign his name with a scribble, rip the check from the book, and hand it to me.

By the third time, we both knew the drill. I'd ball up my fists and refuse to take the check. He'd try to shove it into my pockets, and I'd shove him away—not too hard because, like I said, he was smaller than me. I'd sob and beg and plead for another chance, for him to not give me back the fifty dollars—money I desperately needed, but not as much as I needed to not be without him. I'd try to sell myself back to him, like a used vacuum cleaner. I was sturdy, I was reliable. His family and friends loved me. He wouldn't have to get used to someone new. He could take me anywhere. I knew where the wiper fluid went in cars and he didn't.

I was never able to persuade Andy that I was worthy of his love, however, and he would leave me for a few days until he was ready to take me back, during which time I'd cry, listen to REM's "Everybody Hurts" and Elton John's "Sorry Seems to Be the Hardest Word," chain-smoke Marlboro Ultra-Lights, and live on a diet of pure cane sugar in my postage stamp–sized apartment, my friends at work all trying to lift my spirits by reminding me what an asshole Andy was.

It was mostly Kara who kept me going when Andy wrote out his fifty-dollar check for the last time and told me we were through. She was a rock for me as the subsequent days turned into weeks and Thanksgiving turned into Hanukkah, then Christmas, and finally New Year's Eve, when I realized Andy was never coming back.

My brother Jeff, albeit a long-distance one, was my other rock. He'd moved to LA by this time and would suggest when I called him in tears that, like him, I should pursue a career in comedy. He even offered to get me started by paying for a sketch comedy writing class at Chicago City Limits, which was in midtown near my office. I considered it but declined, telling him what I believed was true—that the most I could aspire to comedy-wise was maybe the third funniest person in stock photography.

Jeff knew I was better than that and never stopped making the offer—not even in February, when Andy returned out of nowhere, wanting to get back together. He'd made a mistake, he said, and he told me I looked thinner. I wondered if he needed money, and how much thinner? Mostly, I was thrilled.

But I'd come a long way, I believed (or wanted to). So, buoyed by the strength Kara and Jeff and my other friends had instilled in me, and with a glimmer of a "fuck you," I told Andy we were done.

This made Andy want me that much more, and he started to stalk me. It was 1997—a "pre-stalking" era, so it was an unusual thing to happen unless you were famous.

For weeks I'd have a giant dude from my office walk me to the street past my diminutive ex, who waited outside the building every night, after which Andy would follow me for blocks—pleading with me to take him back. The next morning, I'd find him waiting inside my subway station, all the way across town from his place on the West Side.

I stayed strong, though, and grew increasingly turned off by him. At least, that's what I convinced myself. Truth was, I was only pretending to be terrified and tormented by this man who I could almost certainly kick the shit out of. I didn't fully grasp the depths of my delusion, however, until one evening when he suddenly wasn't outside my office. He wasn't at my subway station the next day, either—and I let two trains go by, just in case he was running late.

When he failed to show up that night, I called him to make sure he was okay (again, early stalking days—no one knew what they were doing).

He answered his phone. I told him I noticed he wasn't following me and asked if everything was okay.

"Yeah," he said, "I just decided I don't want to be with you."

I was stunned. "So, you're breaking up with me again?"

"Guess so," he told me.

In a sudden panic, I realized that this gave me no satisfaction—which it should have were I actually over him. On the contrary, I felt tears welling as I heard myself asking this asshole what I had done wrong to no longer be worth stalking.

"Nothing," he said. "I just realized I can't be with you, and no man ever could."

Once again, I had become unlovable. Only this time I wasn't even lovable from a hundred feet away. I could have called it and should have. But there was something worse than being led on by Andy. This time, I'd strung myself along. My humiliation was complete.

Or so I thought. A few months later, Kara and I went to see John Irving, a favorite author of Andy's and mine, read from *A Widow for One Year* at Barnes and Noble. Outside the reading, I ran into Andy for the first time since our breakup. He was on a date. With his new boyfriend, named Andrew. Because, of course.

"I don't get headaches anymore!" he told me cheerily, in a newly more relaxed voice that oddly suited his higher pitch.

Everything made sense in that moment, actually. Andy had always vocally hated gay men—no doubt because they knew what he didn't know himself, or did know and didn't want them to know, or didn't want to know himself. Gay men used to hit on him in my presence—after all, how could a girl he was with possibly be his girlfriend? Those men knew: Andy was clearly gay. And, when he said he couldn't be with me and no man ever could, what he meant was, no gay man ever could. God, I hope that's what he meant.

I'D WASTED ALL those years. He'd wasted all those headaches. Irrationally, even though maintaining a physical attraction between us was obviously impossible, I wished I could have done it. Plus, I was jealous that he'd met someone already.

Jeff tried to boost my spirits, telling me it was all "great material" and I should "use" it for my career in comedy. I wanted him to "use" a hammer to break his own legs. He was obsessed with me having a fulfilling career. It was getting annoying.

Kara took a different approach, which was how I found myself sitting on a packed meat-plane next to Julia Roberts in search of my "new beginning."

SINCE WE WERE pretty much still pre–reality TV (aside from MTV's *Real World*), I didn't have an accurate picture of what life at a Mexican resort filled with single people would be like. I just imagined getting there and falling in love with someone who would find the "breakup bangs" I'd given myself adorable, a guy who would be hot but also successful, and never once ask me for fifty dollars, and if he did, have the decency to never pay me back. And also, he would be straight. We would spend the better part of the week together, a couple on the beach, making everyone sick. Only interested in each other, we'd huddle together in our private cabana and in corners. I'd think nothing of doing overly familiar things, like, putting sunscreen on his back and picking a hard-to-get piece of lettuce out of his teeth. We'd have private jokes and have nicknames for each other by day three. We'd drink from each other's glasses without wiping the straw off before taking a sip. I'd get his cold. He'd think my sniffling was the cutest. We'd share a cab back to the city when we got home, I'd start spending so many nights at his two-bedroom apartment in a doorman building that it would make no sense to keep my own place, which was basically a fire escape with a bathroom. Many years later, we'd regale our grandchildren with the story of how we met at Club Med. The Way Life Should Be. Adorable. Take that, Andy and Andrew.

The airport in Mexico, it turned out, was no doubt the inspiration for every Mexican drug cartel movie where innocent, lonely women just trying to get over their ex-boyfriends and maybe have a cocktail always leave with their heads sawed off and their bodies stuffed with cocaine. Kara didn't share the same worry. Why would she? In those movies, Julia Roberts makes it out alive along with the only good-looking guy in the cast—both of them with their hair perfectly coiffed.

We got to the resort, where a giant wooden sign with the words "Club Med, The Way Life Should Be, Playa Blanca" hung on the gates. I figured someone had a tremendous sense of irony in naming the place, as it was clear from jump there was no playa and nothing about this—what appeared to be at first glance—shithole looked particularly blanca, which explained the discounted price and the "oodles of availability" quoted us by our travel agent.

The palm trees and plants had been recently watered—in anticipation of new arrivals, I guessed—and the air was still heavy with humidity that reeked of sweat, hair gel, and despair. Hopefully not all mine. Dale's temperamental hair exploded into an afro within the thirty seconds it took for us to hustle into the lobby while our luggage was unloaded. Once inside, we were greeted by the Gentils Organisateurs (Gracious/Nice Organizers). Unlike the female GOs, who were average looking and on the stocky side but super athletic and buff, the male GOs were each a page out of a calendar. Tan and fit, great hair, great smiles, not one ugly dude among them. All I could think was how much Andy would have loved the place.

We found our luggage and made our way to our room, where meager accommodations were the name of the game. Two full-sized beds were separated by a teeny nightstand that was almost dwarfed by the indigenous bug giving birth in the lamp affixed to the top. There was a bathroom, a closet, and a bureau, on which there was no TV.

No TV.

This was bad.

As I tried frantically to reach someone on the phone, which reeked of sunblock, I watched Kara unpack her camera equipment, bathing suits, and her "fall"—a precursor to extensions that you'd clip into your hair. Kara had it made at a fancy salon and it was . . . everything. Listening to the phone ring, watching Kara gingerly hang up her extra hair in a room with no TV, I noticed Kara had a genuinely amazing body and started to wonder if our friendship would actually survive the trip.

Abandoning the phone, I decided to go down and complain in person—but not before a snack; my blood sugar plummeting, I was desperate for a candy fix. I grabbed my bag and threw it on my bed. It was only then that I noticed a damp, dark stain across the bottom and up the sides of my luggage. Apparently, my bag had been set in a puddle of water by one of the very hot GOs Andy would love more than me. My heart in my throat, I unzipped the suitcase and pulled out a dripping wet Duane Reade bag in which my entire candy supply had started to dissolve (the Circus Peanuts) and congeal (the Jujyfruits).

Even Kara gasped. I was about to be trapped for seven days on an island with Julia Roberts and without both TV and my candy. This was officially worse than fat camp—at least there, someone had some spare gummy bears sewn into the sole of their shoes or Tootsie Rolls stuffed in a hollowed-out teddy bear.

We both knew neither one of us could live like that. My "new beginning" could not be sugar free.

Springing into action to triage my dying candy, Kara broke out her blow dryer while I scooped the dissolving clump of Circus Peanuts from the bag and laid them out on a towel. With the humidity working against us, our patient was disintegrating by the second, changing color from a light toxic orange to a darker toxic orange. Rigor mortis was setting in, and all the shouting and blow drying in the world couldn't halt its demise. I knew that because both of those things were happening.

The Jujyfruits were in even worse shape. Joined in a clump, the box had bled onto them and the colors were running together—not even the minty greens, which I usually threw away, were salvageable. Apparently, the water in Mexico was noxious enough—even the rain—to make short work on candy designed to withstand a nuclear winter. Which I was about to face at Club Med, The Way Life Should Be.

In a self-destructive rage, I flushed my candy corpses down the toilet. Kara was now legitimately nervous enough to go after them as they made endless circles around the drain of our low-flow toilet and I sat on my bed in actual tears.

"What's awlda commotion?"

Alysse, now in a hot pink cover-up, Gucci sandals, giant sunglasses, and sunhat, stood in our open doorway with a completely frizzed-out Dale behind her, gaping at the two of us.

"My . . . candy got ruined," I sputtered.

"Oh my gawwwwwd," Dale gasped.

"I know," I moaned. "No TVs."

"No," Dale said, and pointed to Kara. "I just can't gettovah how much you look like Julia Rob-bits!"

SOME PEOPLE PEAK in high school or college. Or when they move away from home. Or get married or divorced. Or never.

Kara peaked at Club Med, The Way Life Should Be, Playa Blanca.

Her high-pitched laugh that began with a scream wasn't irritating south of the border, it was infectious. The way she said "unregardless" instead of "regardless" was "adorable," regardless of the fact that it made her illiterate. The fact that she pronounced "windmill" as "windmeal" was also not a problem (which she pronounced "prollem"). Her shoulder tattoo of the Chinese symbol for strength with a lotus flower in the middle was also a popular topic of philosophical discussion and examination. Normally just a pretty girl on any rush-hour subway, here Kara blossomed into an exotic new species of New York orchid.

That she didn't know how to swim at the age of twenty-eight was the cutest thing ever, even though it "flustrated" her to no end and to the adoration of most of the male GOs and nearly all the guests. Anytime Kara attempted to doggy-paddle at the deep end of the pool, the unenchanted—and I'll grant you, there were very few of us—were shit out of luck if we needed anything, from a towel to a handgun, from the GOs. Staff and guests alike would convene at the side of the pool to cheer their darling on as she conquered her inner demons and outer accent.

Kara's ability to tie a maraschino cherry stem into a knot with her tongue was also a crowd pleaser. "Do it again!" one male GO shouted, elbowing me in the head to get a closer look. And no one seemed impressed by the fact that my teeth were stained permanently red from the four pounds of maraschino cherries I'd scarfed down just to elevate my blood sugar into Circus Peanut range.

She was resort royalty, incapable of putting a tiptoed foot wrong. And lucky me, she was my roommate.

Sidekick to the pretty girl was a familiar role—Rhoda to Mary, Ethel to Lucy, Laverne to Shirley. In my mental sitcoms, I'd always cast myself to facilitate the dreams of my more attractive partner in crime, cracking hilarious jokes in the process, deflecting the fact that my life didn't matter as much. My character probably wouldn't even have a standing "apartment set" on the soundstage—hey, no one ever made the trip to Potsie's house on *Happy Days*, so why bother building a place for me? Of course, at some point, someone would have to build a corner of my bedroom or bathroom, for that one episode where I'd, I don't know, refuse to leave my house because I was so depressed about the fact that I didn't matter, and the cast of characters would have to come pry me out of a ball—proving that even though I was less attractive, I still deserved love (friendship-love, that is).

Meanwhile, here I was . . . the less-attractive friend to Julia Roberts.

To her credit, Julia (sorry—Kara) was worried about me. At first, that was due to my lack of creature comforts—in the absence of my TV and candy, and, as I learned later that first night, Diet Coke ("No Cokas Light," we were told), my Club Med, The Way Life Should Be experience quickly took on all the comfort and pleasure of a rehab. Living on vegetables and fruit, I spent the first few days limp on a couch by the bar, weak from unrefined sugar (I'd burned through the maraschino cherry supply pretty quickly) and listening to Alysse complain about everything from the dearth of male options for her and Dale to the lack of air-conditioning.

By the third day, Kara's concern for me graduated from genuinely appreciated by me to personally humiliating for me. For Kara had fallen in love on Day One with Pete, a fellow "adorable" from Philadelphia.

"I thought you weren't interested in meeting a guy," I'd said to her the second night as I watched her clipping in her fall before dinner. "You said you just wanted to take pictures of flowers."

Kara shrugged her perfect combination of toned yet boney shoulders, which she was just "born with," and said she was just having fun, that she didn't care where it went.

Where "it" ended up going, however, night after night, was just outside our room.

As stalwart a friend as Julia would be, Kara refused to leave her sidekick alone (much as I begged her to), which meant that I and everyone within eye- and/or earshot of the hallway outside our door were subjected to Kara and Chris's "good night" marathon make-out sessions. The two of them took it to the very brink of penetration. There weren't enough flimsy pillows in the place to drown out the mouth sounds and moans, the giggles and the "but you're so beautiful, I just want to be inside you"s emanating from the other side of my door (I pretty much wanted to be inside a well).

Not that I'd given up on meeting someone myself. That's what I was there for—A New Beginning. Each bus that entered the gates of Club Med Playa Blanca, The Way Life Should Be, came bearing new hope for me. New Jersey rolled in, and I convinced myself that I could date a guy from Jersey; it was a stone's throw from New York, and he'd no doubt want to stay in the city most nights anyway. Then Boston and Pennsylvania and Rhode Island would pull up, and I contemplated the thrill and freedom a long-distance relationship could afford, the veggie burgers on Amtrak, the frequent-flyer miles adding up to a free first-class honeymoon at—where else?—Club Med, The Way Life Should Be.

But there was no one. Even the rare cute guy wasn't interested in me, only Kara—attached or not. Even Alysse, who grew considerably browner by the second (1997 was also before skin cancer was a thing), wanted to know everything there was to know about Kara, so she could set her up when we all went back to the Cokas Light–filled world. Despite that, I liked Alysse a lot—there was something very maternal about her—especially the way she worried about the sunburn I'd gotten on my lips, which caused them to blister and then, well, pretty much peel off, exposing an alarmingly fragile, paper-thin layer of lip skin, making it impossible for me to close my mouth all the way.

While Kara went off to the disco with Pete (where her aggressive, jerking, and bobbing dance moves were not only adored but actually copied), I sat on the couches by the bar with the other Club Med Playa Blanca, The Way Life Should Be, party poopers. By Day Four, like anyone else with Stockholm syndrome, I was starting to enjoy my nightly routine, and my fellow wallflowers were looking better. A flirtation had even begun to bud between myself and one of the hairy gentlemen from the plane—maybe my New Beginning was hiding underneath a carpet of back hair. My confidence was growing almost as fast as my new lip skin.

That night, just as I was close to accepting his invitation for a late-night swim, Kara suddenly stormed past the bar, her heels in her hand, her mascara running, her fall . . . falling. I got up to follow, but not before seeing Pete emerge from the disco with the assistance of a GO.

"Bat-shit bitch threw a glass at me," he was saying. "She cut my fucking foot!"

Apparently, Kara's inability to handle either liquor or rejection very well, un-regardless of the fact that she didn't "care where her relationship went," wasn't as adorable as her mouse-like sneezing fits or cherry stem tying skills.

We now know, courtesy of reality TV, just what sort of fuckathon goes on at beach resorts packed to the rafters with horny singles and tequila. We all know that even Julia Roberts has to put out at some point, or her leading man is going to sleep with one or six of the other available bachelorettes. Which is apparently what had happened.

So, with one screaming tantrum accompanied by a well-aimed wineglass, Kara went from the Golden Girl to radioactive, more feared than the bird-sized blind bugs that darted around slamming into everyone. Naturally, as her roommate, I became toxic by proxy. For the last two days of the trip, Kara and I were an island unto ourselves, with only Alysse and Dale remaining loyal.

As we all finally headed home, I took some comfort in the fact that my inability to deal with the money system—cash was converted to beads or some shit I didn't understand—had left me with all of the three hundred dollars I'd brought with me, which coincidentally was all the money I had to my name. I'd also clearly lost some weight, cut off from my mainland Cokas Light and Circus Peanuts supplies. My lips seemed to have grown back a pinker color. I wondered how much a fall like Kara's would set me back, but Kara had become unstable to the point at which asking her if she wanted her smoked almonds on the plane home was enough to drive her to tears, so I let that one go.

Back at JFK, Kara took off for Brooklyn, where she lived. I shared a cab back to Manhattan with Dale and Alysse. Dale was first to be dropped off, just a few blocks from her buddy, and in that short run to Alysse's place, I decided to just come out and ask her the question that I hadn't had the nerve to ask on the flight down.

"So, who is it you think I look like?" I asked.

Alysse hesitated. I assured her it didn't matter who it was, that I just really wanted to know. I mean, what else could go wrong?

She made a face and then apologetically said, "Molly Ringwald."

"Molly Ringwald, the actress?!" I exclaimed.

Alysse laughed. "No, the podiatrist," she said. "Yes, of course the actress!"

"But . . . she's pretty," I sputtered.

"So are you, honey," she said.

So are you.

I asked her why she didn't want to tell me that first day.

"You nevah know how people are gonna react." She shrugged. "I mean—she's no Julia Robbits."

Alysse gave me her number. I put it in my Coach wallet with my total wealth and spent the rest of the ride home truly and finally uplifted. My Club Med Playa Blanca, The Way Life Should Be, mother figure thought I was pretty. I was totally going to call her.

It wasn't until I was back home a full ten minutes, rejoicing in the tiny splendor, generic bugs, and the stale Jujyfruits I had in my fridge, that I realized I'd left my wallet in the cab.

I stayed up all night frantically calling the taxi company to see if it had been turned in (it hadn't). The next morning, I went back to work, walking downtown because I was broke until payday.

Entering the bullpen, my coworkers saw me and all cheered.

"There she is!"

"She's back!"

"Tan and rested!"

"Was it amazing?!"

"What happened to your lips?"

All the faces, so happy to see me. So hopeful. As hopeful as I'd been a short week ago.

I collapsed in my chair and burst into tears.

It was terrible, watching their faces fall, feeling their vicarious disappointment. But I couldn't stop myself—the tears I'd been keeping in for two months freed me, and I started to go into exactly how terrible it was. Moment by moment, insult by insult. Windmeal by windmeal.

And something amazing happened.

By the time I'd finished reenacting performing CPR on my dying candy, my entire office—from sales to IT to shipping to two messenger guys who had just wandered in—were standing or sitting around me, laughing their asses off. And they weren't there because I was next to the fax machine (except for Wasim, who was waiting for a release from London to come through)—they'd stuck around because they wanted to hear more. I made them laugh.

I was funny. I mean, I'd already known I was a good sidekick, but now I had a crowd of my own. A rapt audience.

Before heading back to her desk, my friend Joanna hugged me. "You really should be writing this shit down," she said.

At that moment, I decided to try. I was going to take that class at Chicago City Limits my brother was insisting I take.

And a new beginning started for me for real.

Water Is for Writers

My first marriage was a work marriage—a writing partnership, which in many ways is the same as a real marriage. We shared a paycheck, a job, success, failure, both good news and bad, criticism, a mind, and three beautiful children (our scripts). We represented each other on the page and in the writers' room. In sickness and in health.

Until the death of our joint career did us part.

Samantha and I met in a Beginning Sitcom Writing class at the New School in Manhattan. I gravitated toward Samantha right away because she had similar features as my childhood best friend, Rachel: thick brown hair cut in a short bob, green eyes, and the overall appearance of a college futon—sort of generally soft and messy but comfortable. After class, we would walk to the subway together, decompressing and debating whether or not our teacher,

Mort Scharfman—who claimed to have written for the greatest sitcoms of all time—had in fact actually written for *All in the Family*, *Three's Company*, *The Mary Tyler Moore Show*, *The Odd Couple*, *Good Times*, and *The Jeffersons*. As this was long before Google, there were no immediate answers, so we decided he was definitely lying. He had to be—no one had a résumé like the one he boasted, and if they had, they certainly wouldn't be spending their Tuesday nights trying to explain story structure to a bunch of New Yorkers who thought they were the next Seinfelds.

The last night of the class, at the top of the subway steps, Samantha and I said our good-byes and good lucks and went our separate ways. But halfway down the stairs, just as the 4 train was pulling into the station and I was about to make a run for it, I heard Samantha call out, "Elizabeth—would you want to be writing partners?!"

I turned back to see that she hadn't moved.

She smiled and shrugged. "Maybe we can have a huge career like Mort Scharfman!" she said.

When I'd first decided to embark on a career in TV writing, my brother, Jeff, had suggested I get a writing partner. It would help me get a job on a show, he said: producers get two writers for the price of one, and they love a bargain. It was also good to have someone to share the workload with, so you didn't have to go it alone.

Jeff had a partner, and it worked for him—at the time, they were writing for this new show called *Friends*, which seemed like it might stay on the air for a couple of seasons. I figured that if Jeff— the smart one out of the two of us—needed a writing partner, then I certainly did, too.

Samantha was waiting for my answer, and the train was pulling in, so I said, "Sure, why not?!"

Ten months later, with a sample *Frasier* script that we'd

written together in hand, we set out for Los Angeles in search of representation. It was all happening. I let go of my studio apartment—a fifth-floor walk-up that boasted clanking heaters, half-painted walls, and a laundry room rapist. I also let go of Josh, a guy I was kind of seeing (the word *boyfriend* made him uncomfortable but getting blackout drunk and vomiting off the side of the Staten Island Ferry didn't). The morning I left, I'd hoped he'd leap off his bottom bunk and run to my place, where, of course, my cab would be waiting, steam rising from the street (because that would be more dramatic, and I'm a visual person). I imagined Josh would cry—no, he'd sob—and yes, beg me to stay, vowing to get an actual job and give up on his college improv troupe ever making it big because, face it, what improv troupe makes it big? He'd stop helping his "friend" Heidi (yes, they'd slept together) rearrange her furniture every Friday night. At that point, I'd tell him it was too late and get into the cab. He'd chase me for blocks before giving up but not before shouting, "I may have been too lazy to walk you home at three a.m., but I'm going to go all the way to California and fight for you, Liz!"

None of that happened. He never even called to see if I got to California okay.

Samantha, on the other hand, was leaving her longtime girlfriend Judy, their poodle Dante, and the two-bedroom condo they owned in Westchester. Judy, the plan went, would come out with the dog soon as Samantha got settled in LA.

Judy didn't like me. I'd heard her say so back when we were still in New York. Samantha and I had been working on our script at their place one night and, as had been happening with rising frequency, Samantha and Judy were arguing behind their closed bedroom door. Their bathroom was next door and had perfect lighting for picking my face, as well as very thin walls.

Scanning my cheek in their medicine cabinet mirror, I heard Judy say she was angry at Samantha because her boots had tracked mud into the apartment. All three of us knowing that it's never about mud on boots, the fight quickly devolved into what was really wrong.

Their voices became muffled whisper-shouts, much harder to hear. I opened the medicine chest to get a closer listen, moving various pill bottles—nothing I wanted—out of the way and stuck my head inside as far as it would go. And that's when I heard it:

"You don't think I'm attracted to Liz, do you?" Samantha was asking, in complete disbelief.

Silence. I pressed my ear farther into the mirror, possibly breaking one or more tiny ear bones. The accusation hurt—but not as much as the fact that Samantha sounded almost . . . repulsed by me.

"Liz? Are you kidding me?!?" Samantha now whisper-shouted with more disbelief and disgust that was now unmistakable.

I closed the medicine chest and looked at myself in a whole new fluorescent light. Was I some sort of monster? Apparently, I was, because Judy quickly apologized for being "crazy to think it was possible" and then blamed her hormones, which I thought was a real low blow. And for the record, Judy wasn't exactly my type, either. She wore scarves, too much eye shadow, and pumps—even with jeans. If Samantha was a college futon, Judy was a wicker chair—stiff, uncomfortable, dated, only went well with other wicker, and very, very not funny.

"I don't even *like* her," Judy said, now out in the hallway. "I don't *have* to like her."

I went to join Samantha in the living room but not before stealing two of her blood pressure pills, just because you could probably miss one day without incident and I was feeling spiteful. As soon as I exited the bathroom, Dante—possibly smelling my low self-esteem—jumped up and humped my leg relentlessly. Prying him off me with all of my strength, I shot Judy and Samantha each a smug look as if to say, "not everyone finds me repulsive."

It was pretty clear why Judy didn't like me. I was a permanent fixture in her home while her girlfriend and I wrote that *Frasier* sample script. I was there on nights, weekends, and even for a holiday party Samantha and I threw for each other—including a shrimp platter for twenty-four that we polished off without her. But I think what Judy hated most about me—other than my looks—was that I was the personification of Samantha's dream of becoming a comedy writer. Thanks to me, and aided by the connections we'd have in my brother, they would both have to uproot their lives. Judy would have to leave her job, as well as the synagogue where she'd advanced to the front row of the choir, and all of their friends, including their dog groomer with whom they'd become close during Dante's bout with dog psoriasis. Meanwhile, Samantha and I would be sharing a full-sized bed in Jeff's guest room in the Hollywood Hills—though Judy seemed unthreatened by that.

Our first night on Woodrow Wilson Drive, Samantha and I lay awake, shoulder to shoulder in silence, staring at the ceiling— neither of us able to sleep, each clutching for dear life the security blankets (hers a torn piece of a T-shirt, mine a pillowcase) that we'd brought from home. We were filled with fear and dread and what I imagine people are filled with after they kill someone in the heat of the moment or decide to move cross country to pursue an almost impossible career with someone they really don't know all that well, who, as a grown woman, still carries a security blanket.

We rented a car and bought a gigantic cheap cell phone to share (they were still new at the time). Almost immediately, the thing was blowing up with calls from talent agencies wanting to meet us, either because they needed to sign the brain trust behind the *Frasier* sample in which the highfalutin Frasier found out he was good at the blue-collar sport of bowling or because word was out that Jeff and his writing partner were looking for new representation and they wanted to get in good with him.

I was guessing the latter. But a break is a break, and we quickly signed with senior agents at one of the biggest agencies, the one that brought out the biggest fruit platter and coffee tray just for us. I mean, what could I say? We loved food on a platter! This ultimately made our work-marriage official. From that point on, we went by Astrof-Sideman. We were promised many, many offers from shows and a long and prosperous future in TV. It almost seemed too good to be true.

It was.

STAFFING SEASON (THE time when shows hire their writers) began, and our agents sent us out on meetings with studio and network execs, who serve as gatekeepers for the actual shows. Even the most stable couple would buckle under the stress of driving around a foreign city with massive traffic. With a giant map spread across the dashboard (pre-GPS times) and not so much as a fraction of a sense of direction between us, we were constantly late and arguing more and more, our bickering turning into screaming matches that went on all the way up to studio gates. We'd gotten along great in the bubble of Samantha's condo in New York, but, like an omelet or French fries, our relationship didn't travel well. It was safe to say the Astrof-Sideman honeymoon was over almost as soon as it began.

Even worse—despite all the meetings, we didn't wind up with a job. Soon it was May, and we found ourselves having to wait another ten months for the next TV staffing season.

I was devastated, desperate, and angry. I wondered—could the reason we weren't getting staffed have been Samantha's shrill voice, which I'd only just started to notice? Or was it the way she cracked her knuckles on her thighs in meetings—both hands at once crunching, then the thumbs—all right in the middle of someone (usually me) talking? Or maybe it was the way her exhales sounded like a city bus coming to a slow, labored stop. Or the matronly dresses she wore. I had one very hip accessory—a Kate Spade backpack. It had been a gift from a friend in New York who worked in the showroom. I always made sure it was visible in meetings, as if to say, "She might look like a middle-aged preschool teacher, but I'm cool. I can compensate, trust me. Trust us."

Nobody did and so, with our *Frasier* sample, we applied to the esteemed Warner Bros. Television Writers' Workshop, which was nearly impossible to get into. But if we got in, it was basically guaranteed to help us get a job the following season.

Meanwhile, Samantha found a grown-up apartment for her, Judy, and their dog. I found a studio apartment much like the one I had in New York—minus the laundry room rapist, but also minus the laundry room. Samantha and I continued to work, this time on a *Dharma & Greg* sample. Judy continued to hate me. And I continued to wonder what about me was so unattractive to the both of them.

To make my rent, I managed to burn through several day jobs— one of them quite literally. My brother's friend had hired me to deliver summer camp flyers to public schools all over Los Angeles. One particularly hot December afternoon on my way to my last school for the day, in somewhere called Santa Clarita, way north on something called the 405 freeway, I parked my car at St. William-Something School and flicked my ninetieth cigarette out the window (I was a chain-smoker now, because it's not cool to eat in LA).

By now I had my own giant cell phone, and, as I got out of the car, it rang. It was our agency. Please be a job offer, I prayed. A meeting, a fruit platter . . . anything!

It wasn't a fruit platter. Our agents, it turned out, were dropping us. Jeff and his partner had signed with another agency, and our agency had coincidentally decided that Astrof-Sideman wasn't a "good fit" anymore.

"Fuck a dick!" I remember screaming in the parking lot of St. William-Something after which, more than a little violently, I pushed the front seat forward and went to grab my box of flyers. That was when, out of the corner of my eye, I saw the filter end of the Camel Light I thought I had tossed out the window. It was sticking halfway out of my Kate Spade backpack.

"No," I said. As in no, the cigarette was simply perched there, and hadn't in fact burned a hole right through the front pocket of the only nice thing I had to my name.

But, not no, yes. It had. Yes. The nylon charred beyond repair, my bag was garbage.

I cursed myself and my disgusting smoking habit, vowed to quit, then immediately lit another cigarette. Picking up the open box of flyers, I walked slowly, sadly, toward the school, hoping, someday, all the laughing, playing, happy kids' lives would wind up sucking as much as mine did. And that every one of them would scream "fuck a dick" in a Catholic school parking lot.

The wind picked up just then, blowing my flyers out of the box—one by one at first but then in tens and twenties. One flew up and stuck to my face, covering my right eye for at least thirty seconds before whipping past me. By the time I got to the steps, the box was almost empty. Turning back toward the car, I saw the lawn was covered in flyers.

Stepping on them on my way back to the car, my cigarette down to the filter, I finally faced facts: What the fuck I was doing in Los Angeles? Did I even want to be a writer? We didn't even have an agent, anymore.

I missed New York—the seasons, the average-looking people . . . I even missed Josh.

I wanted to go home. I wanted to quit.

But when you have a mother who never finished anything—not even raising her children—quitting is not an option that comes easily.

So, instead, I persevered. And also prayed that a sea monster would rise out of the Pacific and eat California. Or that an earthquake would swallow us all up. Along with my mother. Especially my mother—though she was not yet living in California.

Samantha and I continued to work on our *Dharma & Greg* sample, which was way less fun than our *Frasier*. The stakes were higher, now that we'd moved cross country. Still, Samantha remained positive that something would come along. Optimism: another thing I started to dislike about her. Only a month or so went by until finally, after a long day of dog walking and telemarketing, my giant cell phone rang with good news—Samantha and I had been accepted into the Warner Bros. Television Writers' Workshop.

Something had come along. Again, I figured it was probably my brother working on a Warner Bros. show and not the brilliance of our *Frasier* script that got us in, but also again, I wasn't going to complain. This business was proving to be as brutal as I'd feared, and when one nepotism door closes, another opens. Samantha was thrilled. Judy was livid.

The first night of class, we walked into a huge conference room with a giant square light-oak table at the center, and were told it was where the casts of Warner Bros. shows like *Friends* and *Everybody Loves Raymond* read aloud their scripts for the coming week of production. I was on hallowed ground and completely awestruck.

I was also intimidated. I knew I could never have done this alone, so I was happy to have Samantha next to me, a second security blanket, as I set my Kate Spade bag down on the table burn-hole-side down.

Samantha and I had made it to this point. We had survived our growing pains and even a few knock-down, drag-out fights. Even very insulting accusations involving Judy missing two blood pressure pills.

"This is cool." I smiled and squeezed her shoulder—in a genuinely appreciative way.

Before class started one of the students, a young guy in his mid-twenties named (of course) Brett, casually reached for a bottle of water that was sitting on a credenza off to the side.

"Water is for writers!" boomed a male voice. We all jumped, turned, and saw David Sacks, the Warner Bros. executive who ran the program, standing in the doorway—this was his entrance. And his "welcome" speech.

He meant that water was for the real writers—the actual working writers who would be coming to speak to us nobodies. Brett pulled his hand away as if the water were a hot stove—or water that was, well, meant for real writers. Everyone stared wide-eyed, glad that they hadn't made the same mistake of being thirsty.

Once David had made it clear that we were nothing here, he told us that out of the twenty-eight people in the program, only about three would go on to have successful writing careers. This was very Marines-like and a far cry from what Mort Scharfman predicted for us back at the New School. Shame on Mort for lying about our chances as well as his credits. For leading me on.

In addition to Brett, who was now packing up his shit (thin skin much?), our group included the requisite pompous and just-out-of-Harvard bro team, as well as a super-focused and red-faced guy from Texas who wore cowboy boots and chewed on a pen like

it was straw. There was also a young mom who'd given birth literally the day before and couldn't entirely sit down, a non-surgically
enhanced blond girl who was blessed with both looks and a sense of
humor, as well as a middle-aged stay-at-home dad who just wanted
to get out of the house and/or get laid.

The odds that Samantha and I would move forward from this
point, I realized, were slim. But sitting at that table, for the first time
since coming to LA, I somehow actually felt we would. We had to.

The program was a six-week course in which we'd write a sample
script for a Warner Bros. show. Samantha and I decided without even
conferring that our script would be an *Everybody Loves Raymond*.
David would act as our boss and ultimately decide if we were worthy
of being staffed on one of their shows. If we were worthy of the water.

Samantha and I had written our *Frasier* sample script at our lei-
sure over the course of a year. Now Astorf-Sideman had a deadline.
And I had four jobs.

We worked constantly. I called in sick to my three other jobs,
Samantha stood up to Judy when she wanted to go furniture shopping or "have a life" . . . and in record time, we came away with a
script we were proud of. Jeff didn't have time to read it, but his "I
bet it's great!" was enough for me. I was excited. Confident even.

David Sacks hated it. Haaaated it. The story didn't work. The
jokes weren't right. The characters had no "drive." "Raymond would
never say that" was scrawled across every individual page.

We still had another chance to salvage it—the second draft.
But we needed to rethink the whole thing. Worse—we only had a
weekend to do it.

We left the writers' building that Thursday night completely
rattled, too embarrassed to even look at each other.

I was the first one to talk. "We can work at my place this weekend," I said. "I'll get candy and stuff."

"I can't," Samantha said, which I took to mean that she was doing the Atkins diet and would be eating a rotisserie chicken using my carpet as a plate. Without a plate.

But this was crisis time. "That's okay," I offered. "I'll get the chickens. Whatever you need."

"No, I mean I'm going to New Mexico with Judy," Samantha told me, almost defiantly. "It's not necessary to work this hard."

I stopped in my tracks and turned to her. I had no words. It was inconceivable.

Then, I had words.

"Are you fucking kidding me?" I shouted. "We have to rewrite a whole script in two days! You cannot go on vacation! This is what we moved here for! I have a Kate Spade bag that is just exposed fiberglass at this point!"

I lowered my voice and continued, quietly but firmly, "Tell Judy you can't go." Then I got menacing, "I'll. Get. Chicken." I walked off to my car, angry but happy that I'd set her straight.

And so it was that Friday afternoon, in giant "fuck you" fashion, Samantha left for New Mexico—clearly, very clearly, choosing her girlfriend over me, over our career. She left me a message saying she needed to have a life. She needed to get away. She said something about her mental health, and that was it.

She wanted a life.

This was my life.

I was on my own.

I was terrified.

But quitting was still not an option.

Forty-eight hours after I locked myself in my apartment, I emerged from a cloud of smoke, a pile of empty coffee and Big Gulp cups, candy wrappers, chicken and a plate (in case she came to her senses), Pirate's Booty crumbs, and cigarette ashes. I had a stye, the beginnings of emphysema, legs that wouldn't straighten all the way from sitting for so long, and a second draft.

I didn't allow myself even a glimmer of positivity this time. I couldn't allow even Jeff's "I'm sure they'll love it" to give me hope. The script was not good at all.

David Sacks loved it. Looooved it.

I breathed a giant, smoke-filled sigh of relief. Samantha was thankful, a little contrite, and very rested. I pushed down any feelings of hating her fucking guts. I had to, because with our *Everybody Loves Raymond* script, we ended up beating the odds and were one of the three people to get a job out of the Warner Bros. program. It was us, the cowboy, and the new mom, whose battle with postpartum had added a great depth to her *Will & Grace* sample.

We landed on a Warner Bros. show for NBC called *Jesse*, starring Christina Applegate. It was a dream come true. I was working on a staff with ten other writers and writing teams. I laughed all day and got paid for it. A writers' room, I realized, was where I was meant to be, and I was happy.

The only problem was I couldn't look at Samantha without becoming enraged.

As hard as I tried, I couldn't get past the fact that I had gotten us there, alone. We were Astrof-Sideman, but Astrof had done all the heavy lifting while Sideman cracked under pressure and went on a boondoggle. I didn't feel like she deserved to be there. Or have half of my paycheck. And my resentment began to eat away at me. Everything out of her mouth made me cringe or white-knuckle whatever surface I could find.

I separated myself more and more, leaving her to twist instead of pretending my thoughts and lines were our thoughts and our lines. I began to be included in late rewrites, when she was sent home. We grew more and more distant. We barely spoke.

Until halfway through the season, when we were thrown back together to write our own episode. Writing a solo episode was a great opportunity, but I took no pleasure from the news.

I dreaded being around her so much. I wanted to write it my way. Samantha felt my impatience as well as my hatred. She couldn't miss it—I was an asshole, and she knew why. She tried to make it up to me. She tried to make me . . . love her again.

She even suggested couples counseling, promising that she could get a good rate from the one she and Judy saw. (They were having trouble, too, it turned out. I'm not going to lie, this made me happy.) But I'd accrued so much debt from my first year in LA, I couldn't even afford a couch—I was currently using one I'd dragged in from off the curb and the family of birds that had been living in it hated me now.

I was not paying for couples counseling. Not for her. Not for us.

After *Jesse* wrapped for the season, we learned that the show wasn't going to be renewed, and we needed to get another job. We needed to write another sample.

Other writers on the show told me confidentially that I should go out on my own. My brother told me the same.

"You'll be great," he said.

I wanted to branch out badly. But the only way it was going to happen would be if Samantha either dropped dead or dumped me. I wasn't going to be the one to end our marriage.

Never a quitter, I stayed in bad relationships. I always had. Josh was just the latest in a long line of bad boyfriends and losers I couldn't break up with.

The guy who shared a one-bedroom apartment with nine other guys in a fire-hazard situation.

The painfully immature man-baby who kept a Polaroid picture in his wallet of a shit he'd taken because he was so proud of it.

The guy who, after a fun dinner out, pulled me toward him in a passionate embrace, at which point a glass he'd stolen from the restaurant fell from his jacket and smashed on the ground (the most upsetting part was that he didn't think to steal a matching glass for me).

The guy who invited me to a barbecue and told me to bring my own meat.

The widower who wanted to get married right away until he met someone who looked even more like his dead wife than I did.

The guy who took me to Central Park on my birthday with a filthy rolled-up tube sock, where he'd stored a joint for us to share and who smoked the whole thing without sharing.

Andy, who I wanted to hate but couldn't.

Josh. I hated Josh.

In each instance, I didn't do the breaking up. What if it turned out that I was wrong to feel the way I felt? What if this was what I deserved? What I was worthy of?

What if I couldn't write on my own? What if Samantha was the talented one, and the rewrite I'd done was a fluke? What if I was a fraud? What if I never worked again?

On our last day of *Jesse*, I walked into our office, where she was cleaning off her desk. She looked up at me. "What's up?" she asked, looking angelic, actually.

I flashed back to that night on the subway steps, the last night of that bogus class with that bogus teacher, Mort. That night in New York when she'd "proposed" to me, asking me to be her writing partner.

Samantha was the reason I'd come to LA—I never would have done it on my own. I would never have had the guts. If she hadn't bailed on me in the Warner Bros. program, I may never have known what I was capable of.

And she was a good friend. She was a partner. She was my work-wife. I owed so much to her. My resentment had driven a wedge between us.

But in that space, I found my own voice.

She helped me find it, and now I was going to use it.

"I want to break up," I started, and it was over.

My first breakup.

After that, I felt a relief I'd never felt before. A weight had been lifted. If I never worked again, it was worth this feeling of freedom.

FIFTEEN YEARS LATER, on the Warner Bros. lot, in that conference room where it all began, I took my seat at the square oak table behind a placard that read "*2 Broke Girls* Executive Producer Liz Astrof" and opened a bottle of water.

I heard an old voice in my head say, "Water is for writers," and laughed. I was a writer. And then I chugged it, just in case anyone tried to take it away.

End note: Mort Scharfman, it turns out, did in fact write for *All in the Family, Three's Company, The Mary Tyler Moore Show, The Odd Couple, Good Times*, and *The Jeffersons*, to name but a few of his credits. As for David Sacks—I have no idea where he is. I do know that Samantha went on to be a renowned child psychologist in Los Angeles. She and Judy are still together—and still not attracted to me.

It's Not Brain Surgery

I was always running. Always moving. Always in motion, fearing that if I stopped, I would never start again.

I was just one afternoon nap away from disappearing under a pile of blankets for days, just one unfinished script away from never finishing anything again, one missed workout from letting myself turn to jelly, just one ignored load of laundry away from living in filth. It was a slippery slope to becoming my mother.

So, I kept running. Kept moving.

I ran circles around my husband Todd—literally. I was like a whirling dervish, a blur. I did the laundry, the food shopping, I organized our shit, made our plans, made our dog's plans, and I mainly supported us financially. And I was super cool about it.

Until one Saturday almost a year into our marriage.

I was leaving for my first workout of the day and took in my husband sitting on the couch, a crushed velvet throw over his shoulders (a wedding gift), eating cereal out of a large salad bowl (a wedding gift) with a giant serving spoon (a wedding gift), and realized that I still needed to write our wedding thank-you notes. I'd never finished the ones from my Bat Mitzvah, and several relatives had died never having known if I'd gotten their checks. It had been rude of me and was also probably why my great-aunt Frances, heir to the Maidenform Bra fortune, left me out of her will. Which I didn't want to see happen again.

But I barely had time to write a phone number, much less seventy-three note cards. I was swamped taking care of myself and Todd, who I was starting to suspect was taking advantage of me. He seemed pretty comfortable not having much to do most days and spending his weekends relaxing with Olive—who he surprised me with after rescuing her from the pound and who became our first (and favorite) child—so, to be fair, it wasn't like he was doing nothing for us.

Still, I got so angry that day at his perpetual state of Zen that I slammed one of the doors in our apartment. But because of its 1920s charm, our door frames were warped, and the door just sort of floated almost-closed and then floated back open, forcing me to announce, "I slammed a door!" When that failed to raise interest, I took a pack of Life Savers and angrily threw it on the floor. But our apartment also had charming 1920s floors that were so soft and uneven that the Life Savers just landed almost soundlessly and rolled downhill to our bedroom.

"I threw something!" I called. When even that didn't rouse my husband, I finally marched into the living room and told him in no uncertain terms that it was time he got off his ass and helped out.

"Like with what?" he asked. "Every time I try to do anything, you just tell me—"

"'I've got it,' I know." It was true—I even took care of his sentences for him. I took care of everything.

There were times, like any new bride, I asked myself, "Whyyyyy did I marry this person?!" I wondered if I'd sold myself short by not marrying a successful comedy writer. But living with a neurotic guy who's constantly worried that every joke, every idea, every job is his last would be exhausting. It would be like marrying me . . . and who needed that? Or maybe I should have married a businessman, like a banker or a hedge fund manager. I didn't know anything about finances—even my own—and I probably wouldn't understand most of what he was talking about a lot of the time, so I'd be bored. But he'd pay for my life.

Todd, on the other hand, didn't even know what the Dow was (shouldn't one person in a couple know what the Dow is?!). But he knew every line of *National Lampoon's Vacation*—one of my favorite movies. He could also recite, word for word, the entire opening scene in *Airplane 2*. Which is in jive, by the way.

I didn't set out to marry Todd, but I knew early on that I would. About a month after we started dating, we had plans on a Saturday night. He was going to pick me up around eight. He never called or texted that entire day to confirm. Well. I certainly wasn't going to call him! Morning turned to afternoon, then evening—and still no word from Todd. He was blowing me off. That bastard. It was for the best, I reasoned—I was nearing thirty, and Todd was five years younger (four from October 'til January). He wasn't serious enough about his career, either—he was laid back and liked having fun. I clearly needed to focus on meeting a successful businessman.

In spite of Todd not living up to my "nearing thirty" standards, I was hurt that he was planning to let me down. So, I did what I always did when a guy treated me like shit—I went to my brother. I got in my car and cried all the way to Jeff's house and up the walkway to the front door. But just as I was about to ring the doorbell, I stopped. If I cried to Jeff about Todd, I realized, my brother would hate him, and I didn't want him to hate Todd. I wanted Jeff to like him. So, in an unprecedented move, I turned around and cried back to my car.

I got home to find Todd waiting. He was there to pick me up. He hadn't been blowing me off—he'd just made the wild assumption that since he said he'd pick me up around eight, that he would pick me up around eight. And it was exactly around eight. I could trust him. And so could Jeff.

And standing in our living room about a year into our marriage, when he got up to clean the dishes and I made him sit back down—I realized that was exactly how I wanted my marriage to be. I wanted—I *needed*—to be beholden to no one, completely self-sufficient so that in case my husband got sick or left me or suddenly dropped dead, I wouldn't be slowed down in any way.

I could keep running.

Todd was happy to oblige my not wanting to be taken care of—even at those times when I was at my most vulnerable, which was during one of the explosive headaches that would descend on me when I laughed really hard.

"My head, my head, my head, my head . . ." I would say.

The most he would do to help—the most I wanted him to do, and he knew it—was pause the TV and wait patiently for me to finish massaging away the pain in my temples so we could get back to *Jackass* or whatever juvenile obsession of ours had set off the throbbing. He knew I needed to do my own temple massaging; I didn't want to be touched on my temples by anyone. Even him.

Todd was concerned about my headaches, though, and was forever suggesting I go to a doctor, to which I'd suggest he turn the TV up. I was fine. Also, I didn't have time to go to the doctor. Also, they were just headaches, and I probably just had a low threshold for searing pain around my temples. I thought maybe they were caused by eye strain—I read from a monitor all day. Or grinding my teeth at night. I had a night guard, but after I neglected to wear it for a week, it shriveled up into a useless $500 rubber ball that I gave to Olive to chew. Her teeth started to improve, though.

Unfortunately, spending my days in a room full of comedy writers was making my head hurt more. I was working on *The King of Queens*, a funny show with funny writers, and it was literally killing me. I would go into every laughing fit hoping the headaches wouldn't appear this time, and every laughing fit ended with me massaging my temples, inhaling sharp breaths, wincing, and waiting it out, trying not to let anyone at work see. But they were getting harder to conceal.

One day (well, morning), during a 3:00 a.m. rewrite session, a writer was telling a hysterically funny story about his mother. It was so funny that I almost lost consciousness from the pain, sliding off my chair and under the table so no one would be bothered if I blacked out. My friend Melissa poked her head under the table and passed me a Post-it with her doctor's number on it.

"Go. See. Him," she commanded. "You need to do something about those headaches."

"I'm fine," I whimpered, trying not to throw up. The headaches were starting to make me nauseous, too, and the fear of throwing up makes me . . . well, throw up. So, I went to see him.

DR. SUNG WAS in his forties, handsome and dapper in a white dress shirt and tie. An Asian American George Clooney, I'd say. His good looks, combined with the fact that he didn't take insurance or validate parking, assured me that he was a great doctor.

He checked my eyes, my ears, my glands, and throat and listened intently while I described my headaches. I made lots of jokes, deflecting. I wanted him to like me and, in the moments when I didn't have the headaches—which were most moments—I'd honestly forget how bad they were.

At the end of my appointment, he walked me out to the receptionist, prescribed anti-inflammatories, and then, when I wasn't looking, put his dapper hand on top of mine, which was resting on the counter. As Todd could attest, my usual reaction to sudden affection is to flinch or jerk away or assume a fighting stance with karate chop arms. I chalk it up to not being hugged as a child. But this happened too quickly for me to react, and before I knew it, his hand was there, resting atop mine. It was soft and reassuring. I was unsure whether I was supposed to put mine on top of his, huddle style. How does hand-touching work?

He looked me in the eyes and said, "You're going to be just fine, okay?"

"Okay," I said, desperate to move my hand—this kindness, much less from an older father-type figure, was almost too much for me.

Several *okay*s later, I was out the door. I had a good feeling about the anti-inflammatories.

Parking was really expensive.

The anti-inflammatories didn't work, and the throbbing was now happening not only when I laughed but also when I coughed, when I sneezed, when I rose from a forward-fold in yoga, and when I lifted my head off my pillow too fast. It got to the point that, when I woke up, I'd have to keep my head down and roll off my bed to get on all fours before slowly standing up, without letting my head know I was lifting it.

But they were still just headaches—and a small price to pay, I reasoned, for a pretty happy life.

Nonetheless, I went back to Dr. Sung.

I sat on the edge of the exam room table, watching him—think. Thinking. Thinking. He thought *so* much. He twisted his mouth from side to side and recommended an MRI, "just to be on the safe side."

He had his receptionist schedule the procedure, along with a follow-up appointment with him—again, just to be on the safe side. Before walking off and leaving me to pay my out-of-pocket fee, he looked me in both eyes and told me I was okay.

"Okay?" He put his hand on mine, like he always did.

"Okay," I said, feeling the weight of his hand on mine. Grounding me . . .? Sure, why not.

"Okay." He gave my hand a squeeze and let go.

By now, *The King of Queens* was on hiatus. After punishingly long hours filled with painful, throbbing laughter, the time off was glorious; so I, of course, packed my days with activities, errands, exercising, and writing my screenplay. (If you live in LA, you have to be working on a screenplay. It's the law.)

Always running, always busy. Even lying in an MRI machine for an hour seemed indulgent, so I put it off and put it off and kind of forgot about it, even with my headaches getting worse and worse. Until one day, I had my bag dumped out on the floor of Starbucks looking for my wallet and found the referral for the MRI. Standing quickly to apologize to the person behind me in line, my head throbbed, and I made an appointment for the next day. The MRI was lovely, I have to say, and I'm no doctor, but the *tappity-tap* sounds the machine was making made me feel like everything was going to be just fine.

When I went to the follow-up with Dr. Sung the next week, the nurse showed me into his personal office instead of sending me into an exam room. Made sense—I'd already been examined. I felt very important. And fancy.

Dr. Sung was sitting behind a big, wooden L-shaped desk, writing something down. Behind him was a matching wall unit filled with pictures of his family—his wife and two mini Asian American George Clooney–looking kids, smiling.

"Hey, Liz, sit down," he said. There was something different in his singsong voice—it was more . . . consoling than usual.

I sat in one of the leather chairs facing his desk and was going to ask him about his kids, when his door closed without him getting up.

My jaw dropped—how did he do that? He must have had one of those buttons under his desk. This was a VERY good doctor, indeed.

He clasped his hands together, pursed his lips, pointed his chin down, and raised his eyes at me.

"They found something . . ." he started.

I was stunned. I hadn't even considered that he might have brought me there to tell me I had a tumor—that I was dying.

Which was what I must have said, because "No, you don't have a tumor" was the next reassuring sentence out of his mouth.

I wasn't dying.

"The MRI did show something called 'Chiari malformation' . . . okay?"

Dr. Sung handed me the piece of paper he was writing on. It read: Dr. Wesley King, Neurosurgeon.

Surgeon? I thought I didn't have a tumor!

He told me Dr. King is one of three people in the country who specialized in my type of (gulp) malformation.

"Because it's so easy to correct? Is that why they don't need a lot of people?" I joked, hopefully.

I followed Dr. Sung out to the receptionist's desk, where he stood next to me and, like a dapper boss-doctor, told her to make an appointment for me with Dr. Wesley King, Neurosurgeon, for that afternoon. He was going to squeeze me in.

Dr. Sung turned to me, looked me in the eyes, and put his hand on mine. I went for it and placed mine on his, trapping it there. We stayed like this for a good minute until he finally, earnestly said, "You're a nice gal, okay?"

Oh, Jesus.

"Dr. Sung called me a nice gal!" I shrieked into Todd's voice-mail, frantically. "Where ARE you?! Why aren't you answering your phone?!" In the time it took my husband to get back to his desk from the bathroom, I'd left him the same message. Six times.

He insisted on meeting me at Dr. King's office—I told him he didn't have to. I didn't need him to. He was adamant about it—almost sexy in his bossiness—so I let him.

Dr. King was young, confident, muscular, and good looking. A black George Clooney, I'd say. He didn't validate parking either, so this was clearly another good doctor.

First, we made small talk, joking around as I like to do. He was a consultant on a friend's medical drama series—even the brain surgeons in LA are in the business.

"You must hear a lot of people say, 'It's not brain surgery,'" Todd joked. "And then you say, 'It is brain surgery.'"

We all laughed. I said, "Ow."

We talked about my headaches. I shared how they had started about the time I'd gotten engaged. "If that's not a sign, amiright?" I laughed. Dr. King laughed. Todd shook his head, amused but not really.

Dr. King asked if I'd been jolted in the past few years—any car accidents or whiplash. That can sometimes cause people with a Chiari malformation to become symptomatic. I thought about it and then remembered being rear-ended a few years earlier. I'd been on my way to a boot camp class before work and was stopped at a red light when a guy in a giant pickup truck slammed into me. I remembered being furious because if you didn't get to class on time, you didn't get a treadmill, and then it was just lunges and free weights, and there was really no point in even going. I quickly got the guy's info and drove off. A few blocks later, at another red light, a woman in the car next to me had honked and gestured for me to roll my window down. "Ma'am, I think your car is on fire," she'd said, pointing.

Aside from not getting a treadmill and totaling my car and having to deal with a lot of jokes about being "rear-ended" at work that day, I'd figured that was the end of that.

That, however, happened to have also been the beginning of the headaches, I suddenly realized.

Dr. King assured me that even though he was a surgeon, he rarely had to perform surgery. Brain surgery is always the last resort in treatment. I was relieved. For being at the brain surgeon's office, we were having a good time so far.

He stepped out to look at my MRI, returning in what seemed like seconds and putting the image of my brain up on a lightbox. He wanted to explain my condition to me. Problem was, I was starting to black out.

I have this other condition—which may be related, now that I think about it—whereby whenever anyone explains something important to me, like directions, instructions, or brain defects, the pressure to listen is so great that all I hear is the theme song from the 1980s sitcom *The Facts of Life*. It just starts playing in my head over whatever it is they're saying. It's the reason I get lost so often. So, while Dr. King was pointing to the image of my brain on the lightbox . . . all I heard was "You take the good, you take the bad, you take them both, and there you have the facts of life . . . The facts of life . . ."

Fortunately, Todd was in the room and heard about how in a normal brain the *cerebellar tonsils* rest at the top of the spine. When we laugh or cough or sneeze or strain, *cerebrospinal fluid* within the brain and spinal cord that helps cushion them from injury flows down into the spinal column. But with a Chiari malformation, this balanced flow is disrupted. The obstructed fluid forces its way like a water hammer through the *foramen magnum*. Pushing the tonsils down even farther, the fluid exerts pressure on the brain stem, compromising normal functions of the brain and/or spinal cord.

That's what was happening to me.

Something was happening to me!

It explained much more than the headaches. It explained why I always veered to the right—why I couldn't swim laps because I'd go right into the side of the pool. Why I always needed people to walk on my left side, so I didn't bump into them. Why I got into so many bike accidents, and the tingling in my hands and feet, and the and the migraines where I would go to speak and gibberish would just come out.

Todd asked what could be done. Physical therapy? Acupuncture? A drug?

"I need to perform surgery," Dr. King said, as if it was the first resort and not the last.

"But it's not brain surgery," I said.

"Actually, it's brain and spine surgery," said the doctor who had just finished saying he rarely performed surgery. Cue *The Facts of Life* theme song again.

According to Todd, a team of people were going to go in and remove my top vertebrae and drain my spinal fluid through the opening, after which Dr. King would go in to shrink or cut out the part of my cerebellar tonsils that were blocking my spinal canal before reinserting the vertebrae.

I was not expecting this. Todd was not expecting this. Dr. Wesley King, Neurosurgeon, clearly wasn't expecting it, either. After such a nice start.

After such a nice life.

Before I could even process the news, my body was reacting, the tears streaming down my face. Todd put his hand on my back, unannounced. I didn't even mind that it was hot—his hands get hot, I usually get mad. But instead I leaned into it. Dr. King put his hand on my leg, a lot like Dr. Sung's hand squeeze, so that was nice. I leaned into that, too.

I asked what would happen if I didn't have surgery—they were just headaches, after all, and I had to start back on *The King of Queens* in a couple of weeks.

Dr. King told me he liked that show, and then said that without surgery, the brain stem would eventually move down into the spine so far that it would create a space and become inoperable. And then if I were to get rear-ended again, or even have a bad coughing fit, I could have a stroke and die. Paralysis was also a definite possibility.

At least that's what he told Todd while I was on the second chorus of *The Facts of Life*.

Walking to the elevator, stunned, Todd turned to me and said, "I wish it was me instead of you."

"So do I," I said, and started to cry again.

TIMES LIKE THESE, a girl would usually call her mother, who would fly out to be by her daughter's side—supporting her, holding her hand, protecting her, and letting her know she was going to be okay because mama was there. She'd pet her daughter's head and help her on and off with her clothes after the surgery while her head was in a giant cast.

I guessed. When it comes to mother-daughter scenarios that don't involve identity theft and kidnapping, I only know what I've seen in movies.

I went for second and third and fourth opinions. Every doctor said the same thing, "Brain surgery is the very last option." Then they would look at my MRIs and say, "You need brain surgery."

I told my father first.

"It's not brain surgery!" he joke-screamed at me, because he was worried.

"It is brain surgery," I said back.

I called my brother second.

"It's not brain surgery!" he joke-screamed at me, because he was worried, too. Then he had to go lie down because the mention of even a hangnail makes him squeamish.

My father called six times that first night to yell at me and tell me I was fine. And then another three times to ask me to spell the name of what I had again. And twice to warn me not to Google it.

It was too late for that. I'd already pored over pictures of mangled spines and stories of people with Chiari malformations in wheel-chairs and helmets, ramps built onto their houses, paralyzed . . .

I also learned that it was a form of spina bifida—holy shit, there were marches for people like me! When it's found in babies, they operate right away because it can cause intellectual developmental disorders. Which is how I also learned that Chiari malformation is congenital, caused by poor nutrition and poor prenatal care.

I was born with it. My brain hadn't formed properly—or completely—because of my mother. Because she didn't take care of herself. I, like everything else she started, was unfinished. She'd abandoned me before she even abandoned me.

The thought blew me away. Women in her generation smoked and drank their way through their pregnancies, and their kids turned out fine or at worst, alcoholics. What the fuck had my mother been doing? Or *not* doing—did she not eat one apple in nine months, or take one fucking vitamin??? My mother's body was so unsafe, I'd wound up with a brain abnormality—which, to be fair, was a damn sight better off than my twin sister, who'd died in there.

I pictured my mother's womb as a burned-out building in a really dangerous neighborhood. At night—always night. Maybe one streetlight? Littered with garbage, sirens wailing in the distance, and two little, defenseless, innocent fetuses, huddled together, starving, bopping around, looking for an all-night bodega or church . . .

I could not believe that as much as I had spent my life trying to outrun her, always moving, always running, my mother was—quite literally—stuck in my head.

I was *not* calling my mother.

THE SURGERY TO have my mother cut out of my brain was scheduled to take place the following week, on the day of Todd's and my one-year anniversary. "In sickness and in health" had come a lot earlier than we thought.

There was something oddly freeing about it all. Everything was beyond my control. I didn't have any decisions to make—they had all been made for me. I had to surrender. Rest. I was going to have to slow down and stop running. Or die.

I had to let Todd take care of me. I couldn't take care of myself. I finally, truly needed him.

And he came through in spades. In a deck of spades, actually. He was by my side for the blood tests and pre-op appointments, and for everything from late-night Boggle when I couldn't sleep to sitting on the shower floor with me when I was terrified. He met it all with his signature calm, absorbing my fear and panic.

He even absorbed my relatives, answering every one of their calls.

"Tell Aunt Pearl thank you for the coffee maker she got us for our wedding!" I'd call. "Tell Aunt Iris thank you for the blender they got us for our wedding! And we're so glad they could celebrate with us!"

Brain (and neck) surgery was one hell of a way to get out of writing thank-you notes, but it had its perks.

My dad and Cathy weren't sure when to come out. They were trying to plan their trip in a way that circumvented the hospital entirely, my father insisting all the while, "It's not like it's brain surgery." At some point, we stopped arguing with him.

Daily, Todd would hold my MRIs up to our living room window and explain my condition to people.

"See . . .? That's where it's stuffed into her spine." He'd point like a doctor. A Jewish George Clooney, I'd say. Jeff did his best but had to go lie down every time Todd got to the word *fluid*.

I suddenly appreciated everything life had to offer. Flowers blooming, birds chirping, the Hollywood Bowl—an outdoor concert venue that I had always refused to go to because the stacked parking gave me massive anxiety. But at that point I would have given anything to be healthy enough to deal with being blocked in by forty cars, unable to leave the Hollywood Bowl.

The night before the surgery, my suitcase packed, I cuddled up to Olive and said my good-byes just in case. I wanted to make sure Todd was going to be taken care of if I died, so I went through my phone to find him a new mate.

"How about Alison?" I asked my husband, scrolling through my contacts. "Actually, wait—no, she hates dogs. How about

Debbie? You sat next to her at my birthday and had stuff to talk about."

Todd said he didn't want to date any of my friends.

"What about Julie? She has family money."

"She's cute, but no," he said, which made me furious—I couldn't believe he waited until I was about to have brain surgery to tell me he wanted to fuck Julie.

Now that he was in love with Julie, I couldn't decide whether I wanted to watch over Todd as a ghost or not. I definitely would not be attending my funeral. I wouldn't want to see that first time Todd was able to smile after they'd put me in the ground. Or the first time he took his wedding ring off. How long before he and Julie would hook up? How long before they got married? How long before Olive thought Julie was her mother? How long before she was licking medicinal cracked heel cream off of Julie's feet?! It was all too much. Now I was desperate to stay alive just to make sure life didn't go on without me.

SIX O'CLOCK THE next morning, after no sleep and a silent drive, Todd and I arrived at the hospital. We went to the eighth floor, where all the serious surgeries happened. It was empty except for a few people slumped in chairs, trying to get comfortable, some still there from the night before and a couple of early arrivals like us. I was nervous, shaking. This was becoming real. I signed a "Do Not Resuscitate" form, which brooked no argument from Todd, and I didn't even have enough time to be mad before I got my hospital bracelet and my gown.

A nurse came to get me. I left Todd for the first time in a week. For some reason, I assumed he'd be coming with me, like a couples' massage, but very different. Before I walked off for what

I figured might be the last time, I turned to him and said, "Happy anniversary."

"Happy anniversary," he said back.

Once on the gurney, they wheeled me into the operating room, where people bustled around preparing to go inside my head. Just another day at work.

Dr. King came in to see me and asked if I was ready.

"It's not brain surgery, right?" I joked, my lip quivering, changing my mind about all of it. They were just headaches that could eventually kill me but still . . .

The anesthesiologist told me to count backward from one hundred.

Next thing I knew, I opened my eyes. My mouth was dry, I was groggy, my head was heavy. I was in a bed with a yellow curtain around it. In the corner, I saw a man in a black suit and hat, standing there, watching me.

I naturally assumed he was death, come to get me.

"Elizabeth?" he said in a thick accent of some kind. I couldn't make it out because I was dead.

"No," I mumbled. "She's not here." I closed my eyes, maybe he'd go away . . .

"Elizabeth," he said again.

"Wrong person," I answered, disguising my voice as much as I could on a morphine drip.

"It's Jonathan," the man said. "Your brother's rabbi. I came to say hello."

The next time I opened my eyes, Todd was standing over me, smiling.

"I made it," I said.

"You made it," he said. He told me that Dr. King said it went really well and that when he got in there, they saw that the situation was worse than the MRI showed—nearly inoperable. Oh, and that I had a beautiful cerebellum. I gotta admit, I was flattered.

My brother came in, one eye open and trained on the ceiling, afraid he'd pass out from what he imagined would be my head wrapped, cartoon-style, in a huge white bandage with a giant bloodstain on it. But he stayed.

I drifted into and out of sleep. Our cousin Pam came by. "Thank you for the pillow shams you got us for our wedding," I slurred, adding, "oh no, wait, you got us the candlesticks."

My friend Amy passed through. I told her she looked skinny, knowing she'd gone out of her way to come by.

The five hours immediately following the surgery passed in what I soon understood was a morphine-induced bliss. What followed was seventy-two hours of the opposite of bliss; the worst and most blinding pain I've ever felt in my life before or since, including childbirth.

My brain was swelling, and my head was exploding, making me puke the only thing that was left in my system—acid. The blood on my brain from surgery caused incessant hiccups that made my head hurt even more. I barely clocked Dr. Sung coming in and out, squeezing my hand and telling me I'd be "okay, okay?" I don't remember saying "okay." I was not okay.

It was hell. After they took my catheter out, I couldn't pee on my own, so my whole body filled up with fluid—I looked like a Thanksgiving Day parade float. I had a giant neck brace and two holes in my head where a metal halo had been screwed in to keep it straight during surgery. I was a wreck and completely exhausted.

Todd had gotten a sign-in book for visitors. He set the flowers and balloons people sent and dropped off so I could see them whenever I woke up and made a list of who sent what, so I could not send them thank-you notes.

On day two, Dr. Wesley King came by, joined by Dr. Sung. I could now see them more clearly and had the strength to place my hand on the side of my bed, open, ready for squeezing. They wanted me to get up and walk. Just down the hall. We made it almost to the hallway.

Impossible. For someone who'd always been running, two steps suddenly sounded like torture. But Todd helped me out of bed. Holding my IV rack with one hand and Todd's arm with the other, we set out for the hallway. We almost made it there.

After that, I fell asleep and when I woke up, Todd wasn't there. I called for the nurse. "Excuse me? My husband's dead," I croaked out.

She told me he'd just run home to get some stuff. He was gone for all of twenty minutes, and I missed him terribly. I was overwhelmed with relief when he came back. My brain was swollen, but not too swollen for me to realize that "in sickness" I had developed an unhealthy attachment to Todd. I had slowed down long enough for him to catch up, and now, if he were to leave me or drop dead, I would be leveled. I was beholden.

After a few days, I was able to enjoy an episode of *Oprah* and pee on my own—two clear signs to Dr. Sung, Dr. King, and my health insurance company that I was ready to leave the hospital. With eighteen stitches in the back of my head, the giant neck brace, and the two beginning-to-heal holes in my head, I went home with Todd, to the apartment I thought I'd never see again.

Unable to run, I got into bed in the middle of the afternoon, where we finally celebrated our one-year anniversary by watching *Jackass* without having to pause for headaches.

Julie and I are no longer friends, for reasons that are clear to her.

Are You There, God . . .?
It's Me, Jeff's Sister

It's 6:33 p.m. on a Friday evening and I'm pacing frantically in a supermarket parking lot, looking up at the sky, searching for patches of blue sky that will tell me if the sun has begun to set because if it has—even a little bit—it will be Shabbat, and my brother won't be allowed to receive voicemails, emails, or texts until sundown tomorrow.

This is just one of the many, many rules I've gotten used to over the fifteen years during which Jeff and his wife Stephanie have grown increasingly religious to the point of what is now Orthodox Judaism.

The list of rules is long and has—as far as I can tell—very little to do with actual religion, especially on Shabbat.

To the uninitiated (and even if you think you know how crazy Orthodoxy can get), these are just some of the things that are considered "work" from Happy Hour Friday to Saturday at wine o'clock:

- Tearing paper: So that if I bring a birthday present over for my nephew's birthday, he has to wait until sundown to open it.
- Spending money or accepting food that was bought with money spent by a Jewish person on the Sabbath (i.e., me) or arrived in a vehicle (driven by me): So that the cupcakes I bring for my nephew on his birthday go to the nanny. Who can't be paid that day, because Jeff can't spend money.
- Pushing buttons and using electricity: So that when it's so dark at my brother's house at noon on a Saturday that my two-year-old daughter falls headfirst down the stairs, we have to wait until the third star is in the sky to turn on a goddamn light to see if she cracked her head open.
- Operating a phone: Also out of the question. So should we ascertain that my two-year-old daughter has in fact cracked her head open, nobody can call an ambulance or doctor anyway.
- Driving: So that when we can't call an ambulance, and I'm busy cradling my daughter's dented head and holding down a flap of her skin, no one *else* can take us to the hospital.
- Holding down a flap of skin: After much consultation, this is also determined to be "work."

YOU'D THINK TELEVISION wouldn't stop for crap like this, right? That Jeff would find it impossible to get a job when he's only available 24/6 . . . Right?

Wrong. Instead, studios and networks make allowances for him, and he makes it work. He's that talented. He's that valuable. Not to mention the fact that it would be religious-based discrimination. Literally no one was on my side.

Unfortunately, fate loves a challenge, and on this particular Friday my brother's lifestyle was finally being put to the test in the time-sensitive form of a #MeToo accusation. And no matter how talented or valuable he was, Jeff needed to hear about this and act on it. Fast.

Jeff had gotten a deal to develop shows at Warner Bros. That meant job security for two years—something as rare in our business as, frankly, a comedy writer in LA living in an Orthodox neighborhood in a house that's been blessed by a rabbi with a blowtorch. The news of his deal had made the industry trades, which was great. The only problem is that online versions of the trades have comments sections where jealous, angry, and bitter people spend their working hours anonymously spewing resentment.

That Jeff's good fortune drew every unsuccessful writer-troll out of the ooze was expected and not taken too seriously by anyone but Jeff who, like anyone else, didn't want to hear he's a "hack" or, even worse, "lucky."

I was in the checkout line flipping through the latest issue of *US Weekly*, when I got a text from my friend Danielle, who'd worked with Jeff many times. That comment about your brother is a joke, right? she asked. It has to be.

I quickly looked online and saw that in between the "Hack!" and "Awesome News!" comments was one from an anonymous woman, saying that Jeff had harassed her and other women in the past.

To me and fellow writers, judging from the rush of texts I was suddenly getting—more and more asking "Is this a joke?"— the thought of Jeff harassing a woman was and is absurd. When the #MeToo movement first gained momentum, and more and more men we knew professionally were being outed as predators, Jeff and I would joke about how the closest my brother had ever come to misconduct was asking his assistant to wake him up from a nap by sticking her head in the door and yelling, "Jeff! Wake up!" and possibly poking his shoulder with a book if that didn't work.

I'd known from my own experience as a female comedy writer that there was a standard of lewd behavior we'd all been exposed to. Comedy rooms were notoriously like frat houses where one or two or (at most) three female writers were forever subjected to conversations about what the guys would "do to" the actresses on the show, or what they'd done the night before to their girlfriends, or to themselves (the most likely scenario of all). The X-rated doodles on their legal pads and on the dry-erase board where we came up with stories . . . it was all par for the course.

And I can't say I wouldn't laugh a lot, because I did. I knew these guys, and they were like brothers to me—disgusting, loyal, flawed brothers. For a very long time, that mentality was what you signed up for, as a woman in comedy.

But since #MeToo, I'd started seeing things a little bit differently. There was in fact an "over the line"—blurry as that line could be at times. Maybe, just maybe, Jeff—the last person I would imagine, or *he* would imagine—could have harassed someone by stepping over the blurry line into something that would qualify as a #MeToo charge.

I didn't know. What I did know, however, was a major rule in Orthodox Judaism stipulated that a married man is forbidden to physically touch a woman other than his wife or family. I learned this one day a few years previous when Jeff had been about to be greeted by Kristin, a close mutual friend of ours. He flat-out rejected her outstretched arms as she was coming in for a hug, opting to wave from a short distance away instead.

"You won't even hug Kristin anymore?!" I remembered shouting at him, as if hugging Kristin would have solved world hunger. Now, I found myself thankful for what I'd previously regarded among friends as a "stupid rule."

Despite the anonymous nature of the comment in the trades, this was nonetheless a bona fide in-print accusation of my brother being a serial harasser. True or false, it could be career-ending all the same. It needed to be dealt with immediately—Sabbath or no Sabbath. Moses or whoever would surely understand.

Jeff had yet to return any of my thirty texts. My calls kept going to voicemail, and now his mailbox was full—with voicemails from me. I knew he hadn't heard about the charge because if he had, I would have gotten even more texts and calls from him. Jeff is admittedly impulsive, reactive, and emotional—one mediocre review, one network note on a script, one unreturned phone call or email, and Jeff comes unglued. He couldn't handle the slightest criticism, never mind a #MeToo allegation.

This was going to send him over the edge. And I needed to get the news to him before Shabbat . . .

I found a big patch of blue sky and was about to breathe a sigh of relief—he could call me back—when a pinkish, orange-lit cloud floated by. Just like that, it was too late—the sun had begun to set, and Jeff was off-grid.

Now I'd have to drive all the way to his house, in rush-hour traffic, to give him the horrible news.

On my way there, I was in crisis mode, leaving messages for his agent, his lawyer, friends of mine in the know—anyone who might have an idea about what could be done. Could we get that comment removed from the website? How should we manage this?

How would we keep Jeff from winding up in a jail cell next to Harvey Weinstein—or worse, writing kids' shows?

I was furious with everyone who didn't seem to have a solution at the ready. Mostly, though, I was angry at Jeff—that in this day and age and in a time when everyone (me) was going to the mattresses for him, he wasn't picking up his phone. He'd simply dropped off the face of the earth while his world was crashing around him.

It's like I was in Flintstone times, except even they were evolved enough to get on an elephant tusk and make a call when they had to.

I had never been able to wrap my head around the fact that my brother had chosen this lifestyle. People who knew Jeff would always ask me, "Did you guys grow up religious?"

"No!" I'd shout. "He caught it as an adult!" I spoke of it as if it was a "condition." We grew up Reform Jews, which meant we were only Jewish on the major holidays. Bar and Bat Mitzvahs weren't so much a rite of passage as a reason for our parents to show off to their peers with ice sculptures, chopped-liver swans, and overwhelmed centerpieces.

My dad was religious only in that when the Mets were losing or our dog had shit in the house, he'd shout "Jesus Christ Almighty!" Also, when my mother left us, he raised his fists in the air and appealed "God . . . Whyyyy?" But that wasn't so much about the end of their marriage as it was about my mom having taken off in his brand-new Coupe de Ville along with all their savings.

Early signs of Jeff's devotion, on the other hand, were pretty obvious. When we did have to go to synagogue, I'd pass my time counting light fixtures, spotting obvious toupees, nose jobs, and face-lifts in the crowd, and making endless trips to the bathroom. Jeff would follow along in his prayer book, sing along with the songs, and try to read the Hebrew. He also didn't cry and fake an aneurysm or coma every Wednesday when we had to go to Hebrew school. I think he even . . . liked it.

His real transition from what I used to regard as "Reformed Reform Judaism" into Orthodoxy began with his wife, Stephanie. She was born a non-Jew—though Jeff would say she was born with a Jewish soul, to which I would say, "Maybe she got mine." Jeff was crazy in love with her, and she with him. Before they (predictably) got engaged, Jeff's one request was that Stephanie convert to Judaism, so their kids could be raised Jewish. She agreed and, as they were in that stage of a relationship in which you still want to be around each other a lot, Jeff took the conversion classes with her. These classes, it turned out, were where things took a major turn for the religious.

The classes inspired them to start taking part in Jewish rituals like Shabbat dinner on Friday nights. It was kind of adorable at the time, but I kept waiting for Jeff to tire of his latest fad. Whenever Jeff was into something new, he was all in—everything from yoga to spinning, from Pinkberry to rock climbing and all the way up to dating hot girls who were psychos. Each time, a new trend would replace the current one in fairly short order. I figured Orthodox Judaism—to my mind, the weirdest trend yet—was no different.

But I was wrong. So wrong.

Instead of his yarmulke joining the cycling shoes, carabiners, and yoga mats banished to the trunk of his car, Jeff and Stephanie joined an Orthodox temple. They traded their old friends for more religious ones and started singing a lot. The magazines in their house went from good literature like *InStyle* and *People* to more limited fare like *Jewish News* and *Israeli Times*. Every flat surface in their house soon had a prayer book on it, in case someone needed to pray immediately.

Jeff started wearing a black hat in public and a yarmulke full-time. They started separating milk and meat and only ate kosher food. As nothing in my house was blessed by anyone, Jeff's family could only eat there if they brought their own food, utensils, and plates—even, on one memorable Thanksgiving, their own turkey.

Finally, and in an act of full immersion into a world I couldn't or wouldn't comprehend, my brother moved his family to an entirely Orthodox neighborhood, detaching his personal life from the secular world and, in a very real way, from me.

My brother. The one who had hidden under the bed with me whenever our mother went on a rampage. The one who had saved my life when I was eight and fell down our marble stairs as I was trying to pet our dog Schnoodle with one hand and balance a plate of food in the other. The person who would reassure me that screaming at my son in a public pool for soft-touching me is still better than what our parents did to us, and the person I would reassure back that squeezing his son's shoulder in a movie theater to get him to stop making loud clucking sounds wasn't abuse.

We were and would remain best friends. That is, until from Fridays at sundown to Saturdays at sundown and for most of the month of October, when a lot of Jewish holidays take place (none of which is Halloween, which they don't celebrate anymore). That was when he'd leave me for . . . God.

I'd lost my brother to religion.

He had always been my rock. My hero. And now he prayed at every meal, kept separate plates for milk and meat—(NEVER the two shall touch)—and used pre-torn toilet paper on Shabbat. My hero was . . . crazier than me.

I used to challenge him on his beliefs, about the trajectory his faith was taking him. Thinking the whole thing was still up for debate, I questioned his devotion to a God that allowed to happen things like 9/11 and the Holocaust and genocide and cancer and baby deaths and making you love dogs with all your heart and soul when they're only going to live for twelve years.

"I mean, come on . . ." I remember saying. "You really wanna give up shellfish for this guy? You believe in all this?"

"I do." He didn't hesitate. "Because to not believe in God is so much worse. To not believe there's something bigger than us—that there's not something after this life like the heaven that waits for you—it's no way to live."

I was stunned to learn that my brother believed in heaven, a place I'd always regarded as reserved for Catholics. They got Christmas, Easter eggs, jelly beans, and heaven. Jews got smelly food, Hanukkah, and an undecorated wooden box in the ground when they died.

I was never meant to go to heaven anyway—I'd counted on as much from the time I cheated on tests, stole change from my dad, pulled hard currency from Cathy's wallet, biting into one of her gold ball necklaces to see if it was solid gold or not. It was not.

Then there was the summer I worked at TCBY, where I lied about the waffle machine being broken out of laziness and where, when skinny girls would come in and order the fat-free hot fudge, I'd give them the regular. I was also definitely responsible for the deficit in inventory my boss faced, seeing as I was always making myself pies on which I'd write "You are fat" or just "PIG" in frosting before scarfing them down in the employee bathroom.

My adult life was hardly sin-free, either. I lied to my kids constantly and parked in the red zone at Starbucks if I was in a hurry. I've lost count of the number of times I abandoned full grocery carts in the middle of checkout lines at the supermarket—to say nothing of my ignoring the "No Grazing" signs posted over the bulk bins (signs I'm pretty sure were inspired by my grazing).

I'm a serial and unrepentant sinner. And there my brother was telling me how my actions had consequences that went beyond just needing to atone once a year. Which I don't even do.

In a voice that was serious and calm and a tad too religious-y, he tried to explain that heaven was real and suggested condescendingly that I broaden my horizons on the subject by watching Meryl Streep and Albert Brooks in *Defending Your Life*, and while I felt I technically won that argument by informing him that *Defending Your Life* was not a documentary (I think), my brother held fast to the heaven thing. Based on my heathen, shrimp-eating, TV-watching-on-Shabbat, shoulder-baring-shirt-wearing lifestyle—it sounded like I wouldn't be meeting Jeff or Meryl Streep in heaven.

FOR THE MOST part, Jeff and I avoided the topic of religion after that last conversation—he felt I was judgmental, and I felt it was really, really stupid. I avoided religious people of any stripe. They pissed me off. It was my own act of protest against God getting his/ her tenterhooks on my brother. I actually went to great lengths to narrow my eyes at them. I think once I even hissed at a clump of temple-goers. Under my breath. In case God was listening.

Yet despite my animosity, I was becoming aware that "believers" were showing up at important times in my life—Orthodox Jews in particular. They came out of the woodwork to help me. Worse, they were good people.

The first time I noticed was when I very, very, totally accidentally hit a pedestrian with my car. I was driving the kids and we were singing "Happy Birthday" to Cathy—well, into Dad and Cathy's answering machine. Phoebe was refusing to join in, and as I turned back to yell at her to sing—"It's your grandmother's birthday, goddamnit"—I heard that unmistakable *thunk* of my car hitting something . . . human. I didn't want my kids to wind up with PTSD or a pill problem, though, so I needed to remain calm.

I failed.

"I HIT A PERSON!" I shouted at the top of my lungs and pulled over, hoping I wouldn't hit anyone on the way to the curb and dropping the phone, leaving about five minutes of subsequent commotion on my parents' answering machine tape (which my dad promptly smashed to pieces with a hammer in his basement, just in case the recording could be counted as evidence).

The woman I hit was in her twenties, with ripped jeans that may have been ripped before—it was hard to tell. My jeans were ripped, after all, and I'd never been hit by a car, but hers were ripped and she had been hit by a car. By my car. By me. I HIT A PERSON! She hadn't broken anything, the grill of my car having absorbed most of her impact. She would be okay, thank (okay) God. Her elbow dent and raspberry nail polish were embedded in my hood. I'd drive that crime scene around for the next three months—a reminder that I HIT A PERSON!

Immediately, people poured out of the nearby coffee place and office buildings to see what had happened. Of course, they quite rightfully tended to her first, since she was the victim and everything. I was pretty shook up, too, though, and was no doubt crying and possibly hyperventilating as I checked on my oblivious kids, thank (okay) God, and tried to call Todd because the kids needed to get to school and someone was saying something about—holy shit—cops.

"It happens!" said a very kind-looking man walking toward me. It does?!

He told me he saw the accident and that he knew I wasn't texting or speeding, that I was just . . . not a very good driver. And he stuck around until the policewoman showed up and told her the same thing (female cops are not huggers, by the way), after which this angel of a man gave me the number of a lawyer, should I have need of one. He wasn't even the lawyer on the card. He was just being nice! He even hugged me before turning to go—which was when I saw his yarmulke.

He was an Orthodox Jew. He'd be in heaven with my brother and Meryl Streep. I extra-doubted I was ever getting there, now that I had HIT A PERSON. I suddenly felt a need to take advantage of my brother's (and by association, my own) position in the Orthodox community and . . . name drop.

"Do you know my brother, Jeff?!" I called, hopefully, proudly. "He's Orthodox, too!"

The man didn't know my brother Jeff, but I could swear he liked me more just knowing I was Jeff's sister.

My son's psychiatrist was another Orthodox Intervention. Already at the end of my rope, having tried dozens of therapies and therapists for Jesse—none of which had provided him relief from his anxiety so far—I arrived at this new shrink's office an emotional wreck with very little trust and with shame to spare.

Within moments of first meeting Jesse, this extraordinarily kind man demonstrated a soothing confidence that immediately minimized both Jesse's anxiety and my own hysteria about it. Leaning forward in his chair to write the prescription that would save my child (and Todd and me), I was able to see the wooden Star of David around the doctor's neck, though it wasn't until he walked us to the door that I finally noticed the tzitzit of the prayer shawl he wore beneath his civvies.

"My brother Jeff is Orthodox . . . So. You know . . ." I mentioned casually. "His name is Jeff . . .?"

He didn't seem to know my brother either, but I was pretty sure I could now count on him to answer his phone at eleven on a Tuesday night should I accidentally leave Jesse's anxiety pills in a Starbucks bathroom. Chances were, I'd need him to, since I had done exactly that many more times than once.

Then there was the entire Hasidic family who came to my aid on a flight to LA from New York, where we'd gone for a family wedding. Four-year-old Phoebe, overtired and oversugared, had spilled juice all over herself ten minutes after takeoff and then, somewhere over Kansas with hours to go, had wakened me and everyone else on board with a meltdown and her (only) backup outfit soaked in pee.

I was begging flight attendants for a spare blanket and dousing Phoebe in mouthwash when an Orthodox man in full regalia— right down to the hat and *payot*—walked up the aisle, holding a Torah-looking book. He had sensed (or perhaps smelled) my trouble.

"Does she need clothes?" he asked. When I nodded, he turned a few rows behind. "Rivka!"

A young woman in a wig appeared and, a few Yiddish words later, I had my pick of children's outfit sizes from her suitcase (apparently most of the kids on the flight were theirs).

Phoebe was thrilled—it was the first floor-length skirt she'd ever worn. I was humbled. Yet opportunistic.

"My brother and sister-in-law would love this outfit, since they're Orthodox . . . the cousin of Hasidic . . . ism . . ." I gushed, wrestling the long-sleeved shirt over Phoebe's head. "His name is Jeff—maybe you know him . . .?"

They didn't know Jeff but said we could keep the clothes anyway.

I was completely blown away by the kindness of all these strangers. But I wouldn't dare share these experiences with my brother, of course. The last thing I needed was for Jeff to feel validated and justified with his immersion into what I still looked upon as a cult.

I would also never tell him how I exploited his connection to God for my own personal gain—hoping nepotism was as standard in religion as it is in the entertainment business. Besides, I was careful to use it sparingly and only for important shit.

"Are you there, God . . .? It's Jeff's sister . . ." I'd start, looking heavenward. "I know I'm not in touch with you a ton, but you guys are pals . . . so, would it be possible to make my bosses like my script and not give me a big rewrite? I really want to go to yoga this week. Also, there's this sweater I need to go on sale. Also, that person I hit? Can you make her okay?" I HIT A PERSON!

IN THE CAR now, heading over to Little Israel, I checked my phone every five seconds to see if there was any movement on the #MeToo situation. I lost Internet service for a whole twenty-five seconds and, in that time, there'd been no news or solutions offered.

I decided to use this time wisely.

"Are you there, God . . .? It's Jeff's sister . . ." I said to the roof of my car, wondering how jelly got there. "Can you please make sure Jeff doesn't get in trouble and have to write Saturday-morning cartoons for the rest of his career? I mean, it's kind of your fault for making him not look at the Internet after sundown—what kind of stupid rule is that? You invented the Internet! And now you're going to smite him. Or maybe it's 'smote' him—you know which one I mean—and why do they have to wear wool all the time, anyway? You know it gets hot here—you made it hot here! Didn't you?"

I was getting angry. Fuck, I may have gone too far. Even I knew that you don't yell at God.

I checked my phone again to see if the slanderous comment in the trades was still posted.

It was. Shit. And now it had two "likes"! People were liking the accusation!

I was now barreling through Jeff's neighborhood, careful not to hit anyone—because if you do that twice, you're definitely that person. I was the only car on the road, a sea of Orthodox Jews lining the sidewalks headed north, on a pilgrimage to synagogue. I searched for my long-lost brother among the men in black hats.

It had been fifteen years later, and I still couldn't understand why, if you weren't born into the Orthodox life, anyone would ever willingly submit themselves to it. Why would you impose such restrictions on yourself? What if, by the time you died, heaven no longer existed? What if it did, but it was overrated? Or it was nothing like *Defending Your Life*—nothing is ever like it is in the movies! It would have all been for nothing!

I knew Jeff understood why the restrictions were imposed. But I didn't want to hear the reasons. There was a time when Jeff tried to persuade Todd and me to follow his family into the fold. He'd been successful winning me over in the past, after all. With just a "Hey, Liz, you've gotta try this," he'd gotten me to move to LA and pursue a career in comedy writing, got me into yoga and this boot camp run by ex-marines where they make you cry and carry giant rocks uphill wearing a wet bathing suit, but there was no way I was going to feel anything beyond a cultural connection to Judaism, certainly not enough to give up using electricity and driving on Shabbat!

And he'll be thankful I didn't, I thought as I drove. When he found out what had happened, he was going to lose his shit. I'd have to pry him out of a ball while shoving kosher Tums down his throat—or maybe he'd want the real thing, even if it had gelatin in it (also unholy, for some reason)! He'd see what was important, yes, he would, and he'd break the rules, get on the phone, and start doing damage control. Maybe he'd even throw his black hat in the air like Mary Tyler Moore did in the opening credits! Free at last!

I would help him. I would be there for him, like he'd been for me so many times before. I wanted him to know I was panicking for him. His heathen sister wouldn't leave his side.

After this crisis, he would be "normal" again. Like me.

Suddenly I spotted him. I couldn't miss him, he was the same Jeff I'd always known—a little on the shorter side, kind of stocky, shoulders a little hunched. Walking with that little skip in his step, head tilted at an angle, his mouth curling up at the sides, smiling, like he was about to say or just said something he thought was funny. He looked happy, fulfilled—calm, even. He still thought everything was okay, that this lifestyle of his was acceptable, even in the entertainment industry. Basking in the glow of the day's big announcement.

I almost felt bad telling him what had transpired. It was going to crush him. He wouldn't be going to heaven if the accusation was at all true. Just before I pulled over, Jeff's agent called.

"I'm on it," I said, before he could get a word in. "I'm here, I see him. Hang on, I'll just tell him about the comment, I'll even hold the phone, so he can talk to you without touching—"

"He already knows," his agent assured me. "He saw it. It was published right before he went off the grid." While nothing had been resolved, he went on to explain that Jeff had understood and said he had to go because it was almost sundown, and he'd call after Shabbat.

I finally understood the restrictions. The rules. The "no Internet." All at once, I got it.

Orthodox Judaism was Jeff's salvation, his escape. No matter what was going on, no matter how crucial or mentally consuming, come Friday at sundown he checked out for twenty-five hours; he had to.

He had to take himself out of the chaos, the gut-wrenching stress, and ground himself in his family and tradition and something more reliable than a business where entire careers can be destroyed by as little as a false Internet comment—in this case, it turned out, made up by a male ex-assistant who wanted to get Jeff back for firing him for due cause. The comment was taken down almost immediately because it was false.

Jeff needed this break from the chaos. The thing I thought made him crazy actually made him sane. He was content. This was how he took care of himself. His people were kind and good. How annoying.

And before he saw me, I got out of there and gave him a break.

From me, too.

Until sundown Saturday.

Tim Allen Tried to Kill Me

I was working on a show called *Last Man Standing*, starring Tim Allen. It was the first season, and Tim was making his return to half-hour TV for the first time since *Home Improvement*. In June, we began preproduction—that's the eight-week period when the writers get a head start on coming up with stories and writing scripts before shooting starts and the shit hits the fan. We decide on season arcs for the characters—where we see them going emotionally, how we want them to grow and change, and how they will interact with each other—all in the funniest, most over-the-top but never-seen-before-on-TV way possible.

Preproduction always feels like the honeymoon phase of a new TV show, with everyone still getting to know each other, on our best behavior, laughing at each other's jokes, not talking over one another yet. It's also too early in the season to take notice of weird nose whistles, or twitching, or lip-smacking habits, or my giant guttural laugh, which, after those first few months and endless days (and nights) around a conference room table together, will drive us to the brink of insanity and/or homicide.

In late July, we were nearing the end of preproduction and things were going smoothly. Then I was blindsided.

I was sitting at my desk, minding my own business, Facebook-stalking high school friends, when our head writer, Jake, walked into my office. We all really liked Jake—he was super laid-back, and though he was in his fifties, his thick black hair and daily uniform of Levi's, sneakers, and old T-shirts made him seem eternally boyish and, up until that very moment (for me), a really cool guy.

"Tim wants a few of the writers to come to his lake house in Colorado for three days before we start production," he said tentatively.

"That sounds horrible," I laughed. "Have fun."

"You're coming," he said, "and it *will* be horrible."

I said I couldn't possibly go—I had to be home for my kids. Jake reminded me that my self-proclaimed Stay-at-Work Mom status kind of blew that excuse. He also reminded me that back in the first week of preproduction, I had heartily volunteered to take any show-running responsibilities off of his shoulders. Not fair! Jake had been in this business long enough to know that any promises made in the throes of preproduction honeymoon bliss were never to be taken seriously. Anyway, I'd meant that I would help out with approving actor hair and makeup and do wardrobe checks—stuff that can be done on a set. In California.

Jake's maniacal laugh as he walked out of my office pretty much said it all. I was screwed.

Granted, the childhood me would have been very thrilled that her adult self would know a star like Tim Allen, to say nothing of getting invited to his house in Colorado. But years in the business take the shine off stars, and I'd long stopped seeing actors of any stature as anything but people—flawed people—like the rest of us. No longer luminaries on billboards and in magazines, stars become the reason you work through the night to change jokes or—because they wield enough power and hate a storyline—the reason you can find yourself going to Colorado during your precious free time.

My dread kept pace with the details. Not only was I going to be spending three days with Tim Allen, I was going to be the only woman on the trip, and the people I was going with were all but strangers. Jake, who I knew a little; and Keith, an L.L.Bean–looking upper-level writer who struck me as just a little too muscular to be in comedy. Keith loved to talk about two things: himself and the fact that he'd single-handedly convinced Tim Allen to come back to television. So, this was all his fault. There was also Mitch—a comedy veteran whom I'd heard of for years but had never gotten to work with. Mitch was a sweet, intellectual type with glasses and collared shirts who'd just gotten back from an actual honeymoon (with his second wife) and got great pleasure from big words, the *New York Times* crossword puzzle, and his own jokes. I liked him in spite of all those qualities.

And then me.

Magical.

And also a little disturbing. Because while we knew we were going to Tim's lake house in Colorado, no one knew quite where that was. Like the location, the purpose of the trip was also undisclosed.

Now, I'd worked on many shows where the actors would sometimes hang out with the writers. Kevin James would play poker with some of the guys. Christine Baranski liked to join us for drinks after show nights. Leah Remini invited me to her daughter's first

birthday party and also offered to put me on a diet (though technically that was more of an insult than a "social" thing).

But a trip? To Colorado? I couldn't understand why on earth
Tim, who'd repeatedly told us he didn't know why he wanted to be
back in TV, wanted to spend any downtime with the people he was
back in TV with.

The idea was floated that maybe, since Tim was born and raised
in Colorado—and the show was set there—he wanted to give us
some insight into the place. The theory was shot down—isn't that
what pictures are for? Had anyone ever been sent somewhere on a
sitcom fact-finding mission?

No. As a creative group, we put our heads together and came up
with the only logical reason for the trip: he was going to hunt and
kill us for sport.

It made perfect sense given what we did know, starting with
Tim having been rumored to be a survivalist. As in stockpiling
supplies—guns, rubber tubing, duct tape, plastic bags, rope—for end
times. I felt like there would be sandpaper, too; I don't know why.

We also knew we were flying to Colorado commercial but
supposedly coming home by private jet. That clinched it for me
personally—there was no way I was making it home alive because
not one psychic had ever told me I was going to fly on a private jet,
and I'd asked at least a dozen. So.

Plus, one thing we all knew for certain: Tim wasn't happy with
the work we'd done so far on the show, from the stories we were
planning to the scripts we were drafting to the general direction the
show was taking. We based this fact on his grumbling, "I don't want
to do this shit" during one of his rare visits to the writers' room.

Tim was grumpy and rich—a lethal combination. He could
easily cover up a murder or four. No one would ever believe that
Buzz Lightyear killed four people.

Hence, we were going to die.

Our work sessions started to devolve into spitballing sessions about how we would meet our respective ends.

"First, he's going to subject us to severe vituperation . . ." Mitch started, and by the time I had looked up the word (it means "scolding"), I'd missed the rest of what he said.

"Liz will end up running through the forest in a wedding dress at some point," Keith cracked, a grim, unnecessary reminder that my wedding dress wouldn't have fit me anymore.

A week before the trip, word got to us via Tim's assistant that he was planning the menu and needed to know if we'd all be able to eat spaghetti and meatballs on our first night there. He needed to know a week in advance.

"Poison" immediately moved to the top of our "Method of Choice" list. I'd be safe, I announced, because I didn't eat fish sticks for Kevin James, and I sure as hell wasn't about to take on carbs for Tim Allen. Mitch was disappointed in the cyanide-laced meatball method. He was now holding out for being garroted. Another word I had to look up ("strangulation"; he really could have just said that, prissy jerk).

Jake predicted that the food would drug us, not poison us, and that Tim would sit us all up at computers and make us put his jokes in all the scripts. Jake was our head writer for good reason.

Keith reminded us that Tim liked guns.

"He told me when I brought him back to doing TV that he loved shooting," he said. "I think he'll take us out execution style—Liz first because of her laugh," which ended my honeymoon with Keith. I hoped he was the first to go.

Jake suggested we didn't turn on each other until we were hanging from four separate trees, which again was why he was the boss.

The scenarios escalated in violence. You may think it ludicrous that facing a weekend where a metaphorical axe could certainly fall on our jobs had simply led to morbid hyperbole on our part. We wanted to believe we were just kidding, too. But there were way too many unknowns, and we were left to fill in the blanks. As writers, we were creative people with wild imaginations, and we'd all lived in LA way too damned long to not know that anything really and truly could happen. In a world ruled by fantasy, sleep deprivation, and drugs of every stripe, the possibility of our imminent demise grew more and more plausible as the weekend approached.

The day we left, we had to be at the airport at 5:00 a.m. I kissed my kids good-bye and whispered in their ears that I loved them and that no matter who their new mommy was, she could never replace me. I told Todd I loved him and, as I always do when I travel alone or go under light anesthesia or leave for an angry survivalist's home somewhere in Colorado, we still didn't know, left him with a list of friends who thought he was great and a list of friends who didn't really care for him. Why waste his time? And we were off.

In Denver, we were met at the airport by a guy named Mike who was there to take us to Tim's undisclosed-location lake house. I suspected Tim didn't want to be seen with the victims, though Mike seemed sweet enough. "Let's see how sweet he is when he's hog-tying us," Mitch whispered and chuckled alone. At least that time he used a term I understood.

We drove several hours over something called "the treacherous pass" in the Colorado Rockies that Tim had instructed Mike to show us. Obviously, this was where our body parts would end up. Keith regaled Mike with the story of how he'd brought Tim back to TV. I mouthed along and I wished for death sooner rather than later.

We finally got to Tim's house. Where it was, I still don't know. Mike drove down a narrow road that turned into gravel and, just beyond a really fucking creepy totem pole with a yellow and purple devil-like face painted on the top (a clue?), there sat a beautiful, red country home. Beyond it was the most exquisite view of blue sky, green mountains, and a lake with boats surrounded by idyllic-looking houses. It was beautiful, and I hoped I got killed last.

"It's about time ya assholes got here!" Tim was standing on the porch, smirking. He looked different outside of work—was he relaxed . . . or was he kill-y? I didn't know him well enough to tell the difference.

He'd worked out where we would stay, with Mitch and Keith sleeping in the main house with him. "Liz, Jake—you're sleeping in the guesthouse," he said, and pointed to a window above the garage. A window I'd no doubt be dangling from, at some point.

Jake and I went to check out our quarters and were surprised to see that the décor was more *Town and Country* than *Helter Skelter*. His very-obviously-absent-from-this-gathering wife had done a great job decorating, bless her probably-dead heart. I wondered what drawer or closet her body was stuffed in and if it was her wedding dress I'd have to fit into, because I hadn't even been able to zip mine up halfway when I tried it on the night before—just to see. Maybe his wife would appear when we least expected it, wielding a hatchet at some point? I'd be lying if I said it wasn't a little bit exciting knowing that I was going to die though not knowing how.

The property was surrounded on three sides by woods—perfect for running away. And so I had to give Jake the disturbing news that I had a bad knee and couldn't run. Not even for my life. Jake told me that if we were being chased by Tim, he'd gladly hit me over the head with a shovel and end it there for me. Again, that was why he was the boss. He was also getting handsomer by the minute. His dark hair that had gotten shockingly grayer since leaving LA (which happens in horror movies), his deep brown eyes, the five o'clock shadow and stained T-shirt . . . it was all doing it for me. Probably one of those things where you fell in love with your fellow hostages. That kind of drama was the last thing we needed, though, so I reminded myself that he drove a PT Cruiser—my deal-breaker car—and moved on.

Soon it was time for dinner. Yes, *that* dinner. We went back to the main house and met Carol, a compact, blond, and insanely muscular woman who Tim referred to as his "cook." Or was she his poison/martial arts expert? She looked like she could hold me down with one finger.

Before dinner, Tim wanted to give us a tour of the house. We followed him up a staircase to a bright and airy hallway lined with large framed photos of Tim's (late?) wife and his daughters. Tim barked out which rooms were which, and which rooms were off limits. But I was too consumed by the photos to pay much attention. They were beautifully done, and I needed to get the name of the photographer. Were I to survive, I definitely wanted her to do our holiday cards. The year before, I'd skimped and used a photo from my phone and an online stationer. For some reason, the poor resolution gave Phoebe a slight Hitler mustache. Had I been paying attention and seen it, I might not have sent those cards out like that. Especially not to our Holocaust-survivor relatives. I needed to up my game this year. Again—if I lived.

Before I knew it, Tim and everyone were heading back downstairs. I followed them to the dining room. Tim told us to sit. One by one, Carol delivered bowls of the famous poisoned spaghetti and meatballs we'd all signed off on the week before (even though I vowed not to eat it). It certainly looked and smelled amazing, all saucy and delicious. And my nerves, the lake air, the drive—it all made me very hungry.

I moved the food around my bowl, a craft I learned during my one-year stint as a budding anorexic. But just like my anorexia, my willpower was also short lived. Besides, if this turned out to be a "last supper" kind of deal, I'd be really upset with myself for not enjoying that meal. I considered the fact that I might be trying to fit into a wedding dress later that night. But the guys were scarfing it all down with reckless abandon, and I didn't want to be the only one conscious for the slayings.

So I finished my bowl and two more bowls. And licked the pot when Carol wasn't looking.

Later, sleepy but post-carb sleepy not drugged sleepy, back at the guesthouse, I went to my room and got ready for bed. I changed into the pajamas I'd bought just for the trip, ones the salesgirl agreed would be "totally cute" for either lounging or being found dead in.

I was helping myself to some of the luxurious lotion I'd discovered in the bathroom when I heard it—the unmistakable sound of footsteps crunching on gravel. Coming closer and closer and closer, getting louder and louder and louder. I stood at the sink, frozen.

The footsteps stopped, followed by a silence even louder than the crunching. I could hear the front door downstairs, and I screamed, "I'm up here . . .!" I don't know why, I just did. Maybe I wanted to get it over with.

Heavy footsteps bounded up the stairs, and I heard Jake calling my name. Tim had requested our presence back in the house.

I gave myself one more squirt of the lotion (it was so luxurious) and followed Jake, actually bothered that I had to walk to the house to be killed and that Tim couldn't come to me. I wasn't sure if it was weird for my coworkers to see me in my pajamas, but then again, they were going to see me with my brain outside my head, so who gave a shit.

In the den, now dimly lit for some reason, though there were two large white couches and plenty of space, Mitch, Keith, and our driver,

Mike, were all three sitting on one small love seat. All three in paja-mas. I don't even think Mike was staying on the property. Tim stood behind them, the chef conspicuously absent. Jake boldly took a seat on one of the larger couches, and I waited for my seating assignment.

"Sit anywhere," Tim said.

Fuck. What did he mean by that? Why didn't he care? Why was he so . . . normal on potentially the last night of our lives?

I sat next to Jake. I was starting to get feelings again.

Tim picked up a TV remote and pointed it at the TV. He set-tled into a giant chaise and told us we'd be watching the Elton John concert on HBO with him. So basically, "Candle in the Wind" was going to drown out our screams for help. Made sense.

While Tim Allen watched Elton John, we watched Tim Allen and the doors and Mike. It was the longest and most tense two hours of Elton John in history. When it was over, Tim did the expected. He said good night and went up to bed.

He was fucking with us, for sure.

I mean, why else were we there but to be murdered? He didn't like any of us—as far as we could tell. And we hadn't even talked about work. There was not one bit of vituperatics, or whatever the fuck Mitch had predicted.

I had planned on staying awake all night, but once I lay down on those 6,000-thread-count sheets, I must've passed out. I woke up, still alive, in the middle of the night to go to the bathroom. But my door wouldn't open. The knob wouldn't move. I was locked in.

It. Was. Happening.

I was terrified. I went to text Todd, but there was no cell recep-tion. Of course.

I frantically pounded on the wall that separated me and Jake.

"Jake—I can't get out!" I shouted.

No answer. I wondered if Tim had already gotten to him, if I was screaming to a corpse. I quickly brought a chair over to the window, but it was too high for me to jump or even to dangle from. And now, I had to pee really, really badly. I cursed the decision to have a vaginal delivery with Phoebe, which had left me unable to cough without peeing a little ever since, and now my situation was dire. I didn't want to ruin my new pajamas, with pee or with blood.

With one hand, I held myself and with the other tried the door one last time. It opened easily. I was flush with relief. It turned out the lotion I'd become obsessed with had made my hands soft and slippery, and the knob just hadn't turned. I wondered if that was part of the plan: it rubs the lotion on its skin or else it gets the hose . . .

Once back in bed, still terrified, I decided to stay up the rest of the night. And then fell asleep.

I woke up, alive again, at a post-children all-time-late hour of ten o'clock. Rested and relaxed, I was examining my refreshed eyes in the mirror when Jake came in.

"He can see us," he whispered.

"What?"

"I was down at the house," Jake explained, "and Tim said to me, 'Shame you and Liz haven't used the coffee pot in your room . . .'" His eyes scanned the room as he whispered, "He has cameras on us."

At once, Jake and I looked out into the little kitchen and saw the coffee pot on the counter, still in its box. Holy shit.

It. Was. Happening. Again.

"We need to get out of here," I said to Jake. "But first he has to see us make coffee." Also, I wanted the coffee. (Kona beans.)

But Jake had more bad news: Tim was taking us out on his boat to show us Lake Wherever-We-Were.

I didn't want to die in the lake for the same reason I didn't want to swim in the lake—I don't like fish touching me. Fish grossed me out. And I wouldn't be able to get away from them because I'd be dead.

But next thing I knew, the five of us were getting on this very sleek cigarette of a boat, Mitch somehow with that day's *New York Times* under his arm, Keith with a shit-eating grin on his face because he'd gotten to tell someone at the dock how he'd brought Tim Allen back to TV, and Jake tweeting about how much he missed his old job on *30 Rock*—which was only going to anger Tim even more, for chrissakes, didn't he know that? We were given life vests and, as I checked mine for tiny pinpricks, we took off.

Tim was very proud of his boat. As he should have been; it was really nice. He gave us all the statistics on it—where he got it, how long he'd had it, what he did to maintain it, but all I heard was "I'm going to kill you, I'm going to kill you, just wait 'til I kill you, I'm rich and have nothing better to do than kill you, hope you like fish touching you because I'm going to kill you."

Jake whispered to me that I should pay attention, that we'd be tested on Tim's facts later, and whoever got the answers wrong would be the first to go. I shouted into the wind that I didn't test well as we sped through the water, the tip of the boat in the air as Tim turned back from the helm and called, "This is where I throw the bodies!"

We looked at each other and back at him. Tim cackled. I laughed with him, matching his cackle, my laugh echoing off the lake and the houses and the nearby town and the lake again and the houses. God, I hoped Keith was wrong about Tim hating my laugh, because moments later, it was still bouncing around us. And, God, I also hoped Keith went first.

It. Was. Happening. For real this time. We might not know how we were going yet, but at least we knew where we should have our loved ones tell the cops to look for our bodies.

* * *

EVENTUALLY WE DOCKED, being not dead, and headed back to the house (he was definitely still fucking with us). Tromping back up the gravel drive—and I swear to fucking God this is true—that totem pole devil-face that had greeted us the day before looked right at me.

In an instant, my mind shifted gears from *Silence of the Lambs* and *Cabin in the Woods* and kicked clean through the *Poltergeist* goalposts. Maybe we were on an Indian burial ground and the man we knew as "Tim" was in fact possessed. That was it. I had to get in touch with Todd and the kids. I had to. What if, while I was here rubbing great lotion all over, Phoebe was being sucked into our TV back home? Shit!

Problem was there was no cell phone reception anywhere in the guesthouse. Tim was off changing his clothes, or getting his rubber tubing in order, or putting on his ski mask, so I walked my phone around the main house looking for any possible signal.

I finally found a room—a pretty guest room of sorts, with more of those great pictures of his children and (dead) wife—where I got two cellphone bars if I stood a certain way and didn't move.

"I'm still alive," I said breathlessly into the phone when Todd answered. "Are *you*? Are the kids?"

"Ingrid Millman doesn't like me?" Todd asked.

I realized he was referring to the list I'd left of the friends who didn't like him/find him attractive.

"Ingrid just thinks you're grumpy from that time she was over and you were in a bad mood," I said.

"I was picking up dog shit off the floor," he said defensively.

My frustration mounted with my panic. "Maybe she'll give you another chance," I said, then, "Listen—can you trace this call?"

"What about Dale? I'm always nice to her."

"I know, Todd," I told him, "but she said she could never kiss you, which honestly, was more insulting to me because I do kiss you."

"You don't kiss me that much."

Jesus.

"Look," I blurted, "if I make it out of here, I'll kiss you, okay? Now can you call the police? He told us he's going to throw us in the lake!"

"Is the house nice?"

"It's stunning, and they have this great photographer, and we had this awesome dinner, and the bed is so comfortable, and I've never slept so well, and there's coffee in the room, and you'll see it all on the news—now, listen . . ."

He was listening. My throat tightened. What did people say when they were saying good-bye forever?! In my case, given what Todd has had to put up with, it probably should have been "Congratulations."

I spoke calmly. I reminded Todd that Jesse's social skills group was meeting on Saturdays now and told him to make sure he didn't miss even one, I didn't want him to grow up to be weird. And Phoebe was growing out of her Crocs, her toe was poking the front. And she needed a new sunhat, the one she was wearing itched her, and I told him to get the pink mark on Jesse's leg checked, it had been there for a week, and to also try and get him to eat grapes because—

"This is the one room I said not to go in!"

I looked around only to find Tim standing in the doorway, red faced, fists clenched.

The. One. Room. He. Said. Not. To. Go. In.

What had I done?!

"Todd. It's happening," I said. "Good-bye."

I cut the call and bolted out of the room. I'd been so engrossed in their photos that I missed Tim telling us not to go into this one room that was definitely his body-hiding room, duh, which was such a me thing to do.

Tim followed. "Liz," he said, "come take a walk with me."

This was it. It. Was. Happening.

Just please don't make me get into a wedding dress, was all I could think, suddenly. *I'm so bloated.*

I called to the others, who were relaxing in the living room, of all things. Clueless.

"Bye, guys," I said meaningfully, and followed Tim outside to my certain death but not before checking the band of my underwear to make sure I was wearing ones I wanted to die in. I wasn't. And, my thong was on backwards. The fact that I hadn't noticed was almost as disturbing as the fact that I didn't have time to turn it around. My body's description in the paper would be "Woman too stupid to know which way is front of thong and too misshapen to notice found in unnamed lake."

We headed into the woods. Tim led me to a river lined with rocks. And then we walked. In silence at first.

"Is your full name Elizabeth?" he finally asked.

"Yes," I said cheerfully. "Like your daughter!" That had to count for something.

"I never liked that name," he grumbled.

"I'll change it," I said.

"I'm so angry."

The words tumbled out of me. "Jake approves the scripts and the stories—I'm with you, Tim, I think they're bad! And Keith brought you back to TV, not me, if anything I didn't think it was a good idea at all, and Mitch called you stalwart, whatever that means—"

"I'm angry that my father died," Tim said.

Oh.

"Did you . . . kill him?" I asked.

He looked at me, a little strangely. "I was six."

I told him I was sorry about his dad and that if it made him feel any better, my mom left me when I was six. But I was happy she left, so maybe that was different.

"You weren't happy," he snapped.

Normally, you'd want to agree with a potential murderer. But I couldn't—I just couldn't agree that I was sad that my mom left, because the best childhood memory I have of her is her absence.

He accused me of lying. I accused him back of being wrong.

Unbelievably, both of us got madder and madder. He insisted I had fond memories. I insisted that she was a crazy bitch, and then the madder I got, the more I wondered if I was going to kill Tim Allen and not the other way around.

I finally asked him why he was so sure I had good memories of my mother. He said there was no way I could be such a high-functioning person and such a good mother if I didn't have any good memories of my own.

"'High functioning'?" I was stunned. "Me?"

I told him how I sent out a holiday card where Phoebe had a Hitler mustache and that I have to wear my house keys around my neck because I lose them so often, that my son has had to use underwear from my gym bag to wipe his nose more than once because I never have tissues in my car.

That I was a Stay-at-Work Mom who is terrified of ruining her children, which is why I stay at work. But also, I don't always *want* to go home—which is also why I stay at work.

He told me that he'd heard what I had said to Todd (another name he hated) back in that room I wasn't supposed to go in— everything I'd said about my kids, how I wanted them to be taken care of. Then Tim Allen told me what an awesome mother I was and how lucky my kids were and how cool it was that their mom was a comedy writer. On and on and on.

Then he said I was funny. Tim Allen said I was funny.

As jaded as I am, even I had to admit, that was pretty cool. Okay, maybe I still got a little starstruck.

So, between the delicious food, the cozy bed, the gorgeous lotion, the boat ride, the pretty great Elton John concert, the calling me a good mother and funny and smart and that private jet ride all those psychics were wrong about, our prediction came through.

Tim Allen tried to kill me.

With kindness.

And in that, he succeeded.

The Love Bracelet

On a recent birthday, as my gift, Todd got me a tour of the ice cream factory that makes my favorite low-carb, low-calorie, low-fat ice cream. He did this because I shame-eat the stuff in the dark over the sink at night. They don't generally give tours, because who the hell actually wants to be faced with nine-hundred-gallon steel vats full of the ice cream they shame-eat in the dark? But Todd made a bunch of phone calls, told someone in charge exactly how much we've spent on the stuff, and now we were not only going, I was getting my own branded apron.

On the drive over, I asked him, "What—am I Augustus Gloomp or something? Do you have some Willy Wonka fetish you've been waiting for my birthday to share?"

"I don't have a Willy Wonka fetish," Todd said. "And it's Augustus Gloop. I thought it would be fun . . . Forget it."

Todd's mad.

I Google. It is Gloop—he's right. Now I'm mad.

But I was already mad. I was decidedly underwhelmed by my gift, and was only going on the tour to find out if they were lying about the fat content. (I'd been gun-shy ever since the *New York Post* reported that Hot and Crusty had lied about the dietary perks of their "light" muffins; it turned out that they were only "light" in color and texture—not calories and fat, as was advertised—which had left me one of countless very angry, very overweight customers.)

It all seemed as if Todd had learned nothing from the birthday present debacle of just a few short years earlier—the one time when, if either of us had been willing to part with our Labrador retriever, Olive, we would have gotten a divorce.

Now, I'm the first one to admit that I'm impossible to please. I don't like getting flowers because they make me sad—the moment they arrive, they begin to die, like people. Which might be why I don't like babies. I can immediately flash forward to what they'll look like brown and dried up, sitting in murky water. The flowers, not the babies. You may as well get me potpourri and skip the grieving process. But I don't like potpourri either. Why get flowers if they're dead?

I don't like being thrown parties for the same reason—the minute a party starts, we're closer to the end of it, like life. I get sad at the beginning of a party so the sadness of it ending isn't a shock to my system.

Clothes are also out—Todd gives me anything that doesn't have an "extra small petite" label, and we're sleeping in separate bedrooms. He can't get me a weekend away for the two of us, either, because that's a gift for him, too, and shouldn't count as a gift for me. Same goes for concert tickets.

So, it's a tradition that every year about a month before my birthday, we'll be getting ready for bed—by this point in our marriage it's open season for clipping toenails (his) and trimming mustaches (mine) in front of each other, so there I'll be, trying to wrangle one stray stubborn hair on my upper lip, when Todd will come in and ask, "What do you want for your birthday?" and I'll say, "Nothing."

And he'll say, "I want to get you something."

And I'll say, "It's fine. Really. Don't get me anything. I'll buy myself something, and we can say it's from you."

Then when my birthday comes, and he gets me what I asked for—nothing—I get to be furious. I'm also exhilarated, because now I get to text my closest friends and my brother to announce how Todd didn't get me anything for my birthday. For at least twenty-four hours (give or take—it all depends what's on the news) people will feel sorry for me. Instead of for "Poor Todd." For one brief day a year, it's "Poor Liz." It's my moment in the sun, until the next year rolls around and we get to do our dance again—the passive-aggressive tango, I call it. Hey, at least I know how twisted I am.

Everything changed the year I was turning forty, however, when, to my mind, the only thing that could have possibly cushioned the blow of a geriatric milestone like the one looming ahead was a Cartier Love Bracelet in yellow gold. Not rose gold, not platinum . . .

I'd wanted one ever since my friend Samantha Bloum's parents got her one for her thirteenth birthday. It was an adult piece of jewelry, but Samantha was big-boned so it wasn't an issue. Her parents adored her, no question. But when it came to Samantha's Bat Mitzvah, her folks went to town, throwing her a bash replete with everything from hip-hop dancers and a face painter to a candy bar with to-go bags. And this was 1989: you couldn't even post about all the good stuff on Instagram. Her parents made speeches about her, and her mother cried in a good way, and I was awestruck—I'd never seen such a public display of love.

The Cartier Love Bracelet was just another bauble that night for Samantha, an extravagance tossed atop extravagances already piled so high that my friend ultimately became ruined by them all, growing up to be as miserable as the men who tried and failed to worship her as much as her ostentatious parents had.

But I was turning forty—an appropriate age for a tribute like a Love Bracelet. From my husband. The father of my children. Plus, I'd spared him the angst of buying me birthday presents from day one—surely, I was worth this one expense, at least on a cumulative level.

So, that year, when Todd came into our bathroom a month before my birthday and found me slathered in face creams and serums ("rescue"-ing, "revive"-ing, "hydrate"-ing and "lift"-ing), I had my answer ready.

Putting toothpaste on his electric toothbrush, Todd asked, "What do you want for your birthday?"

I didn't hesitate, even though he'd switched his toothbrush on, clearly expecting my standard response.

"I want the Cartier Love Bracelet in yellow gold—not rose gold, not platinum!" I shouted, actually excited about something.

Working on his molars, Todd realized he'd missed something over the din of his toothbrush. "Wha—?" he asked.

I waited for him to rinse and spit. "I want the Cartier Love Bracelet in yellow gold," I said slowly. "Not rose gold or platinum."

I ran into the bedroom and returned with an ad I'd torn out of the *New York Times* months earlier in anticipation of this moment. I showed the bracelet to him, so he couldn't get it wrong. Wiping his mouth, he looked at the image as I explained how I couldn't technically buy the bracelet for myself to spare him the stress, because it was called the "love" bracelet and therefore—to my mind and in the Cartier tradition—it needed to be from someone who loved me.

(The Love Bracelet is a bangle that comes in two parts, and the person who buys it for you screws the parts together around your wrist with a little gold screwdriver that comes with it—making you theirs forever until you die, and they saw it off of you. Now you see how creepy Samantha Bloum's Bat Mitzvah gift from her parents really was. Todd knows Samantha, actually. He's been to most of her weddings with me.)

He asked, I answered. I even provided him a picture and explicit instructions.

What could possibly go wrong?

The night before the dreaded birthday, I was in bed spooning Olive when Todd walked in and said he had an important question.

"Me, too," I said. "If it ever looks like Olive is getting really old and sick—will you kill me first?" I'd never survive life without her.

". . . Okay," Todd said, realizing I was serious. "So, my turn: what do you want for your birthday?"

I reminded him that I'd already said I wanted the Cartier Love Bracelet. In yellow gold. Not rose gold. Not platinum.

"What else would you want?" he asked.

"The bracelet," I told him before Olive slobbered a kiss into my mouth.

"But if I didn't get you that," he said, "what else would you want? It's a big birthday, I want you to open something great."

"I want to open the Cartier Love Bracelet in yellow gold," I said, very slowly. "Not rose gold. Not platinum."

Todd nodded as he watched Olive kiss me again. "You know she cleans her ass with that mouth," he reminded me for the thousandth time, failing once again to understand my principle comparing dog's mouths to self-cleaning ovens—which was fine by me, so long as he grasped the fact that he had T-minus twenty-four hours to produce my bling or be euthanized.

It was around midnight on the eve, well actually morning of my birthday, that I got up to pee (for the third time; *It's true*, I thought, *elderly people really do have to go more*). There on my sink were three birthday cards—one from Todd, one from Jesse and Phoebe (as toddler and baby at the time, respectively), and of course one from Olive. And right beside the cards . . . a large-ish, gift-wrapped, not-very-Cartier-shaped rectangular box.

I stared at my present, confused. It had to be a gag. Todd must've put the bracelet in a different box to throw me off. Hilarious. Todd's a funny guy—it's something most people don't realize about my husband right away because I'm the comedy writer, plus I talk over him. But Todd can be very funny. Like he was being now. I wasn't sure if I should unwrap the box, because if it was the bracelet (which I couldn't imagine it not being), I knew I should wait until Todd was awake so I could thank him and he could screw it on my wrist so I'd be his forever or at least until I died before Olive and they had to saw it off of me.

I decided to wait. Even if I opened my gift without him, my delighted squeal was sure to wake him, and we were both so sleep deprived because of our demanding jobs and two kids under three who were sapping the life out of us that to wake him up could truly be considered an actual hate crime.

I shut the light and returned to my bed, vowing to wait 'til the morning to open my present, then I hopped out of bed and raced back into the bathroom. I had to pee again, anyway.

I ripped the paper off of the box, tossing it over my shoulder. Inside was (as you surely have guessed) not a bracelet, but a Kindle.

A Kindle.

Why would Todd get me a Kindle? It was a joke—he was being hilarious again. He had to be playing a sick and perverse joke on me. I went over to his side of the bed and poked his shoulder.

"Todd?" He stirred, rolled over. "Todd . . ."

"Huh?" He was groggy.

I held the Kindle over his head, trying hard to make it not look like a potential murder weapon. "This is a joke, right?"

"Wha—"

"This . . . present. You bought me a Kindle to be funny?"

"You like to read in bed, and this way your light won't keep me up." He rolled back over.

I turned the light on. All the lights on.

He rolled onto his back, opened his heavy-lidded, big brown eyes. Eyes I loved. Eyes that saw a Kindle and told his brain it was something the mother of his children would like for her fortieth birthday.

"I thought you were getting me a Cartier Love Bracelet," I said. "In yellow gold. Not rose gold. Not platinum. Yellow gold."

"It's just a little something from the kids." He yawned.

"Oh!" This wasn't my gift-gift. "That's so cute . . . you're so funny! Okay—Shhh," I soothed. "Go to sleep, sorry to wake."

He grumbled and rolled over as I reminded him that he had to get up with the kids in the morning since it was my birthday. At that point, seeing as I was up, I settled in my armchair with my current read, a giant book called *How We Die* that I'd been saving for a beach vacation.

BY THE EVENING of my birthday, with no bracelet in sight, I was starting to worry. But the morning had been hectic—now that we had two kids, neither of us ever had our hands free, so there was no real time for him to have presented it to me, screwed it on, and made me his forever. Then we both got home late from work; we had to hurry getting ready to make the reservation for my birthday dinner (I wore a shirt that bared my wrist). But when we left the house and he wasn't carrying anything, my worry compounded. Maybe it was in the glove compartment . . .?

Once at the restaurant, Todd pulled up to the valet and hopped out.

"Did you leave anything in the glove compartment?" I asked helpfully, hopefully.

"No." He shrugged.

I followed him inside, wondering where my present could be. That was when I realized that he was wearing a sport jacket, which he never does. I saw him cup his hand between the jacket and his wrist, so as to not let whatever was up there (the bracelet) fall out. He really wanted to surprise me, I thought. It was obvious.

We were seated at a table in a dim, romantically lit corner—the perfect setting for him to pull my Cartier Love Bracelet in yellow gold not rose gold not platinum out from his sleeve. I had never been the girl at the restaurant who got the romantic gift or the engagement ring served to her in a soufflé. I was always the girl two tables away, close enough to see the action but craning my neck to hear exactly what was being said so I could imagine it was being said to me.

But tonight, I would be the girl everyone in the restaurant pretended to be happy for but kind of hated. It was my turn at last.

Todd ordered wine. I normally didn't drink, not after Dr. Oz told Oprah that the fastest way to get fat was alcohol. I was saving my calories for the frozen block of Cool Whip I'd gnaw at in bed later, my legs resting on Olive's back, enjoying the latest murder installment of *Dateline* (remember, it was my birthday, not Todd's). But I didn't want Todd to drink alone, so I ordered a glass for myself. I even suggested we get a bottle. After all, we were both out of the house, away from the babies, and on a real date, just the two of us. We were actually not in sweatpants at seven o'clock at night, but in real grown-up clothes, in a restaurant without a kids' menu or a changing table in the bathroom. I didn't have to fish through my bag for crayons to keep Jesse occupied or pretend I didn't see Phoebe eating straight ketchup because it was keeping her quiet. We wouldn't have to flag down a busboy to drag out a yellow cone and bring us extra napkins after Jesse smelled something green and started projectile vomiting. And Todd would soon present the ultimate token of his love to the mother of those very cherubs.

Before the wine arrived, I got up to go to the ladies' room. I had to pee, obviously, but I also wanted to put on fresh lipstick, so I looked pretty for my present selfies. When I came out, I saw Todd at our table across the room, his jacket off. Bracelet time. I fluffed my hair and looked down at my bare wrist for the last time.

I got back to the table to see two glasses of red wine and no signature red jewelry box.

"Did you order a soufflé?" I asked.

"I figured you'd have Cool Whip with Olive at home," he said.

I scanned the table, then our surrounding tables—even the floor.

"Did you lose something?" Todd asked.

"Did you?" I checked out the waiters' trays.

"No. Sit down."

I sat and was about to ask our waiter if he could turn the lights up when Todd raised his glass. My heart stopped.

"To my wife—" he began. "Happy Birthday . . . I love you!" He started to drink, then stopped, noticing my face had gone dark. "What's wrong?"

"I . . . I thought you had the bracelet up your sleeve."

"What bracelet?"

"The Cartier Love Bracelet," I pressed, like saying it might make it materialize. "In yellow gold, not rose gold, not platinum. I thought you were going to surprise me with it. I thought it was in your jacket sleeve—or is it? Maybe you hid it somewhere to tease me? Because you're hilarious that way?"

"Why would I have a bracelet up my sleeve?" he asked, still holding his glass in the air.

"Why would you wear a sport coat if you're not hiding a bracelet up your sleeve? You're always hot!"

"Excuse me for wanting to look nice for your birthday," he said defensively.

He wasn't excused. I was red. Flushed. Livid. "What bracelet" . . .? How could he not remember? How was that not ALL he'd been thinking about? I'd been living a completely different night than he had—a completely different month than he had.

"Liz . . . I'm not getting you that bracelet," he said.

"Why not?"

"It's really expensive."

"So? It's not like I have any other expensive jewelry. I belong to the cheap gym. They don't even have showers, Todd . . ."

I was standing my ground. Yes, of course Todd was right, it was expensive and extravagant—it was unlike anything he'd ever bought for me. I knew it was a big ask. I mean, it's not like any old bracelet would have spoiled Samantha Bloum for love forever!

But when I added up all the money Todd hadn't spent on birthdays past, he'd saved more than enough to pay for it.

And when I added the fact that we'd never gone to Europe, there was *more* money we hadn't spent.

We also didn't have a horse. Not that we should or would, but if we did, with all the stable rental, carrots, hay, transportation to wherever horses need to go, vet bills . . .

Basically, we were flush with money that we didn't spend on things we never would have spent money on anyway, so I wasn't about to let my husband defend his failure to produce my Cartier Love Bracelet in yellow gold not rose gold and not platinum on fiscal principles.

The waiter came over and started rattling off the specials. I heard "Branzino," but nothing after that. He said he'd be back to take our order and left me to not murder Todd.

"You were supposed to screw it on my wrist, and I'd be yours forever until I died before Olive did, and they'd saw it off of me. I'd be publicly loved," I said, not as quietly as I thought because now the people at the next table were staring (at me). I wasn't "that girl." I was . . . that *other* girl. The nagging wife who criticizes you in public.

"I'll get it for you . . . someday. I'm just not ready to get it for you yet," Todd said.

Wasn't ready? Like I hadn't earned it? I wasn't good enough for it, yet?

"Can I please just make a toast?" He was raising his glass again.

I looked past him, my arms and legs now crossed as tightly as I could manage. I was completely closed off, my body language sky-writing "You can't hurt me." But he had. Like my mother who left and my father whose love was conditional, Todd was withholding his "love" from me. As clichéd as it sounds, that's what this felt like. It reopened an old wound I kept protected and hidden by never asking for anything. By always saying "Don't get me anything," I was able to always remain a step ahead of inevitable disappointment. Sure, I'd be crushed, but on *my* terms. By never asking Todd for anything, he never had to be forced to tell me I wasn't worth anything.

Like he'd just done.

The rest of our precious time away from the kids that night was pretty much spent in silence, except for the clinking of silverware. I didn't talk about the bracelet. I didn't talk about anything. I didn't talk at all. Which is nearly impossible for me.

The silence continued the whole drive home. I hadn't uncrossed my arms and legs and wondered vaguely how I'd walked to the car that way. There'd be no taking pleasure that night in texting my friends about how Todd had let me down—I couldn't even enjoy other people's sympathy, not when I was this humiliated.

Pulling into the driveway, Todd said he felt bad, he was sorry he'd upset me.

I looked at him for the first time since the bracelet hadn't been up his sleeve or in a chocolate soufflé at the restaurant. He *was* sorry? He *felt* bad?

He was making it sound like it was all over—"bygones be bygones" and all that shit. I'd been hoping he'd seen the error in his ways in not thinking I was worthy of a Cartier Love Bracelet in yellow gold, not rose gold, not platinum. But instead, he was sitting there actually waiting for me to take his apology and a Kindle as signs of his esteem.

Without realizing it, I'd built up expectations again—not for some half-assed strategic attempt at remorse but for a pledge of redemption from my bastard husband. I was barely going to be able to eat my frozen block of Cool Whip.

I couldn't just ask again. I couldn't possibly make myself that vulnerable again. I couldn't set my twisted body and brain up to hear that he didn't love me enough again.

But damnit, I still wanted that fucking bracelet.

So, as I opened my car door, I spoke the first words I'd said to him in eleven miles: "Well, don't bother to buy me the bracelet now. It's ruined. I don't even want it anymore."

AS THE WEEKS passed, we once again became engrossed in our kids and our jobs—and Todd went back to being an amazing, loving dad and husband. The bracelet incident slipped into the past.

As much as it could. Truth was, I was still hurt and resentful. Everything about him started to annoy me: the way he stood with one knee a little bent, the way he pronounced the word *lunch* as "lunsh," the fact that he breathed so much. Even the shape of his head—so . . . round. My eyes would narrow, and I'd become angry at the sight and sound of him. Like they say, it's never about leaving the cap off of the toothpaste. And the way he did that bothered me, too.

The Cartier Love Bracelet had driven a yellow gold, not rose gold, not platinum wedge between us.

The next month was February, and Todd suggested we go out for dinner on Valentine's Day to make up for my shitty birthday dinner. The last time we'd celebrated Valentine's Day had been six months into our relationship. Back then, I'd ripped the ass of my favorite pants trying to pull them up—not even along the seam. Just a giant ass rip. I was so upset that I tore them to shreds, and when Todd had arrived at my place, I'd been in a towel, too upset to go out. Pieces of my pants littered the floor.

My secret had been revealed that night, and I remember expecting Todd to just leave upon discovering that I wasn't in fact perfect, but that I came with many flaws, one of which had just gone up a size. Instead, he shrugged and suggested we rent a movie. We ordered Chinese food, and I ate it in front of him. I could be myself around this man, I learned that night. He accepted me. Even loved me.

For both our sakes, I really wanted to get past the bracelet thing. But I also really still wanted the bracelet,

in

yellow

gold.

Not.

Rose.

Gold.

Not.

Platinum.

Goddamnit.

The Sunday before Valentine's Day, Todd told me he needed to run to the Topanga Mall to pick something up. Todd hates malls and never "needs to run" to one, so I went online and saw that the Topanga Mall had a Cartier store.

YES.

"I'm getting it!" I cheered to my six-month-old daughter, who stared at me like she couldn't give a fuck. I poked her belly playfully and told her she would get the bracelet when I was dead, that she might not have cared at the moment, but that someday she'd be standing over my dead body and telling the coroner that before they put me in the oven (Olive and I are being cremated together) the bangle needed to be sawed off of my wrist. She'd take it to her jeweler and have it melted down and turned into earrings she'd lose within a week. I could already tell Phoebe wasn't going to be the type to be careful with jewelry.

On Valentine's Day night, I left a bunch of new clothes all in separately wrapped boxes in that space between our sinks where presents went. I wanted Todd to have something to open, too. He loved them and decided to put them on for dinner. While I was in the shower, I saw him come into the bathroom and take a Cartier bag out from waaay back under his sink and take it into our bedroom. He looked toward the shower to make sure I hadn't seen him, and I turned to face the faucet, smiling widely at the shower wall. Giddy, I barely got the soap out of my hair before I turned off the shower, wrapped a towel around myself, and got out.

"I hope you didn't get me anything for Valentine's Day!" I shouted playfully from behind the closed bathroom door. I winked at myself in the mirror, did a small victory dance, and had started to blow dry my hair when the door swung open and Todd came in, now dressed in the clothes I bought him and carrying the red Cartier bag.

I acted surprised. It was the right thing to do. "To-ooodd . . ." I singsong mock-chided. "I told you not to—"

"It's not the bracelet," he said, putting the bag on the counter.

My shoulders fell. "What is it, then?" I asked, looking at the bag, disgusted, like it had shit on it.

"I got you something else."

"But I don't want anything else."

"Will you just look at it, please?" He took the big red box out of the bag.

I wouldn't just look at it, so he opened the box. Inside was a thin silver necklace. I picked it up, and in the center there was a charm. It was a tiny replica of the Love Bracelet. In silver.

I held it up. "Why would you buy me this?" I asked, incredulous.

"Because I wanted you to have something nice to wear tonight," Todd said.

"But I don't want it."

"Will you just wear it tonight?"

"No." I put it back in the box. "Just . . . no."

"Fine." He left the bathroom, pissed.

I looked down at the silver necklace that had yanked me back down to earth, at the tiny charm that said, "You can have a little love. A replica of love—like 10 percent, but not the whole thing. Not yet. You haven't earned it. Wear it in good health. Enjoy."

I stormed out of the bathroom and threw the box on the bed.

"Return this," I spat. "And get your fucking money back. And do *not* get me the bracelet."

Another silent grown-up-restaurant dinner ensued. The couple next to us got engaged. I hoped they got *E. coli*. That was who I had become. That was what Todd had reduced me to.

The following day, I saw a receipt on Todd's dresser for the necklace.

"You returned it?" I asked him, picking it up.

"Yeah. Got my money back, too," he said and chuckled. "Can't go back to that store again—I had to argue with the guy to get a refund. They've never done that before."

A refund. He fought for a refund?

"Didn't you get me the bracelet?!" I almost screamed.

"You told me not to!"

"I want that bracelet!" I was actually screaming now. "How do you not know that when I said I didn't want it that I wanted it?!"

"You told me to get my money back!" He was screaming too, now.

Oh, no. There was no way *he* was going to get mad at *me*.

"Do not turn this on me, Todd . . ." I started.

"So, then what?" Todd said, flinging up his arms. "Are you saying you want me to turn this on you, is that what you're saying? Because I should be doing the opposite of what you say?"

At that point, the Cartier Love Bracelet in yellow gold, not platinum, not rose gold, had finally lost its beauty. Even if I did get it, it would now be a symbol not of love, but of something I'd horsewhipped Todd into giving me. Which is not the way anyone wants to be loved.

I had to let it go.

So, I let it go. Insofar as I'm capable of letting things like that go.

DAYS LATER, I was in my car when I placed a call to my husband. "I'm on my way to Cartier," I said on speaker, which probably made my voice sound even tighter, more sleep-deprived and hysteria-tinged than it was.

"Liz, don't get it!" he shouted (he was in his car, too). "I'll get it for you!"

"When you're ready?" I asked. "Forget it."

"Liz, it's—"

"I know it's expensive," I cut him off. "It shouldn't matter. Clearly, I'm not a good enough mother or a good enough wife. But if you're waiting for me to get better, for me to 'earn it,' or something, it's probably not going to happen, so forget it! Because I'm an unthinkable age now, and it ain't getting better than this!"

Head rushing at the uncorking of my pent-up rage, I rolled my car into a crosswalk, barely missing several pedestrians. I think they would have understood if they'd known the situation. Lying there in the street, "But . . . you . . . told him what you wanted . . ." one would try to say. "He doesn't deserve . . . you," another would eke out.

There was now silence on the other end of the phone. I assumed I'd lost him and went to cut the call.

"I'm sorry," he said. "I don't know what's wrong with me."

It was the question I'd been asking for nearly two months. Yet hearing him say the words knocked me clean off what had only moments earlier been my high horse.

"There's nothing wrong with you, Todd," I said softly. "Nothing. There's something clearly wrong with me. Don't worry. I'm not going to buy the bracelet. Don't worry."

"Liz—"

"And I don't want it now, I mean it," I assured him, and I pretty much almost completely believed it myself. My disappointment, all this strife, was my fault for asking for something so outrageous.

I hung up and drove home. And by nighttime, as I was very involved in peeling a Bioré strip off my nose, my mind was empty of all things Love Bracelet when Todd came into the bathroom. I felt him standing there, hovering. I didn't speak to him, partly because I had only a three-minute window to slowly but firmly peel the strip off my nose or half my nose skin would come away with it.

Three-quarters of the way through my task, out of the corner of my eye, I saw that he was holding a red Cartier box. For the first time, I genuinely had not been expecting it.

"It's not the bracelet," he said and smiled as he opened the box.

But it was the Cartier Love Bracelet. In yellow gold. Not rose gold. Not platinum. Wordlessly, he placed it on my wrist and screwed it together. I was his forever, until I died before Olive and they sawed it off me.

I looked at the bracelet. I looked at Todd. Then I looked in the mirror—at us, my husband beaming, my Bioré strip dangling. I caught the reflection of the Love Bracelet, glinting radiance off my arm . . .

And realized:

"I think I like the rose gold better."

I've Got This

One Saturday night, I decided Todd and I would take our kids to the outdoor mall in Los Angeles that they love. Jesse was seven and Phoebe was five, which seemed like fine ages to keep them out past nine. But not much past nine, because since birth pretty much around nine-fifteen, Phoebe starts to turn sort of . . . mean. Like a bad drunk after two drinks, she becomes abusive, starts making false accusations, and it gets ugly.

But that still left us plenty of time to have dinner at Wood Ranch BBQ & Grill, then stroll around the mall, enjoying the giant water display in the fountain set to music, and riding the trolley. I might even get to run into Nordstrom's shoe department, quickly, by myself, to see if they had the platform Oxfords I wanted.

How fun. How idyllic. How unlike my own childhood.

A few hours before we left, however, Todd came down with a

stomach virus. Either that, or he ate sushi he'd left in his car all day, so he could get out of the trip. Though that seemed more like a "Liz thing" than a "Todd thing."

His illness forced my hand: Was I going to bail on the opportunity for quality time with my children? Would a "Fun Mommy" do something like that?

Also, I really wanted to see if Nordstrom had those shoes.

"I'll take them to the mall myself!" I blurted against my better judgment.

At first, I was filled with dread—how was I going to handle my own children alone in public at night? This was something that a natural mother could handle with ease. But not me. I'm not a natural mother! I'm not even natural chestnut brown with hints of auburn!

"Get a grip. You can do this," I told myself into the rearview mirror. "You've done much harder things on a daily basis. You run a TV show! You're in charge of fifteen writers and coming up with stories and scripts and jokes in the wee hours of the night. Plus, you can do a handstand!"

"I can do a handstand, too!" Phoebe chimed in from the backseat, startling me. I'd forgotten they were back there. Oy.

We got to the mall, and the fact that we had to park all the way on P12 seemed like the universe's way of telling me to turn back. But I couldn't. There were too many cars behind me.

We weren't out of the car for two seconds before Jesse started worrying that we'd lose the car because I'm forgetful. It was insulting, albeit assertive of him—I didn't tell my mother she was insane when I was seven, but that might be because she was gone by that point.

"We're fine," I assured him. "We're not going to lose the car." Though I was starting to trust his instincts and regard him like one of those prescient seer-children in a creepy Japanese horror film adaptation.

"But what if you do?" he asked, his pitch rising with terror. "You always lose everything."

"I won't lose the car."

"We're going to die here!" He was spiraling now. Which made me spiral.

I grabbed him by the shoulders and shouted into his face, "You're safe!" Which, unsurprisingly, didn't allay his fears.

We finally got to the entrance. Venetian-themed, the mall was all marble and glitz. Shops, restaurants, the fountain—it all awaited us. We just needed to get past the all-but-impenetrable wall of people.

The place was packed. Throngs of teenagers and couples holding hands tightly, making it impossible to navigate past them. Families with double-wide strollers rushed toward us, around us, behind us. Phoebe, already bored, commenced hanging on my arm, her four-year-old weight sending shooting pains up and down my spine and weakening my knees. Jesse, who suffered from crowd aversion, dove under the back of my shirt, pressing his boney head into my back to soothe himself, making moving forward impossible, had it been possible to begin with.

It was a retail hajj, rush hour without the whimsy. The pain was dizzying, I was already dripping with sweat, and we were all of three feet into our trip.

Jesse was right. We were going to die in the mall.

I knew that if we were to have our idyllic night, complete with me running into Nordstrom, quickly, to look for those shoes I wanted, I needed to break out the big guns. Not literally.

I told them that if they were good listeners, they could get whatever they wanted from Dylan's Candy Bar.

"And a toy," Phoebe said.

"No toy," I told her.

"Yes," she insisted.

Jesse emerged from under my shirt, his anxiety eclipsed by his curiosity at seeing how the sudden clash of wills would shake out.

"No toy," I repeated, determined to be strong.

"I want a toy!" the fruit of my loins screamed back at me. It wasn't even seven-thirty yet, and she was turning.

I made a mental note to instruct their nanny, Angela, whom we'd hired to be extra strict so I wouldn't have to be, to teach my daughter not to be a spoiled asshole, and said they could both have a toy because Jesse needed to know he counted, too.

In a clear-headed moment of self-preservation, I decided to bag the sit-down dinner at Wood Ranch Grill. The only thing worse than a thirty-minute wait with two kids is a thirty-minute wait with two kids fighting over the giant light-up beeper thing they make you carry around to let you know your table is ready. I decided not to be a hero and just take the kids to the food court. We could bring our dinners over to the fake grass lawn and look at the fountain at the same time, killing two birds with junk-food sedatives. Then we'd go to Dylan's Candy, I'd run into Nordstrom quick and see if they had those shoes. Then home by nine, to a martini, a true-crime documentary, and bed. And maybe another martini.

We went to Wetzel's Pretzels, and I ordered them everything their mercenary hearts desired. Hot dogs, pretzels, butter nugget things, cinnamon balls. They wanted it, they got it. Because I was "Fun Mommy" and, while I might not always be home to come up with brain-building activities or disinfect boo-boos (also Angela's job), I can buy my children's love on an idyllic Saturday night.

Which I was now about to do.

Except I couldn't find my wallet.

I rooted through my purse, frantically digging through the stray Xanax, gym clothes, gum, loose papers, and other shit, and still couldn't find it. I gave the girl behind the counter the "just a sec" finger, put my bag on the ground, and squatted over it.

"Just getting my wallet!" I singsonged so as not to cause Jesse alarm.

Jesse dove his head back under my shirt, making it hard for me to extend my arms for full bag digging. I dumped out the contents on the concrete and then zoomed in on where my wallet was: on my dresser at home, in my closet, where I had left it.

Fuck. I couldn't wait until the future when I could . . . just beam it to myself. I did find in my bag a squished, wrapper-less muffin and a $20 bill. I ate the muffin, which had a couple of Tic Tacs in it, and nearly $18 of the $20 bought us two pretzel dogs (they should be ashamed). The remaining $1.90 would have to last us until we got home. If I could find the car of course, which, judging from the stricken look on my son's face, he strongly doubted.

We sat on the fake grass away from the crush of people and, while the kids ate, I prayed they didn't get thirsty because water was nine dollars a bottle. I texted Todd about my wallet. He confirmed that it was on my dresser. Thanks. He claimed he was throwing up too much to come to our rescue and added a gagging emoji for effect. I was about to rip him a new one when I spotted a beacon of hope in the form of a mom from our school and her two kids. They would help us. We were a community, after all—at least that's what I heard they tell the parents at every school meeting I miss. This mom would give me cash, and we'd commiserate about what a dumb idea coming to the mall was. We'd maybe even each watch the other's kids while we took turns running into Nordstrom quick.

I went to call her, but her name had escaped me. Barbara? Carol? Judy? I had nothing. I asked the kids her kids' names. They didn't know, and I watched our only hope turn the corner at the

Pottery Barn—our *Carpathia*, leaving me to drown with my two babies and no life vest.

I lectured Jesse and Phoebe about how extremely rude it was to not know the names of the people you see every day and mentally added learning people's names to Angela's Monday to-do list before announcing that we should go home and check on Daddy.

"What about the fountain?" Phoebe asked. "I want to see the fountain."

I told her the fountain was at a different mall, hoping she wouldn't see the giant spurts of colored water shooting into the sky above the crowd. At what age do they start really seeing things? I wondered.

"What about the trolley?" she asked.

"It's broken," I told her, and when the trolley *ding-ding*ed past us, I told her that the people on board were taking it to the Trolley Hospital.

"What hospital?" Jesse asked. He could smell my fear. I think kids can do that, especially Jesse.

"It's . . . in the back." I pointed off at nowhere and halted the interrogation by saying that if there were any more questions we wouldn't go to Dylan's Candy. In the ensuing silence, I wondered what the hell two bucks could possibly buy at Dylan's and prayed the store would be on fire when we got there.

Just then, throwing out the hotdog wrappers, I spotted a five-dollar bill sticking out from under a plate of half-eaten pizza in the garbage can. My eyes went wide with disbelief and excitement. Who throws away five dollars?! Who throws away pizza?! I dove into the trash for the money, thinking *if this is a napkin that looks like a five-dollar bill, I will lose my shit*. Not that I had far to go: I was already neck deep in a trash can. The garbage was wet and hot and smelly, but I powered through for my children.

With my forefinger and thumb, I retrieved the soaking wet bill and, holding it up victoriously, I whooped, singing "Mommy found five dollars in the trash!" accompanied by a sort of Jewish version of an Irish step dance. "Let's go get six dollars and ninety cents worth of candy!"

We made our way to Dylan's Candy, where I was able to talk the kids into the cheapest and possibly most carcinogenic candy, resulting in a respectable-sized bag of crap. I waited until we were in the mall bathroom, however, with a stall door separating us, to break it to them that there would be no toy buying that night. Blissed out on candy, they didn't raise a protest, which emboldened me to press my luck and walk them through Nordstrom quick.

The store was a respite from the crowds. Jesse and Phoebe were happy to sit and eat their cancer candy while I did a sad lap around the shoe department, where I soon spotted my quarry. The platform Oxfords were in stock and absolutely gorgeous. I touched them. I held them. I wanted them so badly. But all I had was seven cents in my bag. It was a fitting end to our excursion.

When you're a working mother, you have precious little time to make it up to your kids, and even though I had the best intentions, I had failed. I had ruined the night: no Grill, no fountain, no trolley, and now I also couldn't have the shoes I wanted. I started to cry. More about the being-a-bad-mother part than the shoes part, but also about the shoes.

I pouted all the way back to the kids and told them we were going home. Without any new shoes for Mommy.

Before we headed outside and back into the crowd, I reflexively pulled the back of my shirt out, making room for Jesse's head.

"That's okay," he said, and pulled his own shirt over his head.

I was confused. "Wait—you don't want to put your head in my shirt?" I asked him.

"Nope," he said from inside. "I'm calling this 'turtling.'"

"He's a turtle!" Phoebe laughed.

He was self-soothing his crowd anxiety. For the first time, he had put his head in his own shirt. Proud as I was of him, it made me melancholy. They were growing up so fast. One minute they were babies who looked to you for comfort, and the next they were—well, turtling.

It was too much for me at that point. I needed to be needed. If not for money, of which I had none, then for the calming pressure I could provide my son's head.

"Turtle me, Jesse," I demanded.

He did. I told Phoebe to pull on my arm. She obliged—even though we were edging closer to nine o'clock, and I could see her eyes starting to narrow.

I was just beginning to feel better. I mean, no one had ever died from not getting platform Oxfords . . . when one of the salesgirls ran over to hand me a Post-it note with a name and a number on it. "I hope you don't mind—" she started to say.

"I already have a therapist," I told her. "Thanks."

"No—that's my number," the girl said. "I babysit. Your kids are amazingly well behaved—I'd love to watch them."

I gestured to Jesse, obediently pressing his head against my spine, and Phoebe people watching—noted a budding staring problem, which she's inherited from me.

"These kids?" I asked her, incredulous.

"Oh, yeah," she answered. "You should see the monsters we get in here."

"Really?! Bad, huh! Like how bad?" I said, hungry for anything terrible she could tell me about other people's kids.

I'd never thought of my kids as examples of "good behavior," but, come to think of it, they actually were good. Out of the three of us, I'd been the only one who'd had a truly extended tantrum the entire time we'd been at the mall, plus I touched garbage and ate a muffin off of the ground. I made a mental note to thank Angela for teaching them how to behave.

But then I thought that maybe the reason they were so good was that this had been just a normal outing with me, their overwhelmed, scattered, disorganized mother. Whether I'd lost our hotel room key at the bottom of the pool, locked my last set of keys inside my car, made us miss a flight because I left our plane tickets at the airport McDonald's, when they were late for school because I accidentally hit that pedestrian . . . thanks to me, they'd grown accustomed to utter chaos—and that, I am convinced, will serve them well in life.

Until I had children of my own, I didn't realize how important it was to have a mother. Not just someone to babysit in a pinch and tell you you're gorgeous even when you're nine months pregnant and pushing 250 pounds, but a constant presence in the lives you bring into the world. That responsibility has long weighed heavily on me, mostly because I'm no more equipped now than I was the day my son was born and I told Todd not to take the tags off.

I had no role model worth emulating in the people who raised me. No road map. No skills. No mother. And it shows. At the very least, I feel it.

Yet as time goes on, I'm starting to think there are a lot of moms like me out there.

Moms who sit in their car a block from home at night, waiting for their kids to go to sleep because the bedtime routine is just too frightening.

Moms who let their kids eat butter for lunch because their own parents sent them to fat camp and gave them body dysmorphia.

Moms who buy car seats based on how well they coordinate

with the car upholstery and who don't know any of the evils of soy milk.

Moms who will climb a fence at their kid's preschool—an actual metal fence—to escape the small talk of the Stay-at-Home Mothers gathered at the entrance gate.

Moms who are more confident running a multinational conglomerate or network TV show than they are getting their kids to brush their teeth.

And it seems that even as I struggle to not become my mother, even as I deal with the complete lack of parenting skills and surplus of PTSD that were the only constants of my childhood, I have become someone my kids like. Someone who they, for some reason, can't get enough of. A source of chaos to be sure, but a consistent one whose love they can always count on. Someone who, when they're old enough to buy my Mother's Day card, won't have to ask the saleslady at CVS where the "Estranged, from All of Us" section is, like I do.

I hope.

WALKING TO THE wrong car on the wrong level of the parking garage, Jesse emerged from inside my shirt, his lips dyed blue from the toxic candy he ate, and said he had the funnest night ever.

"Me too," Phoebe cheered, and asked me to do the "Mommy found five dollars in the trash dance" again.

I danced. And they laughed. And I got Phoebe home by 9:14, seconds before she turned mean.

It wasn't an idyllic Saturday night. But it was perfect for us.

Epilogue:
One Flying Leap

It's impossible for me to get any work done at a trampoline park (I think it's safe to say I'm not alone in this). Something about the loud music pumping over the din of a hundred kids screaming, bouncing, diving into foam cubes, doing flips, and coming within inches of paralyzing themselves makes for a less than ideal mobile office. Yet the trampoline park was my office, one recent Sunday afternoon.

I was on deadline for a script outline that was giving me grief. I was having trouble plotting the story, truly blocked; it's something that happens to writers, pretty much every day—we are stricken with the panic that this script will be the one that outs us as a fraud, the one that proves we just can't do it. I mentally put my house on the market and sell my overpriced sneakers to an online shopping site. If only I could come up with that second act complication, crack the problem by tonight, I could mentally take my house and my sneakers back off the market.

But weekends are when I make up for lost time with my kids and, on this day, I had Phoebe and her friend Kimberly to entertain—it had been either that or take Jesse to a Dodger game. As it turned out, I almost certainly would have gotten more work done there.

Before Kimberly arrived, I told my daughter that I needed to work that afternoon and they'd have to entertain themselves. Phoebe promised me they would.

Mere moments into their playdate, however, Phoebe appeared before me, with Kimberly at her side and holding a box containing a bracelet-making kit she'd gotten for her birthday. These craft-type "presents" are, in my eyes, a hate crime against parents. The box says "5 and up" but really it's "40 and up" because it's the parents who are inevitably tasked with the 25-step directions which are (naturally) in both microscopic print and nine languages. By the time I got to English, I already had a migraine and was ready to start screaming in tongues.

Phoebe's kit contained a hundred little baggies of string, glue, rubber bands, and a contraption used to make the damn things, which was (naturally) broken. There was only enough green string for one of the girls, so of course Phoebe declared that green was her favorite color and threw a fit when Kimberly said green was her favorite color. I dragged Phoebe into the kitchen and told her that I didn't like her spoiled behavior and also that if she agreed to give her friend the string, I would buy her a professionally made green string bracelet later.

Five minutes later, an acrid smell from the kitchen proved that Phoebe was pulling a DIY science experiment that required a plastic container with holes and a warm surface, and that she'd lied about letting me work and was never going to leave me alone unless I got her and her friend out of the house.

My guilt for not spending a quality-time Sunday with my daughter resulted in our making a thirty-minute drive to the crème de la crème of trampoline parks (and there are actually several trampoline parks in Los Angeles, for some godforsaken reason), boasting rope swings, a zip line, seventy trampolines, and a dodgeball court. A ninja warrior course for cherubs—cherubs I desperately needed out of my face.

When we got there, I filled out nine hundred waivers stating that I was totally cool if my kid broke her neck and ended up being rolled out of there on a stretcher, permanently immobile. Yes, yes. Whatever. I needed to get work done. To just get over this hurdle, so I could relax.

I paid the ridiculous fee, bought the girls the necessary socks with "grip" on the bottom, and set them free. Then I took the now-freezing coffee I'd had since the morning—more of a security coffee at this point, all but undrinkable—and sat on one of the couches they have set up for parents in places like that. I planted myself between two almost sleeping parents, opened my laptop, and heard—almost immediately: "Mommy . . .?"

Three other mommies joined me in the slow, dread-filled, "please don't make me get up" turn toward the voice. I drew the short straw.

"Can you watch us?" Phoebe was asking with a pout.

I sighed and told her that I was watching her. Sadly, at nine, she's old enough now to know that if I'm facing away from her—as I was doing—I couldn't see her. I agreed to move to a seat where I could look right at her, and she took off.

For almost exactly a minute.

"Mommy."

I looked up from my computer to see Phoebe hovering two feet in front of me.

"I'm thirsty," she moaned. Phoebe's always thirsty. I've never met a kid who needed more water. Kimberly pulled up beside her, and next thing I knew, I was taking the two of them to the vending machine to get waters. Finally, they went back up to the trampolines, and I took my seat once again and opened my laptop . . . just as Phoebe reappeared. She'd lost Kimberly and needed help finding her.

"Just go find her!" I growled. "Phoebe, I HAVE WORK TO DO!"

"I'm sorry, Mommy!" she fake-cried.

So, we searched among the crowded trampolines, and Phoebe quickly spotted her friend, pointing to a blur in the distance flipping pretty high in the air. Great. I told Phoebe I'd see her later, and I was watching everything she did. I made a break for it.

But before I got far, Phoebe was calling me back. She was standing where I'd left her, refusing to move.

I stormed over to her, if one can storm while bouncing a little on a trampoline floor surface. Through gritted teeth, I told her in no uncertain terms that I had to work, and that I was working for us, and she'd made a promise to me, and that lying was not nice, which was when Kimberly backflipped into view and asked me to watch her do a handspring.

I was becoming irate at this point. I hadn't come there to watch my own daughter do a flip, never mind someone else's kid. But before I could say anything, Kimberly bounced from the platform we were standing on up onto a square springboard, leaping, twisting, and landing on a crash pad about three feet high. Kimberly's one lithe little girl. A star athlete, she has two moms, and her father was chosen at a sperm bank. He was a Harvard graduate and competitive swimmer with model-like features and so sought after that they sat on a waitlist for a year just to get a quarter ounce of his DNA.

Kimberly inherited the best of both parents. She's half-Jewish, half-projectile. Unlike her mothers, though, I didn't pick Phoebe's father from a menu. Instead, I met the other half of Phoebe's DNA at a bar, where we were both tired from standing and found seats next to each other. Go, Phoebe.

I oohed and ahhed at Kimberly's flips and whirls and weightless midair backhand springs, praying I wouldn't have to call her moms and tell them she snapped her neck. After five *Wowww!*s, I felt I was free to go. But then it was Phoebe's turn. I stayed to watch. I was there anyway.

Phoebe stood at the back of the platform to give herself room to run, her shoulders back, eyes narrowed, focused, in a runner's starting position. On the count of three, she took off. Slowly. She plodded forward—hesitantly, clumsily plopping onto the trampoline square, barely propelling herself upwards and, with zero momentum, hit the side of the mat. She righted herself and walked away, defeated.

I flashed back to myself at her age, in gym class, when I would have to mount the pommel horse during calisthenics. The pommel horse was my biggest enemy. We'd line up in the gymnasium in our green nylon gym suits—mine came in a slightly different shade, of course, because they didn't make my size in children's (I still wonder what kind of grown-up wore a gym suit that size and what the hell they did in it).

Mr. Winslow, our PE teacher, was a short and white-haired ball of a man, with a huge gut, giant calves, and a ton of authority. When he blew his whistle, we were supposed to run, jump onto a spring board (the 1970s version of a trampoline), and propel ourselves up, onto, and over the pommel horse. Quickly.

All the rest of the girls in my class would mount the horse with ease and trot on to the next piece of apparatus. I had a different experience.

When my turn came, I would take up position, shoulders back, eyes narrowed, focused, in a runner's starting stance. On the count of three, I'd take off. Slowly. I'd sort of plop onto the springboard and then fall. Just short of the horse. From there, now at a complete stop, I'd sling my leg over the back and with my arms, try to grab on to the underneath of the other side for leverage, and then heave myself on to the top of the horse. Before I could catch my breath, feeling all eyes on me—the whole class would invariably come to a halt at the spectacle of my exertions—I would slide off the other side and, mortified, slowly turn to face my second worst nightmare, the ropes.

I've never thought Phoebe looked much like me. She has dark brown hair, dark, almond-shaped eyes, and olive skin—all from Todd. I, on the other hand, physically gifted her with little more than my body-shape and athletic prowess. Looking at her in that moment—sweating, trying again and again to clear the top of the mat—I wondered if it was a good time to tell her that she didn't stand a chance. That she might as well give up, that she took after me, and we don't "mount" things. Was this the moment, there in the middle of the trampoline park, that I should break the news to my daughter that her mother was eventually put in a special gym class for the athletically challenged—equipped with lower pommel horses and no ropes and balance beams that rested on the floor?

Kimberly was helping/not helping by coaching Phoebe, telling her it was easy, to just do what she herself was doing—as in, basically, fly.

I wanted to tell Kimberly to zip it, that Phoebe couldn't fly. And that Kimberly came from super sperm and that I didn't get to choose Phoebe's skills like Kimberly's mommies did, and no, it's not fair, but there we were.

I needed to distract Phoebe from this personal failure. One that would undoubtedly follow her into adulthood, when she'd be at a trampoline park with her daughter—probably on Mars or somewhere—

and flash back to this day. So, I told Phoebe all the other things she was good at. How she had an original fashion sense and didn't care what other people thought of her mismatched outfits (carefully avoiding mention of the Thanksgiving when she wore a polka-dot skirt and butterfly shirt, and her aunt Barb looked at her too long and I'm pretty sure had a seizure). I told Phoebe how she was great at coloring and a fantastic guest at other people's houses. That she was a kind and loyal friend (except when it came to green string).

A "referee" was hovering, a scowl on her face, glaring at my illegal feet. I was standing on a surface where shoes were forbidden. I told Phoebe I had to go. They were making me. I told her to try diving into the foam block pit—it was impossible to fail at that.

But Phoebe refused to give up. She was so determined. Poor thing.

I really needed to work. I needed an ending to my script. If I could figure out this one piece of the story, if I could just warm my coffee up in a microwave . . .

Walking back to my laptop, this feeling came over me—a mother feeling I'm assuming—that I needed to get back to Phoebe. My work would be there later, though, as the trampoline park had no lockers, my laptop might not.

I couldn't un-slide off of a pommel horse onto the floor, unland on my back, legs in the air like a giant bug. But I could help Phoebe clear her own hurdles. That's what I was here for. And if Phoebe could do this—if she could get over her hump—she might apply it to other things she might not master on the first try or even the fortieth. How great would it be to take that weight off of my daughter's shoulders? To make her lighter? To help her fly like her bioengineered friend?

I bought a pair of twenty-dollar grip-socks, signed a pile of waivers agreeing to not sue if I got paralyzed, and bounced back over (this time with purpose) to where she was, surprising her, myself, and probably the referee.

I was Phoebe's coach now. All business, I told her in a voice slightly deeper than my own to go back farther on the platform, start farther away, then farther still. I told her to jump twice on the trampoline if she had to, to get extra height. She was tired. Honestly, I was, too.

I know you're not supposed to lie to your children, but I do it all the time, so I told Phoebe she could do this. "You can do it. Clear the mat," I said, my voice deeper still. "Do it."

She ran and jumped and fell.

A line was forming behind her. A toddler who had no business being in the "big kid" area and couldn't possibly handle any of it was waiting impatiently for his turn. He started to cry like a three-year-old, which he was. It was distracting, so I told Phoebe to wait and let him go—though not before shooting him a very, very dirty look. To add insult to insult, the little shit sprung into the air from the trampoline, landing feet first on the mat.

Phoebe stared at him, her face getting red. Well, redder.

"Eff him," I said to Phoebe. "He's not even cute."

But I'd noticed something in the toddler's form—like coaches do. When he jumped, he kept his gaze forward instead of down, which was where Phoebe looked when she leapt. Looking forward seemed to help him go farther on the trampoline.

"Look forward," I told Phoebe, "not down!"

The scene was out of *An Officer and a Gentleman* all of a sudden—with my daughter as Casey Seeger and me as whoever Louis Gossett Jr. played. ("Climb that wall, Seeger!" I think I heard myself chant; she didn't catch the reference.) I was serious. Way too serious for a trampoline park on a Sunday afternoon.

"It's all in your head, Phoebe," I enthused, the irony all but dripping off me. "All in your head. If you think you can do it, you'll do it. YOU CAN DO IT. Get out of your own way."

Shoulders back, sweat dripping from her brow and down the side of her face, she looked at me, to make sure I was there. I was there.

I told her "On three" and counted her down.

"One. Two . . ."

She looked at me again.

"Three!"

She took off. Her head up, feet forward this time, she landed on the trampoline with more energy. Her body propelling her up, she pulled her knees into her chest . . .

. . . and landed on the mat with both feet.

She lurched forward, gained her balance, and stood up to her full height.

"YES!" I shouted. "Yes!"

She turned and looked at me, her wide-eyed expression mirroring mine.

Silence . . . and then . . .

A smile spread across her face. A smile filled with breathtakingly beautiful pride. Phoebe, Kimberly, and I cheered and jumped up and down—Kimberly higher than both of us, but that was okay.

I hadn't planned on spending time with Phoebe that day. I'd told her that Mommy had to work. And hoped it would count that I was spending time near her, if not exactly with her. Because I had a deadline. My story needed help.

But the story that really needed help wasn't the script I had writer's block on, it was mine and Phoebe's—and on that score, we'd both come through. She did what I couldn't. She'd broken the curse. A curse I didn't even realize I had put on her.

Isn't that all we want for our children? For them to do better than we did?

My kids are growing up. They're turning into people. Difficult people. Difficult, wonderful people who make me wonder if my dad and Cathy weren't so wrong. Hardwired by my own childhood, I'm tempted to repeat their patterns. But I hold myself back, and in trying to correct their mistakes, I'm making new, different mistakes of my own. And my kids will make their own in trying to correct mine. And so on, and so on.

I have no idea what's to come in our story.

But one thing is certain: I'll be looking forward, not down.

Screwed

For one month during the pandemic, I abandoned my family and had a summer romance. It was in my head, but that didn't make it any less real, any less tangible. The object of my imaginary desire is a doctor. A surgeon. An oral surgeon to be exact, so a dental surgeon, but as important as heart, brain, or otherwise (in my head).

Our meet-cute was a little less than cute, but as with most love stories, fate brought us together when my hair was dirty. It was June 2020. Early enough in the pandemic that people were still hoarding toilet paper, leaving Amazon boxes outside for an EXTRA twenty-four hours before opening them, TikTok videos parodying moms losing their shit over homeschool and voice-overs of dogs complaining about their humans being home all day were becoming less and less funny as lockdown became more and more interminable.

Kids at home, husband at home, myself . . . at home—I was trapped . . . in my own life. For a self-proclaimed "stay-at-work mom," someone who has referred to her son as "the one in the glasses," her daughter as "why is she always mad?" and her husband as "Tom" (he refers to himself as Todd) and all of them as "those people," it was torture. I had nowhere to hide. No pretending to be working late when I was really at yoga at seven on a Monday night, aimlessly walking around the mall, out with friends, or driving just to . . . drive. My car, which was once my kitchen/office/phone booth, sat idly in the driveway collecting dust, saving miles, a constant reminder of what used to be. Lockdown stole my freedom and my identity. I prayed something would get me out of the house. Anything.

It was about 2 a.m.; everyone was asleep, and the house was finally quiet. This was the only time I could actually get any work done. So instead, I was deep in an Instagram wormhole watching my former spin instructor, Joanna B, pre-Covid, jump off a yacht in Capri with her new, independently wealthy girlfriend. Back in the day, before articles started coming out about how spinning gives you big thighs, Joanna B.'s class was so popular you had to get there an hour early to sign up. So popular that one time, the gym was literally *on fire* and not one of us left. Sirens, power went out, firemen coming through with hoses, the whole thing. Not only did none of us leave, people came *into* the studio on the chance someone had given up their bike or passed out from smoke inhalation. I had no idea how good I had it back then, out in public, living my life, gasping for air in a pitch-black room, getting screamed at by my instructor to "climb!" while someone else was giving my kids dinner.

I started to google "celebrities who have died in gym fires," when a dull ache crept up the lower left side of my jaw. I chalked it up to the fact that I'd been plowing through a giant bag of Skinny

Pop and maybe my mouth was fatigued. In the next few minutes the pain went from dull aching to little pulsing stabs, the telltale hammering of an infection. I needed to go to the bathroom to see what was going on. I threw the blankets off me, sending Skinny Pop shards flying onto my two dogs and Todd who was sound asleep, blissfully unaware of what I was going through. This made me angry.

Everything he did made me angry. From the way he ate his lunch on a plate, sitting at the kitchen table and not standing over the sink or garbage because he's filled with shame for taking a break, to his work voice, pleasant and lighthearted but also with an air of authority (*who is that guy!?*), to the way he worked out every day, even changing up his form of cardio, refusing to let his body go like everyone else, to the way he couldn't understand me when I talked with my mouth full. Another thing I noticed that I'd never noticed before: His breathing. He breathed *A LOT*. An inordinate amount. In and out . . . all day and night. Quite frankly, I didn't know how much more of it I could take.

Without even having to turn the big light on in the bathroom, I could tell my cheek on the now relentlessly pulsing left side was swollen. It hung a little lower and looked like I had a big gumball in it, distorting my nose to make it look wider. That whole side of my face looked like a caricature: a louder, more obnoxious, but oddly more confident version of myself. When I looked inside my mouth, it was exactly as I had feared: tooth in question was my back left molar. My "mall tooth."

I had broken it on a caramel Nip back in December 1999 when I first moved to LA. I was on a driving tour of Christmas lights with my brother, Jeff, and his fiancée, Stephanie. They oohed and aahhed and held hands over the center console. Jeff's thumb was caressing the skin between Lisa's thumb and forefinger so aggressively, I expected him to start a fire. I was hoping he would. I was bitter and single and spending Friday night with two very in love people. I stuffed a Nip in my mouth and made the rookie mistake of hastily biting down before the Nip softened and had any give and cracked my molar in half.

I was in major debt and didn't have insurance so the only dentist I could afford was in a seedy mall in the San Fernando Valley. The sign out front was a neon toothbrush with DR. OOTH written in neon toothpaste. You could faintly make out a darkened T if you looked closely enough. Fortunately, the mall was open until eleven for holiday hours so I was able to go that night. Being a former mall rat, myself, getting medical attention across the way from a food court and next to a JC Penney seemed fitting. The filling wasn't pretty, it was definitely not healthy—I'm 99 percent sure whatever plastic goo it was made of seeped into my blood and gave me a fatal disease. But that would be a "later" problem.

My mall tooth outlasted any of my cars, phones, laptops, the mall itself, and all my grandparents. It was always a ticking time bomb and it decided to go off during a global pandemic.

The gum surrounding the area was a brighter shade of pink and puffier than the rest of my gums. I went to touch it with my pointer finger, but my unmanicured, misshapen nail was like a dagger on the tender flesh and even the tiniest bit of pressure sent an electric shock of pain down into my bone that radiated throughout the left side of my body, my face, and even my hair. It was so bad my OCD didn't make me try to re-create it on the other side.

I had to find something to knock me out. I really regretted giving my Vicodin to a friend just because it started making me feel a little suicidal the next day. I regretted giving Todd my last Percocet because he had a migraine, and it was his birthday . . . and that was his present.

I went through my purses, jackets, computer bag, turning every pocket inside out, and finally, in the bottom of an old beach bag that was permanently damp, I found a crumbly yellow pill. There was lint on it, but if I removed it some of the pill would go with it so I ate it. It was, if memory served, a Valium a mom in Phoebe's class brought me back from Mexico when the girls were in first grade. This, of course, made me nostalgic for the days when our kids were young and cute. And I could leave whenever I wanted.

The linty pill parts were no match for my growing infection. The pressure under the filling was unbearable. I needed relief immediately. I woke Todd with what I thought would be a pleasant surprise.

"Here, I need you to rip my mall filling out." I said, holding a pair of pliers close to his face.

Much to my surprise, after spending two months trapped in a house with me, he didn't jump at the chance. He mumbled something about "not wanting that responsibility." Even when, *especially* when, I told him how with my mild heart thingy an infected tooth could kill me.

"Just call the dentist in the morning," he said, still half-asleep.

"I can't call the dentist! We are in the middle of a global pandemic, in case you haven't noticed. They won't be open. *Starbucks* isn't even open! *Starbucks!*"

"Okay. *Don't* call the dentist." He folded his pillow and went back to sleep. But not before looking at the landscape of the bed, covered in popcorn, and making a deeply disgusted face that I did not appreciate.

"Do you have to eat in bed?"

"You know I do."

Another thing that infuriated me—the way he asked me questions he already knew the answers to.

I had no choice. I had to call my dentist and couldn't wait until the morning. Dr. Marvonzo was my first actual grown-up, legit dentist. Her office was very sterile and cold, and she was one of those all-business professionals who didn't like to let on that she had a personal life. Even when she chopped nine inches off her hair and turned it into a reverse bob, she wouldn't acknowledge it when I said it looked nice. Even though it hurt my feelings a little, I did respect her professionalism. Plus, she had a large pour when it came to nitrous. She'd been gunning for my mall tooth since she first laid eyes on it so maybe she'd be excited to finally pluck it out.

Moments later, she called me back. I started to breathe a sigh of relief, but the air hitting my tooth sliced through my gum and brought me to my knees. Moving my mouth as little as possible, I told her the problem and before I could even finish, she said no. She rejected me. Clearly not a girl's girl. Shame on her.

"Everything is shut down. Even Starbucks. I'm so sorry," she said, not sounding quite sorry enough.

"You can't go by *Starbucks*! That's insane. Please?! It's my mall tooth . . ."

"There are just many unknowns. I have young children."

Now she starts talking about her personal life?!

"I have young kids too! I'd be exposing mine too! It's fine. They're resilient!"

"Can I at least send you a picture of my face and then you can decide?" I begged.

She thought about it for a moment and decided instead to send me to someone on the other side of town in Beverly Hills. *Fancyschmancy*, I thought. Dr. Gayfort was seeing patients. On top of that, he was not only a dentist but an *oral surgeon* and as far as I was concerned, a hero.

I needed a ride in case they had to put me under (*God, please let them have to put me under.*). Todd had to stay with our kids because they refuse to be self-sufficient. By the time I was 11, Phoebe's age, I was already stealing cash from my stepmother, riding my bike to the train station, and learning how to smoke. Phoebe doesn't even know what a cigarette is and only rides her bike in the driveway. In full safety gear. I guess we were just more mature.

My friend Stacy agreed to drive me on the condition that we both double masked and held our heads out the window like dogs. The hot mid-June air burning a hole in my forehead did nothing to offset the war that was going on inside my mouth.

Stacy let me out on the sidewalk in front of the building and told me to text her when I knew how long I'd be. Until then, she'd be circling the block in her car.

Once in the elevator, I unmasked myself, allowing my left cheek to continue to swell freely. The metal doors closed, and standing before me, facing me, was the picture of giving up: my reflection. Dear lord. I had sixteen floors to survey the damage lockdown had done.

I had deep creases that went from next to my nose to my chin, smile lines next to my eyes that fanned out like spiderwebs, when there hadn't been a smile in ages, barely the hint of eyebrows, the hair around my temples and forehead was the same gray as my complexion and gave the appearance of a receding hairline. I looked like I was aging naturally.

"You look like you're aging naturally," I said to myself, narrowing my eyes, which I was able to do since the Botox was gone from my system.

The tragedy didn't end with my face. My sweatshirt with the word *Heaven* painted across the chest had a giant hole in the armpit (which explained the breeze) and my sweatpants had a grease stain on the thigh. I had gone out like this.

In fairness to me, I had planned on getting my act together before I went back out in public. I'd get back in jeans, color my hair, stop using my face as a napkin—self-care-type things. CNN said it would be about two years before any sort of normalcy resumed IF we were not all dead before that. Either way, I had time.

A nurse met me at the door and immediately held a thermometer gun to my head. I explained that if my temperature was high, it was because my head was hanging out of the car on the way over. She looked at the gun, shrugged, and walked me through a darkened waiting room with tape stretched over every other seat and a sign that read Do Not Sit Here with a little drawing of the Covid virus beneath it . . . She took me to the back where the offices were and over to a high-tech X-ray machine. It would move around my head in a circle, take X-rays, and probably give me brain cancer (another "later problem"). Then she got me settled in the exam room, where I waited for the doctor.

"Let's see what we have going on here!" Dr. Gayfort said, in a slightly muffled but breezy voice, gliding into the room with purpose, ease, and confidence. Exactly what you want in a doctor when your head is about to burst into flames.

Wearing a hazmat suit complete with a gas mask with little ventilators on the sides, he strode past me and over to a monitor in the corner. He clicked a button and the screen lit up with my X-rays. His hand on his hip (like a boss), he tilted his head one way and then slowly the other.

"It's a mall tooth," I moaned in pain. "Please get it out."

"Oh. Well, it's coming out," he said, turning to me.

A wave of relief, mixed with incomprehensible pain, washed over me.

"You cracked the root. Probably grinding from stress. It's very common right now."

So this was Todd's and the kids' fault? *Those people* did this to me. Todd's breathing, the kids needing to eat lunch *every day* . . . all of it was making my teeth shatter at the roots.

Dr. Gayfort explained that I'd need something called an implant. When the root is cracked, a tooth dies, so they take the whole thing out—the nerve and everything—and put a tiny screw in and then a crown on top of that. Somewhere in his explanation, out of the corner of my eye, I noticed I was wearing Birkenstocks from two different pairs—one black, one brown. The brown was Phoebe's and there was a big puffy blob of cheese on the buckle. God, she was such a pig. Wait. The brown one was mine. I was making her mac 'n' cheese and must've dropped a blob of cheese on my foot. If I were at home and not at the dentist, sorry, *oral surgeon*, I knew for a fact I would have eaten it off my shoe without even thinking about it. I was living like a bear. A bear that had given up and would eat macaroni and cheese off a shoe.

"So, I'll fix you up," Dr. Gayfort said, bringing me back from my shame spiral. He gave my shoulder a gentle squeeze with his double-gloved hand. I tried to flex my arm to show some muscle tone and really hoped my sweatshirt wasn't wet for any reason. The only part of him I could see, through the little window in his gas mask, were a pair of warm, kind brown eyes. I would call him Dr. Kind Eyes.

"You'll need to be put under," Dr. Gayfort said, with an apologetic tone.

This meant heavy drugs. I smiled with half my face. *Thank you God for hearing my prayers*, I said in my head.

The nurse rolled up my sleeve and prepped me for a giant needle filled with my escape. "You can put me the most under it goes. I have a high tolerance for methyl whatever that is," I said, hoping I didn't sound like a drug addict.

The anesthesia did its magic quickly, my pain subsided, I relaxed my death grip on the chair, and while Stacy circled the block, I slept the sleep of a thousand nights. The next thing I knew, my mall tooth was in a hazardous waste bin somewhere and in its place was a blood-soaked piece of gauze . . . and suddenly I was sitting in a comfortable reclining chair in the recovery area. I was groggy and for a moment forgot where I was. It all rushed back to me when Dr. Gayfort came over.

"Gah. Ko uh echer," I said.

"So much better! Good! That's what we want to hear!" He smiled, I think.

Wow, he understood me with my mouth full.

Dr. Kind Eyes didn't take my insurance, but he took my pain away and he came out during Covid to do it. I had a warm feeling about him—it could've been the drugs, but I've been on drugs before, and this wasn't that. Did I have a crush?! Did I have that transference thing people get when they fall in love with their doctor on hospital shows?! Was it real?

"You have someone picking you up, right?" Dr. Gayfort asked.

And he's chivalrous too! What a catch I thought, taking my phone out to text Stacy who'd been circling the block for over two hours.

That night, still swollen, groggy, and stuffed with gauze, it was business as usual at my house. I was in the garage unpacking a box with 25 pounds of sand that Phoebe ordered on my Amazon account and Jesse, against my wishes, was playing video games with a guy named Bomb who sounded no younger than 50, when my phone rang. It was Dr. Kind Eyes.

He called to see how I was doing. *He* actually *wanted* to know how *I* was doing. No one had asked me how I was doing in months . . . years . . . I asked him how *he* was doing, and he only wanted to know how *I* was doing! This man risked his life and left his house in a global pandemic to save my tooth and asked me how *I* was doing. I was able to hear his voice clearly without the gas mask. It was smooth, melodious, and calming. I flashed back to his kind eyes and his nimble double-gloved fingers that fixed me.

My heartbeat sped up, I got a burning twinge in my stomach, and the deep desire to talk in an annoying, soft little baby voice. Was it more than a crush?! It had to be. Dr. Kind Eyes was telling me to make sure I gargled with the medicated rinse they gave me when Phoebe came in to see if her sand had arrived.

"I'm on the phone with the *doctor*!" I whisper-shouted, shooing her out of the garage. Dr. Kind Eyes gave me his cell number (scandalous!!!) and made me promise to call him if the swelling didn't go down or if there was bleeding or severe pain—I could call him at any hour.

"Okayyyyyy, I will, Dr. Kind— Gayfort . . ." I said in an annoying, soft little baby voice.

Now I was half hoping the swelling would stay the same or worsen just so I would have an excuse to call him. Either way, it wasn't over for us. The great thing about losing an entire tooth, including the root, was that the process of getting a new one involves three appointments total. He'd still need to put a little screw in and then a crown would go on top of that. Rosie, his receptionist, was going to call me the next day to set up my next appointment. She was looking at dates in mid-July.

"A *month*?! I won't see him for a month!?" I asked, a little too desperately.

"Your gum needs to heal before he can screw the post in," Rosie said matter-of-factly. "Do you need to see him sooner? Is something wrong?"

Yes, something was wrong. I had a budding romance and if we wait a month for the screw, we'll lose momentum. The blessing in Dr. Kind Eyes wanting to wait was that I had a whole month to work on my appearance. The next time I went into that office he was going to see the unswollen human, not a bear, me. I had an incentive now. I had someone to look good for. Reversing the signs of giving up was going to take a lot of heavy lifting by professionals and we were still in lockdown.

Imagine a montage of me getting underground Prohibition-style beauty treatments over the next four weeks. There was the manicure and pedicure in a friend of a friend's backyard. I had to promise to keep my mouth shut, get a pale color so it wouldn't draw attention, and if anyone asked, I had to say I did my nails myself. To make that more believable the manicurist botched two fingers and a toe. There was the Botox on my cousin's friend's balcony. She did an okay job considering she's a vet tech. I couldn't find anyone to do my hair, so I did the best I could with a can of spray-on color in "warm chestnut" and prayed I wasn't allergic to it. I cut out carbs— replaced my bedtime popcorn with cheese, I put a stop to eating all food off the floor—unless it was healthy ones, and I started to work out. Not as much as Todd, but no one did.

On the long-awaited eve of my next appointment, I was trying to decide on an outfit. I needed to look good half lying down. In the end, I chose a T-shirt with a cartoon of the moon landing on it . . . you know, to look smart, and the only pair of jeans that fit me. They were really sweatpants that looked like they were denim, and you could only tell the difference if you touched them. Possibly the best invention of our time. A few minutes later I got a text reminder from Rosie. They were looking forward to seeing me the following day. Likewise. Likewise.

Stacy agreed to drive me, and this time, the Covid numbers had gone down and she was cool with me keeping my head inside the car.

"Why are you wearing so much makeup to the dentist?" she asked as soon as I got in the car.

"He's an *oral surgeon* and I'm just wearing a little blush, barely anything."

Was it that obvious? I wanted to look natural. I wondered if the fake lashes and the cat eye were a bit much.

I waited for Dr. Kind Eyes in exam room 1, where it all began. This time I brought a *Newsweek* so I could pretend to be reading something smart when he came in and sat in the most flattering position I could find. Legs crossed just below the knee.

Aside from his kind eyes, I still had no idea what he looked like. I purposely didn't google him, as an experiment to see if I could be attracted to someone without ever seeing the middle of his face. The answer so far was an enthusiastic yes!

"Helloooo," Dr. Kind Eyes said, grabbing my file from the folder pocket on the door. My heart skipped a beat and my stomach dropped. I stopped pretend reading and looked up, surprised to see he was stripped down to just a surgical mask, a pair of gloves, and scrubs. He had a neck—no sagging or gross moles; thick salt-and-pepper gray hair parted on the side; and around his kind eyes— tortoise-shell glasses. He was thinner than I remembered, but also a hazmat suit adds pounds.

We made small talk. It turns out we had a lot in common. We were destined to meet—we both lived on the Upper East Side of Manhattan, never at the same time, but still. Eerie.

He laughed (an adorable giggle) when I jokingly asked if the cops would come to him to get my dental records if I was murdered and unrecognizable.

I made a joke about my husband murdering me but backtracked quickly. I didn't want him to think I was hard to live with. I instead said that Todd wasn't mentally great, a bit unstable. He breathes a lot.

The nurse started setting up the IV and the room went quiet. I started second-guessing my choice of shirt. What if he didn't believe the moon landing really happened? What if he was a conspiracist? I folded my arms over my chest, prepared to flip and say I was wearing it ironically—of course we didn't land on the moon! Duh! Idiots! Liberals . . . I guess?

But luckily, not only did he believe we landed on the moon but he told me his mother worked for NASA! What an amazing family of brainiacs. I would learn SO much from them. I wouldn't even have to pretend to read *Newsweek*, or maybe I would read *Newsweek* because I actually *read Newsweek*. The possibilities were endless.

Dr. Kind Eyes sat on a rolling stool and rolled over to me. He asked me to open my mouth so he could take a look. I did as I was told. We were both quiet while he examined me, and I wondered if he felt our chemistry. He stood up and said my gum had healed beautifully. It was healthy and pink and ready for the post that would hold my crown. Maybe it was because of the words (pink and crown) or because it was ridiculously expensive, but it felt very much like a fairy tale. Then, when I was leaving, Rosie told me, in her signature matter-of-fact tone, that my regular dentist would be giving me my crown.

Wait. "What? Why?" I tried to contain my shock and disappointment but it was too fresh. "Why would my regular dentist do it? She's not even a girl's girl!"

"That's just the way it is," Rosie said cheerily. It made no sense, especially given everything we'd been through together, the intimacy we shared, and *why* did he have Rosie tell me and not tell me himself? Was he too much of a coward?

My mood plummeted. So that was it. It was over between us. We were done. No closure, no fairy-tale ending. Unless, of course, he was planning to call me outside the office, or was I supposed to call him? He did give me his cell. Was that a move on his part? I'd never been in this situation before, I didn't know what the rules were. I decided I'd reach out in a week. I'd butt-dial him and that would open the lines of communication.

I didn't have to wait a week. Two days later, on a Friday afternoon, I was eating salad and felt something rolling around in my mouth—was it an earring? I spit it into my hand . . . It was the screw!! It fell out! I would have to go back and get it screwed in again! I was giddy. I was *actually* happy about a dental mishap. I sprayed my head chestnut brown, checked myself for crumbs, and hopped in the car.

Driving over the hill, I felt a tinge of excitement. I figured this would be a nice treat for both of us, even given the circumstances. I tried to imagine the look on the top half of his face when he saw me. Would he get a big smile in his eyes? Or would he get flushed and pink? I purposely didn't call because I wanted to surprise him.

I didn't even wait for the nurse with the thermometer gun to read my temperature, I just entered. He was standing in the waiting room saying goodbye to a female patient (older, not a threat) and saw me. He didn't look as happy and blushy as he looked confused to see me.

"Hiiii. My screw fell out," I said, an unintentional hint of that annoying baby voice making an appearance.

"That's not good," he said, a little taken aback.

"Come on. Let's take a look," he said, nodding toward one of the exam rooms.

I followed him back to our usual room, sat in the chair, and arranged myself cutely.

"I didn't call because I figured you'd want me to come right in . . ."

"Where's the post?" he interrupted.

"What post? Oh! The little screw? I didn't bring it."

"It's a post," he corrected me. "Why didn't you bring it?"

"I didn't think I was supposed to. I'm sorry. I'll bring it next time."

"There shouldn't be a next time. It wasn't supposed to happen this time."

He pulled a new one out of a cabinet and gathered some tools.

He was defensive and prickly. He said this has never happened to him before. He's never had a post come out on a patient. I wasn't blaming him. I was just happy to see him and hoped we could just . . . have a nice time. That was not the case.

"Did you eat something sticky that could've loosened it?" he asked a little accusatorily.

"No, you told me not to eat anything sticky."

"Crunchy?" He wheeled his chair over to me. "Open. Taffy?"

I opened my mouth and shook my head no. I didn't eat anything crunchy OR sticky.

Wait. *Did I?!* I wouldn't put it past myself to purposely eat taffy so the screw would come out, so I would have to see him again. I knew I didn't eat anything sticky. No, I know I didn't.

In the hour or so between when the screw fell out and the time I got there, my hole had started to close. He could barely find it and when he did, he had a hard time getting the screw in. He decided to lose the tools he was using and just use his thumb to get the job done. He felt around in there and unlike the first time, he was rough, I didn't like it. It hurt.

"Ow. Cah gu um ma?"

"Nahhh, you don't need to be numbed. It'll take a second."

"Uch acha ug occhy ," I apologized, even though I did nothing wrong. Something I did a lot back when I only dated narcissists.

Dr. Gayfort went at it from another angle and without warning, pressed down on it hard; one shot of searing pain and it was in. He removed his fingers.

"Owwww," I whimpered, holding my jaw.

"It'll only hurt for a few minutes (a vast understatement). You'll be okay," he said, halfway out the door. He had another patient to get to. I felt spurned. He couldn't even stick around for a few minutes to see if I was okay? Oral surgeon pillow talk? The truth was, though, I couldn't get out of there fast enough either. I was embarrassed for thinking he'd be happy to see me and maybe even insist on giving me my crown even though it's not customary. But no. Not even close.

"Lay off the taffy!" he called behind him.

"He was probably just embarrassed that his screw fell out? That he did a bad job? You know how men have egos," my nonjudgmental-because-she's-having-an-actual-affair friend Joanne said.

"Yeah, you're right. Like he let me down."

"And maybe he doesn't like to be surprised. Maybe he was having a bad day. You don't know his life."

"Do you think I blacked out and ate taffy?"

"Wouldn't put it past you."

I woke up the next morning in severe pain—like the first pain back in June. I looked in the mirror and my face was just as lopsided and swollen as it had been then, if not worse. Can a mall tooth grow back?!?!?! I sent a picture to Dr. Kind Eyes's office and then two minutes later my phone rang—it was Dr. Kind Eyes himself. He told me to come right in. He moved his morning appointments around just for me. He sounded worried this time, instead of angry. Maybe he was just having a bad day yesterday. He told me to bring the original post.

There was an infection. His screw gave me an infection. I guess the equivalent of an STD. But unlike the day before, when I showed up, I could tell he felt bad, and he looked cute when he felt bad—at least from the mask up. He was gentler this time. He numbed me and cleaned the infection.

After I sat up, I felt better. *We* were better. This most certainly brought us closer.

"Hey, where's that post that fell out?"

"Oh. I didn't bring it. I think I lost it," I said, shrugging.

"Really?" he asked incredulously.

"Yeah," I answered, just as incredulously.

"*How* could you lose it?"

"It's a tiny dot of metal."

"Doesn't make it any less important." The edge from yesterday was back in his voice.

"Why do you need it, anyway? Were you going to recycle it? That's pretty unsani—"

"No! I would return it to the manufacturer. Obviously it was faulty."

There he goes blaming other people for his bad screwing.

"I think it was your fault," I said under my breath.

He couldn't wrap his brain around the fact that I couldn't locate a minuscule piece of metal.

Did he think all I had to do all day was sit around staring at a *screw?* That his screw was my only responsibility like some . . . princess?

"It's all you had to do," he said and strode out of the room.

I was seething.

I have a job; I might be in pajamas all day and mostly do puzzles and color in adult coloring books but I *do* work, I'm a writer, I work in my head and when I'm not working in my head, I am homeschooling two kids and making them meals, which it turns out, they need *every day*. I'm a *little* overwhelmed. I lose things all *the time*. Much more important things than tiny screws.

What would he do if he was on a work trip on the other side of the world and I lost his only car key somewhere on a massive soccer field? What if, even after searching and searching every inch of grass, mud, and garbage, the key was nowhere to be found, and I called to wake him up at 4 a.m. his time to tell him I lost his last key? That the kids and I were standing in the dark on an abandoned soccer field . . . again. Would he give me shit because this happens ALL the time, or would he calmly unlock and start the car with an app on his phone like Todd did?

Would he do the right thing and take responsibility for my fuck-up and say, "I should've taken that key with me, so you wouldn't be able to use my car" like Todd did? I don't think so.

Shit. I was thinking about Todd!!

"Get out of my affair, Todd!" I hissed under my breath.

"Just bring the post in when you can. They cost money," Dr. Cheap Eyes said, walking toward another exam room.

"I'll put it in the mail, and for the record, it's a *screw*! And I didn't eat taffy! I think," I called after him.

Leaving the office, I understood why the regular dentist puts the crown in . . . after the screw, everything gets weird.

Acknowledgments

I am eternally grateful and indebted to Anne Bobby. Without you, I would still be trying to figure out what an "overview" for a book proposal is—as well as what exactly a book proposal is. Thank you for your brilliance, talent, handholding, and wicked sense of humor. Thank you for living in my brain with me for so long. I know it could not have been easy. And for that, I am also sorry.

Kristyn Keene at ICM, thank you for taking me on, for your guidance, and for always answering the phone when I called, even while you were on a boat over July fourth weekend.

Huge thanks also to Kate Dresser, my editor at Gallery Books, for making this book happen, for trusting me and supporting me, and for your amazing notes and edits (and for extending my deadlines). Thanks also to the art department for your tireless work and for going in so many different directions.

Dan Norton at ICM and my manager, Robyn Meisinger, thank you for your friendship, but also for understanding how important this book was to me and giving me the time to write it, as well as your support while I did so.

Deepest thanks to Beth Lapidus at the Un Cabaret in Los Angeles, for allowing me to stand on stage and tell my stories there, so I could see what made people laugh, cry, or walk out. I'm grateful also to my cousins Pam and Jerry, Emily, Wayne, Mara, Shira, and everyone else, for sitting through those stories and not walking out.

To the staff at the Coral Tree Café in Encino: thank you for allowing me to park myself at the corner table for twelve hours a day and blatantly ignore the "please don't stay more than 45 minutes" sign, as well as knowing I don't like the salmon's tail, and for looking the other way when I adjust the thermostat.

To Linda, Michelle, Justin, Dina, Betsy, Genna, Stacy, Joanna, Kristin, Bryan, Charlie, Christy, Steph, April, Jonna, Alix, Andrea, Adam, Dana, Catherine, Michele, Laura, Debi, and Ali—thank you for your friendship, love, breathless laughter, endless material, and for allowing me to "run something by you, real quick" always at the most inconvenient times, and never "real quick."

(Kristin, thanks for not getting all spiritual when I just couldn't bear it. Michelle—"*I am we.*")

I love you all. I changed your names. And to Jack, Kevin, and Marsh, for the unforgettable experience we shared. Marsh, you are immensely missed.

Thanks to Ingrid and Betsy W., for giving me a hard deadline to finish my book proposal, and as promised, rewarding me with cupcakes.

Gratitude beyond words to Kiki Harris and the Candiffs—Michele, David, Nicole, Carinne, and Monique—for taking such good care of Jesse, Phoebe, the dogs, the turtles, and the gecko(s). You are our family. I'm sorry.

Samantha Fox, thank you for my sanity and for telling me I'm doing way better than anyone would have expected.

To my Uncle Marty, Aunt Pearl, Uncle Sam, and Aunt Iris and all of my cousins—thank you for the love, support, my favorite childhood memories, and the extra Cool Whip.

To my brother, Jeff, thank you for your friendship, love, mentoring, shared memories, and childhood torment—all of which made it into this book. You still make me feel safe-safe—I love you for that, and for everything.

To my sister-in-law, Shawni, thank you for your kindness, lack of judgment, and patience. Basically, thank you for marrying Jeff.

To my niece, Sasha, and nephew, Caleb, thank you for inspiring me to have my own kids. Without you, there would be no book.

To my dad and beautiful, kind, clean Cathy: thank you for supporting me and raising me with a rich life, a catalog of experience, and the strength to trust my own voice. For your sense of humor, and your appreciation of a good read and a good laugh, I love you and I am truly grateful.

To my husband, Todd, thank you for being our rock. For your endless patience. And for allowing me to go to yoga forty-five minutes away, knowing I'll be gone for at least three hours. Thank you for our children. And our other children—our beloved dogs, Olive, Ellie, and Crash. I am well aware that none of us would be alive without you. Thank you for letting me be me, for letting me tell our stories, exploit you, and tweeze your eyebrows when I've over-tweezed my own. Thank you for laughing with me.

I am forever and ever and ever grateful to Jesse and Phoebe—my children, my muses, my reasons to go home when I eventually do. You have taught me what unconditional love is and that I can be a good mother. I love you more than anything.